BALANCE
POINT

SEARCHING FOR A SPIRITUAL MISSING LINK

BALANCE POINT
SEARCHING FOR A SPIRITUAL MISSING LINK

ISBN: 0-9644258-5-8
Library of Congress Control Number: 00-091803

Want to help spread the message? Please recommend
this book to a friend, donate a copy to your library, or give them as gifts.
Generous discounts are available for quantity purchases.
Just call 1- 800-639-4099.

Acknowledgements
I owe my inspiration for this book to the scientists of the world, the activists, the social workers, educators, farmers, business people, laborers, artists, housewives, parents, students, and media people who are actively trying to avert the rapidly approaching Point of No Return.

A heartfelt thanks to all of you who commented on or edited the manuscripts.

Published by Jenkins Publishing
PO Box 607, Grove City, PA 16127 USA
Phone/Fax: 814-786-8209
web site: www.jenkinspublishing.com
email: mail@jenkinspublishing.com

Other books by Joseph Jenkins:
The Humanure Handbook (1999 — ISBN 09644258-9-0)
The Slate Roof Bible (1997 — ISBN 09644258-0-7)

TO ORDER BOOKS BY JOSEPH JENKINS CALL 1-800-639-4099

All Jenkins Publishing books are available at retail and wholesale rates from our book distributor: Chelsea Green Publishing, PO Box 428, White River Jct., VT 05001; 800-639-4099 (or 802-295-6300), or from your favorite bookstore or library, Ingram, Baker and Taylor, Amazon.com, Barnesandnoble.com, or elsewhere on the world wide web.

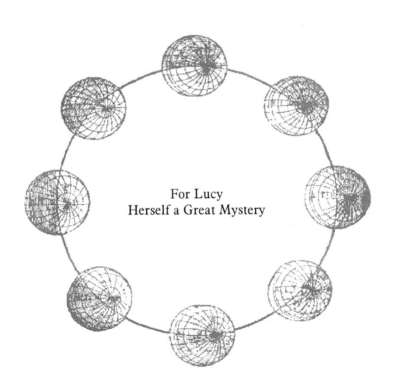

For Lucy
Herself a Great Mystery

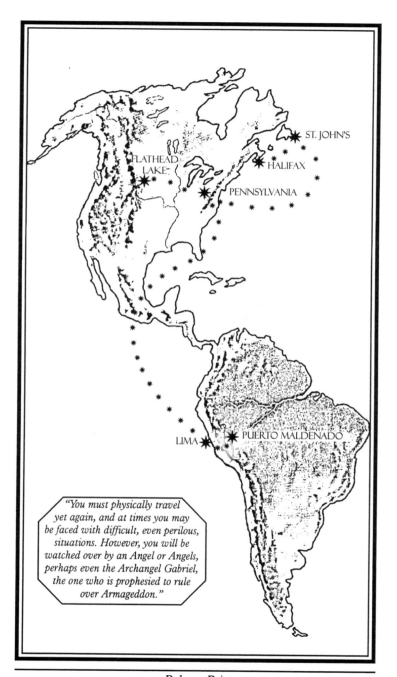

ST. JOHN'S

FLATHEAD LAKE

HALIFAX

PENNSYLVANIA

LIMA   PUERTO MALDENADO

"You must physically travel
yet again, and at times you may
be faced with difficult, even perilous,
situations. However, you will be
watched over by an Angel or Angels,
perhaps even the Archangel Gabriel,
the one who is prophesied to rule
over Armageddon."

Balance Point

CONTENTS

1

The Ego vs. the Eco

Each moment in life marks an invisible boundary between the past and the future. Any of those moments may become a pivotal one that changes your life, veering you off course — sending you into uncharted territory with no hope of ever returning. For me, it occurred on a spring morning in 1999, at my country home in Pennsylvania.

A BROWN DELIVERY TRUCK RATTLED DOWN THE LONG driveway, passing blooming pear trees and scattering ducks off my gravel lane. My barking dog alerted me to the truck's unexpected arrival, and soon the uniformed driver stepped out of the van, ignoring the dog as he had done so many times in the past. The parcel delivery guy always had a smile on his face when he arrived at our door — he knew the dog was friendly and wouldn't bite, and on this glorious morning with the sun streaming through billowy clouds, he was in a good mood.

I stepped out the front screen door to meet him. "You'll have to sign for this one, Mr. Jenkins," he said, pulling out a pen and handing me his clipboard.

"I don't remember ordering anything," I muttered as I scrawled my signature on the dotted line. The man ignored me as he entered data in his electronic notebook, then he handed me a manila envelope, waved goodbye and took off down the lane.

"What's this?" I asked myself out loud, stepping back

into the house. "Annie, did you order anything by mail?" I yelled to my wife, who was in the kitchen washing the breakfast dishes.

"No!"

Well, me neither, I thought to myself, looking closely at the return address on the envelope. This is not good, I thought, walking into the kitchen. "It's from a damn law firm in Montana," I said to Annie. "Ninety-nine percent of those guys give a bad name to the rest of them, you know."

"I've heard that one. Several times." Annie drained the sink.

"Well, it's true."

"What is it? What's in the package?"

I grabbed a paring knife from the drawer, sliced through the top of the envelope, and pulled out an official looking legal document, along with a white, letter-sized envelope. My name and address were neatly written in ink on the front of the letter. I momentarily set it aside, and read the legal document out loud:

Dear Mr. Jenkins,

We regret to inform you of the death of your Great Aunt Lucille Boggs, who passed away suddenly on the 26th of April, 1999, in Missoula, Montana. As per the Statement of Wishes stipulated in her Final Will and Testament, we are forwarding to you the enclosed envelope. She left us with the instructions that you are to receive this envelope without delay in the event of her death. She indicated that this was a matter of utmost urgency, and instructed us to inform you that you should open the envelope immediately.

Very Truly Yours,

Stainbrook and Halforth, Attorneys at Law

"Great Aunt Lucille Boggs? I hardly knew my Aunt Lucy!"

"Just open the envelope!" Annie said in frustration.

"Wait a minute. Why would Aunt Lucy send *me* anything? I've only seen her once in my life, at my grandmother's funeral back in '78. And I didn't even talk to her then!"

Two decades had passed since I last saw my Aunt Lucy. At the time, I didn't realize that it would be our first, and last, meeting. I remembered her as a salt-and-pepper haired lady in a long flowing dress. Her thick hair hung down to her waist, and a garland of fresh flowers crowned her head. She was different from the other family members — her hair shone, she was tanned, with rosy cheeks, and she had a beguiling smile on her face in great contrast to her bent, ashen, and grossly overweight siblings.

Aunt Harriet, with her thick layers of make-up and flaming red hair-do that resembled a plastic bicycle helmet, sat on a chair in the corner of the funeral home scowling at Lucy and muttering something about Lucy being a disgrace to the family, with her flowers and all. Uncle Lou, who sat beside her chomping on a cigar, nodded in agreement. I had just returned from a winter backpacking trip in Mexico and Central America, and I attended the funeral in cut-off jeans and sandals. They talked about me behind my back, too.

I remember standing alone at the side of my grandmother's casket, staring at her shriveled face painted with make-up by the undertaker's brush, her wispy white hair so thin you could see her scalp, her eyes looking like they had been sewn shut. I was thinking about all the years she had blessed my life, the cherry pies she baked, the smell of fresh bread that so often permeated her kitchen, when suddenly Lucy appeared beside me, hands clasped in front of her, head bowed. She casually glanced at me out of the corner of her eye, then suddenly stared at me intently, with a disconcerted look on her face. I looked back at her and started to smile until I noticed the bewilderment in her eyes. She was looking at me like she had just seen a ghost. Suddenly, she took one last look at grandma's corpse, turned on her heels, and whisked out the door of the funeral home. That was the one and only time I ever saw her. Nobody could explain her abrupt departure, and, to the best of my knowledge, none of my relatives ever mentioned her, or even saw her, again.

"Did I ever tell you about the one and only time I met Aunt Lucy?" I asked Annie.

"At the funeral? Yes, I've heard that story. Weird. Open the envelope! I want to see what it is. Maybe she left you some money or something."

"Why would she do that? I was practically a stranger to her." I ripped open the envelope. Two keys spilled out on the floor as I pulled out a hand-written letter. A personal check was stapled to it. The figure on the check practically jumped out at me. "Damn!! Ten thousand bucks! This is a check made out to *me* for ten grand!"

"WHAT? Are you kidding?" Annie asked incredulously, craning her neck to get a look at the check. "Thank you, Aunt Lucy!" she yelled, plucking the check from the letter to inspect it for herself. I grabbed the check back and threw it in the air. *"We're in the money!"* I sang, taking Annie for a quick jig around the kitchen. Then I remembered the letter, which had fallen on the floor in the excitement. "We better see what our dear old generous and wonderful Aunt Lucy has to say," I exclaimed, bending over to retrieve the note. Smiling, I read silently:

Dear Joseph,

A terrible battle is at hand. The forces of the Eco and the Ego have become locked in conflict. No less than the future of our species, in fact the future of the world, is at stake. I have been engaged in the struggle for years, and now the most critical time is at hand. Unfortunately, I fear the worst for myself — I sense impending doom. If I should die suddenly, I have left instructions with a law firm in Bozeman, Montana, to see that you get this letter. You must take my position as a key player in this ordeal. You are not alone — there are many of us spanning the entire planet struggling to avert the upcoming critical time, which I call the Point of No Return. My role is very important, and I have pledged that if I die before my task is completed, I will choose a successor. You have been chosen. Please take this very seriously. I know I can count on you. It is your destiny.

Your instructions are as follows: Proceed to my home on the Flathead Indian Reservation in Montana (see map on other side of this paper). My cottage will hopefully be locked up and undisturbed, awaiting your arrival. In the study (the room with all the books, located in the southwest corner of the house), look under the desk ...

Lucy explained what she wanted me to do, and ended her instructions with the following warning:

Do not share this information with anyone other than the closest of confidants, perhaps your wife. Make sure someone knows you are coming here, in case you do not return (so they can come looking for you).

I have included a check in the amount of ten thousand dollars to cover your expenses. Use the money sparingly. You'll need it.

Make haste.

Lucy

The smile froze on my face. I didn't know what to say. It seemed my dear old Aunt Lucy had something up her sleeve. My destiny, no less.

"You better read this." I handed the letter to Annie, then looked around on the floor for the two keys. Annie read the letter out loud, quickly at first, then slowly, drawing out each word as she spoke, her voice finally becoming a whisper.

She sat down on a kitchen stool and put the letter on her lap. "Is this crazy or what?"

"I don't know. How should I know?" I had found one of

the keys and was crawling around the kitchen floor looking for the other.

"Are you going to do this? I mean, go to an Indian reservation in Montana? You're not, are you? When would you have time to do *that*?"

I just shook my head. I had no intentions whatsoever of going on some wild goose chase. "Hell, no!" I replied, still on my hands and knees.

And then, out of the corner of my eye, I caught the golden glint of a brass key lying just under the edge of the kitchen stove.

Balance Point

2

Lonepine

I TOSSED LUCY'S LETTER AND CHECK INTO A DESK drawer and laid the two brass keys on top of my wardrobe, assuming I would soon forget about both the letter and the keys. The cynic's voice inside me told me my aunt's words were the rantings of a dying person hanging on to reality by a thin thread. Yet, I had nagging doubts. Every time I opened the desk drawer, I spotted the letter and had the urge to read it again. Her penmanship was neat, her grammar was correct, but her message was bizarre, even frightening, and it was frustrating for me to try to make sense of it. I couldn't shake the apparent urgency of her letter.

At night I would dream of Lucy and the look I had seen in her eyes twenty years earlier. In these midnight visitations, we were back at my grandmother's funeral. At the casket's side, Lucy stared at me again as if she were looking at a ghost. Then she quickly pressed two golden keys into the palm of my hand while saying something that I couldn't quite understand. I could see her lips moving, but I could hear no words. She would suddenly vanish in a flash of light and I would wake abruptly, in a cold sweat.

Each morning, after such an encounter, I would go straight to my desk drawer, take out her letter, and again read her words, always pausing when I came to, "Proceed to my home." These four words jumped out at me each time my eyes passed over them, as if they had a life of their own.

Finally, I understood that the words Lucy was speaking to me in my dreams were those same four words — "proceed to my home." She was telling me to go to Montana as she pressed the keys into my hand, night after night. I read her letter a dozen more times before I finally summoned up the will to go.

Needless to say, I remained a skeptic. Megalomaniacs think they're going to save the world and usually they just make a mess of it. For all I knew, Aunt Lucy may have been in that category. She had written something about the future of our entire species being at stake, so when I got to the airport I was amused that my flight had been cancelled. Damn, it's tough to make a trip to save the species when you can't even get on the plane! Nevertheless, I was transferred to another airline, and after being routed through Toronto, I arrived in Missoula drowsy from airport beer, and already six hours late in saving the world. I had ample time to think on the plane, and I managed to conjure up plenty of doubts about what I was doing. Why was I going to Missoula, Montana, in May, when I should have been home taking care of my roofing business? Was I that easily manipulated by letters from deceased strangers and by inexplicable dreams? The roofing season had just begun in Pennsylvania. At this time of year business picks up so much that I hardly have time to read my mail. Taking off on vacation in the spring is virtually unheard of.

But, I *had* deposited the ten thousand dollar check into my bank account before leaving home, and now I felt obligated to carry out Aunt Lucy's instructions. So here I was, at an airport in Missoula, Montana, fifteen hundred miles from home, whether I liked it or not.

I picked up a rental car and headed for a nearby hotel. It was too late to do anything else. After a couple of cocktails at the hotel bar and a few rounds on their gambling machines, I was ready for bed. Getting an early start the next morning seemed like a good strategy since I didn't know where I was going.

The next morning I drove straight to a gas station mini

store, grabbed a cup of coffee and a donut, and bought a road map of Montana. The Indian reservation where Lucy lived was a few hours drive north of Missoula, near Flathead Lake, and with Montana's unlimited interstate speeds, I was soon heading north at a good clip. The ruggedly green Mission Mountains framed the road and made for a beautiful spring drive under an endless azure sky. This was my first time in "Big Sky Country" and I could see the area's appeal — breathtaking mountains, vast expanses of wilderness, plenty of elbow room, and lots of places off the beaten path where one could disappear from the world.

Soon, the dark expanse of the lake came into view and a sprinkling of a village appeared on its south bank. I pulled into the gravel lot of a small, old diner, one of those silver ones that looks like a mobile home. I squeezed through some parked cars and went inside, choosing a booth next to a window with a magnificent view of the lake. The water was a blue carpet stretching wall to wall between the green mountains, extending forever into the distance. Dilapidated fishing boats dotted the lake's edge, bobbing like white driftwood against the shore. A stiff, cold wind had flags on boat masts snapping and dancing.

After ordering a grilled swiss on rye, fries smothered in gravy, and a glass of iced tea, I asked the graying, portly waitress for directions.

"Can you tell me where Lonepine Road is?" I asked.

"Lonepine? You mean the *village* of Lonepine. That's about an hour west of here, north of Camas. I suppose if you drive toward Camas someone out there will be able to tell you where Lonepine Road is. There's no Lonepine Road around here, in Polson."

"Are you absolutely sure?"

She looked at me askance, shook her head, and said, "I've lived here all my life. What're you looking for?"

"Well, I have a map here showing Lonepine Road coming out of a village on the south shore of Flathead Lake." I fumbled in my shirt pocket, unfolded Aunt Lucy's hand drawn map, and placed it on the tabletop, smoothing out its creases.

The waitress leaned down and squinted. "That'd be Polson," she said, pointing at a spot on the map. "That's where you are now."

"I'm looking for a house about 15 miles out," I pointed, "on this road here."

"Let me see that." She took the map in her hands and held it at arm's length. "Why, that's not Lonepine Road. That road has no name. It's just a dirt road that eventually gets you *near* Lonepine, *if* you're dumb enough to drive it that far. I guess I've heard some people call it Lonepine Road, but then it's called a lot of other things too. Used to be called Witch Road or something like that."

"Which Road? Like you're lost?"

"No, Witch Road, like witches live out there." She smiled and nodded. "You're not from around here, are ya?"

"Witches?"

"You know. The kind that fly on brooms. Why, they say there's UFOs out there, too. I don't believe it, but some do. I never go out that way. Militia out there too. No sir, I don't need those kinds of headaches in my life. I got enough crap around here with Harold. He's the manager."

She turned and walked away, refilling the patrons' coffee cups as she passed by.

I scanned a local paper and finished my lunch, which was surprisingly good considering the place was little more than a dive. But my mind kept wandering back to what the gray-haired waitress had said. With the newspaper in front of me, I stared into space, thinking about witches, UFOs and militia. If I'm lucky I'll get out of this place alive. Or maybe not. Maybe I'll be abducted by a UFO. That will really delight my wife. Witches I can probably deal with. Militia? No thanks. I don't think they eat enough brain food. I'll keep my distance if I see any gun-toting nimrods.

I snapped out of my reverie and decided, what the hell, I can find this Lonepine Road or Witch Road or whatever the damn thing was called. Afterall, it was on Lucy's map.

A little sleuthing in the car and I should go right to it. I had to admit that my curiosity was piqued, and since I love a challenge, I paid the bill, left the waitress a five dollar tip, and headed for the car.

Yet my doubts about my aunt's sanity were increasing at every step of this journey. Was she a witch? Did she belong to the militia? Or was she actually an alien, I wondered, sarcastically. At least, thank god, I've avoided Harold, I thought, as I slammed the car door and started the engine.

3

Which Way

THE ROAD WAS PRETTY DAMN ROUGH, AND THE RENTAL car clunked several times as I hit bottom on rocks and potholes. I thought I might blow out a tire at any minute, so I drove slowly, gripping the shaking steering wheel with both hands, crawling along at a snail's pace, veering to the right, then to the left, trying to avoid the worst areas. I didn't meet any oncoming traffic at all — I guess I was the only one foolish enough to be driving on this road-from-hell. Nor did I see any camouflaged brigades marching down the road, or witches flying over on broomsticks. Not even a UFO landing site.

A tense mile or two down the washboard road, a stack of old tires appeared to my left, on the berm. Someone had driven a steel fence stake down through the center of them, apparently to keep the tires from falling over. The words "Witch Way" were scrawled on the side of the stack in white spray paint. That must be what started the rumor about witches. It looked like some lost kid just didn't know how to spell.

Lucy's map showed a trail heading north off Lonepine Road, 6.8 miles from the last intersection, at a "big tree." The side trail was described as a "quarter-mile long dirt track" on the map. At the end of the trail, Lucy had drawn a star with the words "my cottage" beside it. She had indicated that her house wouldn't be visible from the car, and had described it as a "plain, white, one-story house," probably the kind I had seen scattered along the way — typical minimal housing allocated by the federal government to the native Americans on the reservation. What Lucy was doing on an Indian reservation beat the hell out of me.

I carefully monitored my dashboard odometer and slowed the car to a stop when the numbers rolled around to 6.8. There was no big tree, as expected, and no dirt track, just more of the same — potholes, rocks, scrub, and dust under an intense sun that was turning the car into a bake oven. I double-checked the map to make sure I had read the numbers correctly, then I stepped out of the car onto the dusty roadway to look around, shielding my eyes from the sun and squinting into the distance. Not a goddam thing. I was either on the wrong road or Lucy was deranged as hell. What a crock, I thought. Only an idiot would come this far on the strength of a stupid letter and find nothing in the middle of nowhere. If I ever felt like a fool, I certainly did at that moment. Nevertheless, I had nothing to lose by continuing further. I would make one last attempt before turning back.

Another quarter mile down the road, I finally spotted a giant pine tree off to the right. A hand-painted sign that bluntly stated, "Keep Out!" was tacked to its trunk. A dirt trail passed beside the tree, showing two well-worn tire tracks leading back into the brush and up a slight grade toward the distant mountains. I coaxed the car up the narrow lane, bushes scraping against the sides, until I could go no further. Shutting off the engine and stepping into the blazing sunlight, I stretched to get my blood flowing. I leaned against the car and looked around. No house in sight. With the map, letter, and keys in my pocket, I started up the trail on foot.

The sharp peal of a hawk shattered the silence as I clambered up the rutted trail. The dry, stony terrain reminded me of the southern Rockies where I lived when I was a kid. I loved hiking in those mountains then, and even though I was only twelve years old at the time, I would take off on long hikes alone, climbing up into the mountains and exploring the marvels of the desert. I saw many a lizard, horny toad, prairie dog, snake, and desert rat during my forays into the wild, not to mention cacti, which I learned very quickly to avoid. Here in Montana, I poked the thorny bushes with a stick as I passed, searching, as I did during my youth, for snakes and lizards scurrying beneath them.

The sight of a red hex sign out of the corner of my eye jolted me out of my reverie. The sign was fastened to the gable end of a small, white, stucco house, out of reach, but plainly visible over the tops of the tall bushes. Reminiscent of Pennsylvania Dutch hex signs once popular on the old eastern barns, this one was nailed to a board and a red circle was painted around it. My grandmother, the one whose funeral I had attended years ago, had Pennsylvania Dutch ancestry. She used to keep hex signs like this one hanging around her old wooden farmhouse. She said they were for luck — they would keep the evil spirits away.

As I sneaked up on the small dwelling, I noticed immediately that the place was oddly silent; no dogs barked, no cats scampered into hiding upon my approach, no birds scolded my arrival. I tested the front door. It was locked, and the house key Lucy had sent me didn't fit. I peeked in the windows, but couldn't see anything because of the drawn curtains. I skirted around behind the cottage and banged on the back aluminum screen door. I knocked harder and shouted, *"Anyone here!?"* but no one answered. The screen door creaked when I pulled it open. I slipped the brass key into the lock and, to my relief, it easily turned. Well here goes, I thought, as I pushed open the door. A blast of stale air momentarily took my breath away.

All the curtains and blinds were drawn and the interior looked dismal and foreboding. I stood just inside the open door for a while, motionless, listening for any noise at all. Nothing. I felt a light switch on the wall and flipped it on. Still nothing. The electricity must be turned off, I thought. I left the door open behind me and took a few more steps inside. Enough light entered through the doorway that I could see well enough. The place was tidy, although there were dead house plants on the window sills. I took a few more steps and stopped again, frozen in a state of heightened awareness. *"Anyone here?!"* I yelled loudly again. If anyone was there, they surely would have heard me. But no one replied.

The realization that I was probably alone in this house enabled me to relax, and, as my eyes adjusted, I began to poke around. I noticed a lot of Native American artifacts placed neatly throughout the interior. On the wooden fireplace mantle were several kachina spirit dolls, a turtle-shell rattle leaned against a wall on the living room floor, and a couple of hoop drums hung on another wall. An impressive collection of quartz crystals of all sizes and shapes adorned a southern windowsill, including one large, clear chunk of quartz that was carved into a perfect sphere — a crystal ball. Brightly colored glass and wooden beads hung over the doorways. A wolf skin lay draped over an easy chair in the living room, and several partially burnt candles were strategically placed on tables about the house.

Even though I had read Lucy's letter dozens of times, I pulled it from my pocket and read it again to review her instructions.

"In the study (the room with all the books, located in the south west corner of the house), look under the desk."

The floorboards in the hall squeaked under my feet, deafening in the utter silence of this tomb of a house. For all I knew, the place was haunted. I came to the end of the dark hallway and entered a dim room lined with oak bookshelves. The purple velveteen drapes covering the windows were heavy with the smell of books and age. I pushed them back, inviting the sunlight in.

I immediately spotted a wooden desk in the center of the room, obviously the desk I was looking for. It was littered with papers, receipts, and cancelled checks, as if it were still in use. An address book sat amongst the clutter curiously open to "J." When I spotted my name in it, I picked up the little black book, quickly leafed through it, and slipped it into my shirt pocket for safekeeping.

One other curious, dark book lay on the desk top: "Materia Medica" by Maisch, dated 1895. A dried leaf marked a page on "Cinchona — Peruvian Bark." I thumbed through the pages, which described herbs used for medical purposes, then quickly set it back down. I was not in the mood for distractions, wanting to focus on my mission, get it done, and get the hell out of there.

"You will find a red rug on the floor. Move the desk and roll the rug back. There is a trap door here in the floor boards. You will find a metal lockbox there. In it will be instructions. Follow them impeccably."

I pulled the chair out from under the desk to expose the red carpet underneath. Pulling the desk away from the wall wasn't difficult, and the carpet rolled back easily enough, exposing a small trap door in the floor. The floor boards had been cut out and then set back in to make a secret hiding place, but they were fastened tightly with several screws. Luckily, my Swiss Army knife had a screwdriver on it and, with some effort, I got the screws out and pried the hatch up. Underneath lay a shallow depression crudely boxed into the floor joists, a carpentry job that an inexperienced person might have done. Inside was a gray tin box, the container Lucy had promised. I lifted it out, surprised at its lightness. It felt empty.

Fishing around in my pocket for the key, I pulled out the house key first, and finally found the lockbox key. I cleared a spot on top of the desk and set the lockbox down. Sliding a chair up, I sat down at the desk and stared at the box, key in hand. I felt very strange at that moment, far from home, in a foreboding, dark house, sneaking around and prying up floorboards to follow the fanciful wishes of a woman I had never known. I paused for a long moment, full of doubt, then that damned ten grand check went dancing through my head and I knew I had to carry this thing through. I couldn't return Lucy's money very easily, since she was dead. And although I hadn't voluntarily entered into any deal with her, I *had* deposited her check and now felt indebted to keep my end of our "agreement."

The key slipped into the lock, twisted, and the top of the box opened. Resting inside was a single, white, business-sized envelope. Nothing was written on it. I removed the envelope, which felt practically empty, and set it on the desk. Then I shook the box upside down, sure there must be another secret compartment where something important lay. The box just rattled, revealing nothing. I couldn't believe there was nothing else in that box! The envelope, which had not been sealed, contained a business card, a check, and a handwritten note dated April 25, 1999. The note stated:

"Dear Joseph,

"I fear for my life as I write this. If you are reading this now, you have made it this far. Good for you. Here is further incentive for you: I spent nearly thirty years teaching at the University of Montana. My retirement fund has accumulated a sum of about a half million dollars. If you complete my mission for me, it is yours to keep. I have instructed my lawyers, in my will, to hold my estate in escrow for no longer than one year. Within that time, if you have located your personal 'Balance Point,' you may claim the estate."

I could hardly believe it: a half million dollars! The letter, signed by my aunt, went on to briefly explain that she had included a $20,000 check made out to me to cover any expenses I should incur in the execution of her "mission." That was the check in the tin box. Yet, she didn't elaborate on what her mission was. Like her first letter, this one was just as cryptic, and even more maddeningly frustrating. I had no idea what she meant by locating a Balance Point — it sounded like new age blather. She mentioned that she had been a university professor — maybe the Balance Point had something to do with that. Or maybe her "mission" had something to do with her tenure at the university.

I sighed and rested my head in my hands, setting the

letter back down on the desk. Well isn't this something, I thought, laughing out loud. A fat check, like in a treasure hunt, but again with strings attached. Lucy's first note from her lawyers had promised me further instructions in a hidden lockbox, but instead she left me with another obscure and confusing note and a stupid business card. *Business card!* I grabbed the card off the desk and read it with intense interest. Maybe there would be a thread of information here that I could actually *use*. "Better Baby Birthing Clinic, Youngstown, Ohio" was printed in an elegant script. Two women's names, Sandy Riding and Cynthia Bernard, and a phone number were displayed below a logo of a stork holding a baby dangling by a diaper. I turned the card over and recognized Lucy's handwriting. On the back of the card she had written "Sisters of the Sacred Circle," and *nothing* else.

I held the card up to the window light looking for a secret message, or secret ink. I considered constructing anagrams from the words "Sisters of the Sacred Circle," thinking that maybe Lucy was a fanatic for riddles and was trying to make things especially difficult for me. I read and reread both the letter and the card trying to find any clue that I may have overlooked, any hidden communication, any veiled meaning. The more I probed, the more shadowy it all became. Shadowy and dim, like the house I was sitting in. The whole thing was becoming an unintelligible enigma, and I was beginning to get a pounding headache.

I had come fifteen hundred miles to locate instructions hidden in a dead woman's floor, and found nothing but a ridiculous letter and a card for a birthing clinic. There were apparently no instructions here at all. I felt like a fool — again. The twenty thousand dollar check was a pleasant surprise, I admitted, although I had no intention of ever cashing it. This entire affair was just too bizarre, and I had bad feelings about it. I didn't want to get sucked in any deeper than I already was.

As far as I was concerned, there was only one thing I wanted to do at that moment, and that was to go home. I went through the house, carefully putting everything back exactly as I had found it, then hurriedly stepped out the back door into the fresh air and sunlight, locking the door behind me. With the lockbox in hand, I hurried down the rocky, sun-soaked trail toward the rental car. I had been at Lucy's cottage exactly one hour, and that was enough for me.

4

Secret Rendezvous

I TOOK A RED-EYE FLIGHT HOME FROM MONTANA, arriving in Pennsylvania in the wee hours, and slept late the next morning. As soon as I got up, I described the entire episode at Lucy's cottage to my wife over tea at the dining room table. She hung on to my every word, but dismissed my assertion that there were no instructions in the lockbox. She was fascinated by the birthing clinic business card.

"You have to call these people!" Annie insisted. She held the mysterious card in her hand, thinking that maybe if she stared at it long enough, its secrets would be revealed to her. I gazed out the dining room window at the ducks poking their heads underwater in our pond, their rear ends sticking up like fishing bobbers. Maple tree helicopters rained down on the patio outside, and the house wrens, who had recently migrated back to their northern home, were chattering like crazy, their busy song pouring in through an open window. The smell of spring drifted into the house and across the dining room table, perfuming the air.

"Are you listening? You need to call the number on this card." She flung the card across the table as if dealing a poker hand.

"Why should I?" I answered, shrugging my shoulders. "I was obligated to follow Lucy's instructions as stated in her letter. She instructed me to go to her house, find her lockbox, and follow the instructions there. There weren't any instructions there, so now, as far as I'm concerned, I'm off the hook. *Finito*. Done."

"There were no instructions that you are yet *aware* of. That doesn't mean that there were no instructions *at all*. Something must have been extremely important for Lucy to leave you thirty thousand dollars and then promise you another half million. You can't just blow it off because you don't understand what she's trying to tell you."

"Plenty of old women, and men no doubt, leave lots of money to televangelist shysters when they die. That doesn't mean they're not fools," I said pointedly. "It may not bother *those* people's consciences to take money from senile folks, but it bothers *me*. I can't just take an old lady's money and waste my time running around on a wild goose chase. I think I'll donate the money to charity and be done with it."

"Look, you went all the way to Montana and came back with this stuff. You can't ignore it. There *is* a phone number on that business card. The very least you could do is call it. For all you know, it's a disconnected number. If it is, you're home-free. I don't see what the big deal is," Annie said, matter-of-factly, sipping her tea and staring impatiently at me over the rim of her cup. Her slender body was propped on her elbows as her gaze lost focus, perhaps she was imagining what Lucy's "instructions" really did mean. Maybe she was dreaming of what we could do with a half million bucks.

Penelope, our ten year old daughter, was still asleep, tucked in with her menagerie of dolls and stuffed animals in her bed upstairs. With her long, wheaten hair and slight, delicate frame, it was readily apparent that she was indeed her mother's daughter. They both had the same positive dispositions, always with a smile on their faces, laughing when they stubbed a toe, or made a mistake. I, on the other hand, was just the opposite, swearing when I made a mistake and straight-faced most of the time. They say opposites attract, and in this case it was true. Annie and Penny were always fawning over a little kitten, or baby duck. My responsibilities lay with making ends meet, "bringing home the bacon." Being the sole breadwinner in the family, I tended to dwell on my contractual and financial responsibilities, often working seven days a week, as self-employed people do. Annie's job, by choice, was in the home, where she did most of the gardening, child-rearing, cooking, and cleaning. Earning money was never part of her responsibility. It was a partnership that worked for us, and although I played the staunch role of no-nonsense businessman, I sought her counsel whenever I had an important decision to make. She usually offered a fresh insight that was helpful.

"So you really think I should go ahead with this thing? You want me to phone this birthing clinic?"

"Well, you can't just call it quits."

"Alright, then. I'll call right now and get it over with." I grabbed the business card off the table. "Sandy Riding and Cynthia Bernard," I read out loud. "Never heard of 'em."

I grabbed the cordless phone and walked out to the sun porch, wanting to concentrate on the conversation without anyone, even Annie, listening too closely. I punched the number into the phone and waited impatiently while it rang. Secretly, I hoped a recorded voice would answer and tell me the number was no longer in service. It rang a few more times; I heard a click, and, much to my surprise and dismay, a voice at the other end answered.

"Hello?"

"Hello?" I stuttered. "This is Joe Jenkins, calling from Pennsylvania. I'd like to speak with either Sandy Riding or Cynthia Bernard."

"This is Cynthia." The voice at the other end was pleasant and soft.

"Oh. You'll have to excuse me if this call seems a little

odd to you. I got your name and number from my Aunt Lucy Boggs. I know you don't know me, but she sort of asked me to call you, I think."

"Did you say *Jenkins* from Pennsylvania? Oh my god! On the contrary, Mr. Jenkins, I *do* know *of* you. Lucille told me *months* ago that I might expect a call from you someday. This is quite a shock!" After a short pause, Cynthia spoke with an earnest tone. "We should meet as soon as possible."

"What for?"

"Didn't Lucy tell you?"

"Tell me what?" A hush from her end of the line suggested that I must have said the wrong thing. I waited silently, not knowing what to say next.

"Lucille didn't mention *anything* about this?" she asked incredulously.

"Well, she did say some ominous things in a disturbing letter she sent to me, but I didn't understand any of it. Now that she's dead, I obviously can't get her to explain it."

"Lucille's *dead? Oh my god!* I just spoke with her not more than a month ago. When did she die? How?"

"You didn't *know?*" I was surprised by her reaction, and felt awkward that I had become the bearer of bad tidings. "I don't know how she died. Nobody told me how. She wanted me to call you, I think, as part of some instructions she wanted me to follow in the event of her death. Some craziness about a battle with her ego and the world coming to an end. Maybe you know what she was talking about; you probably knew her a lot better than I did, didn't you?"

"I knew her very well," Cynthia replied curtly, in a somber voice.

"Then tell me, was my aunt lucid in her old age? Did she have Alzheimer's or something? You know, I'm kind of a busy guy, and I don't know if I can really do whatever she wanted me to do. Especially since I have *no idea* what it was she wanted anyway."

"We're all busy people, Mr. Jenkins, and —"

"Call me Joe."

"Okay, Joe. Listen. Lucy was one of the most rational and intelligent people I have ever known. I would suggest that you take her recommendations, whatever they are, *very* seriously. If she had asked *me* to do something for her, I would've risked my very life to do it. I'm obviously going to have to convene the Sisters for this. We must meet with you as a group. As soon as possible."

"What for? What sisters?" I asked, turning the card over in my hand. "The Sisters of the Sacred Circle, by any chance?"

"How did you know that?" she inquired warily.

"It's written on the back of your business card that Lucy left for me at her house in Montana."

"Can you come tomorrow night at eight? We'll meet near Youngstown, at a private place in the woods. You'll have to meet me at my house and ride with me in my car or else follow me. It's too difficult to give directions over the phone; you'd get lost."

"And what's the purpose of this, if you don't mind me asking — again?"

"We really shouldn't discuss this over the phone, Joe, but let's just say that you're now bearing a tremendous responsibility, one that you're obviously not aware of, and maybe you shouldn't be at this time. We're pledged to assist you, to help point you in the right direction for your journey. Lucille asked me to do this for you, and we're willing, if you are. You have to trust us."

"What journey? Journey to where? Willing to do *what?*" The stack of roofing jobs which were quickly piling up on my desk flashed through my mind. Then I thought of the thirty thousand dollars and Lucy's letters. I couldn't believe what I seemed to be getting myself sucked into.

"That's what we'll ascertain tomorrow night, at eight. Please be on time," she paused. "Oh, I almost forgot! You should fast the entire day tomorrow, from sun-up. Take nothing into your body except water and natural juices. And tomorrow evening, come alone. And please, don't share what I've told you with anyone. Bring whatever you have that relates to your aunt. Dress for a hike in the woods. And please be on time."

"Let me get this straight. You want me to meet *you*, a total stranger, tomorrow night, at a private place in the country, dressed for a hike in the woods, and you won't tell me *why*?"

"You should already know why. If not, you'll find out tomorrow night."

"With all due respect, this seems a bit far-fetched."

Cynthia replied impatiently, "As I said, Joe, you'll have to trust me. It's the least you can do for your aunt."

"Oh alright, give me the directions." I grudgingly wrote down the directions to Cynthia's house, and placed the phone back on the receiver.

"Guess what, Annie," I yelled through the doorway. "I have to go to Youngstown tomorrow night on a secret rendezvous into the Ohio forests with a bunch of women."

"If it's a secret, then why are you telling me?" she yelled back.

"Damned if you do and damned if you don't," I muttered.

"Can I come?"

"No. It's a *secret*. Anyway, that's one of the conditions. I have to go alone. I'll tell you all about it when I get back."

"How do you know you *will* get back?" Annie replied laughingly, mocking my reluctance to go.

"Don't laugh. I have no idea what I'm getting myself into. Who knows, I may disappear into the woods of Ohio, never to return. Then Lucy's secrets would be lost forever, and me with them. If I do get back, I'll tell you all about it."

Annie stepped up behind me and wrapped her arms around my waist. "You'll return. You never were good at keeping secrets."

5

White Magic

THE NEXT MORNING I WOKE TO A DARK, OVERCAST SKY that burst into a pelting rain by the time I finished my liquid breakfast. I was already concerned about the "appointment" I had scheduled for the evening, and the foreboding, wet, miserable weather had me pacing back and forth in the house, stopping frequently to look out a window. I spent as much time in my office as I could, but seemed to only shuffle papers back and forth, start something then set it aside, and generally remain preoccupied and unfocused on my work. Every so often, I looked out at the garden, wishing I could be pulling weeds out of the broccoli beds or transplanting tomato seedlings, but the rain kept me cooped in.

I was becoming increasingly apprehensive about going to some strange place out in the country, and the gray, oppressive weather seemed to stimulate my imagination in a negative way. I imagined, among other things, a meeting with toothless, tattoo-covered, sex-starved, biker women in the middle of a sea of junk cars and junkyard dogs. The mental image of me sloshing into a deep swamp in the night, beating back mosquitoes and snakes, while a troupe of crazy women led the way with brooms and torches didn't help either.

About the time my imagination would really start to get carried away and I could see myself being jerked through the dark woods on the end of a chain hooked to unmentionable parts of my body, my empty stomach would groan and remind me that I hadn't eaten anything. I had never fasted before, and did my best to alleviate my hunger by sipping on tomato juice. A fat steak would have hit the spot right about lunchtime, but I couldn't eat anything solid, thanks to Cynthia, so I tried to put food out of my mind.

I managed to keep myself busy in my workshop all afternoon, cleaning up from the last woodworking job I had done, and setting up for the next. Finally, around six o'clock, the rain stopped and the sky brightened. Before dark, the clouds parted and the setting sun streamed through the widening gap on the western horizon. The wind shifted out of the north, dropping the temperature to an unseasonable coolness. When I finally gathered my stuff together, said goodbye to Annie, and got in my truck to head west on the interstate highway, I had to lower the sun visor to keep the setting sun from blinding me. The only thing predictable about Pennsylvania weather is its unpredictability.

After an hour and a half of driving, I found Cynthia's place back a narrow country road. A towering oak woods wrapped around her small brown cape cod house; a red barn, sagging with age, sat across the road. A weathered split rail fence extended along the road in front of the barn, and an old black horse stood inside the fence, its shadowy head hanging over the rails, watching me intently as I slowed to a stop.

I swung my truck into what I assumed was Cynthia's driveway, parked alongside a road-beaten Ford van, and made my way up the gravel drive toward the house. "Hello!" shouted a woman's voice. She sat on a porch swing behind an overgrown grape trellis, waving. "Are you Joe? I'm Cynthia Bernard!"

I walked the hundred feet or so up to the house. "Yeah. Hi. That's me." I complimented her on her place, which was quaint and rustic, but impeccably maintained. A porch light revealed white and purple pansies bursting from flower boxes mounted below the porch windows; a newly seeded garden appeared to run the length of one entire side of the house. I could hear goats bleating somewhere out back. Small children peered from behind a window curtain, giggling.

Cynthia was thin and lanky, her flaming red hair tied back into two long pigtails. She reminded me of Pippi Longstocking as she looked me over, then stood up and took my hand as if to shake it, only to gaze straight into my eyes as if looking for something. "Did you have any trouble finding the place?" she asked, letting go of my hand.

"I drove straight here. You give good directions."

"Well, now that you made it this far, would you care for some water or juice?"

"Oh, no, I don't think so. But thanks anyway."

"Well, we should be going anyway," she said. "Want to ride with me? That way we can talk on the way."

I wasn't sure I really wanted to leave the security of my pickup truck, but found myself saying, "Sure, why not?" Initially, we drove in an awkward silence, passing fewer and fewer houses as we progressed deeper into the country-side. I watched the scenery become engulfed in a cloak of darkness as woods finally extended on either side of the road, uninterrupted. We broke the silence with small talk as we began to ask each other questions about our personal lives. Like me, she was married and had several children. Her husband was a carpenter, about my age. She was probably in her early forties, I guessed. I asked her about her birthing clinic.

"I'm a midwife. A lay midwife. Do you know what that is?"

"A midwife delivers babies, right?"

"Well, not exactly," she said with a smile. "We like to say we *catch* babies, we don't deliver them. They deliver themselves. In many instances, we don't even catch the baby, the father does. Then, we're just there to help. But, if the father doesn't want to be involved in the birth, the mother can rely on her lay midwife instead."

"What do you mean — *lay* midwife?"

"That means I'm trained through experience and independent learning rather than through a formal school. I apprenticed under an older lay midwife who's attended over a thousand births; I've attended over 400 births myself. We've never lost a baby. Or a mother either," she said matter-of-factly. "Lay midwifery is one type of midwifery, another is nurse midwifery. That's what Sandy does." Cynthia had both hands on the steering wheel and kept her eyes straight ahead, quickly glancing at me from time to time as she drove on the narrow, winding road.

"Sandy Riding?"

"Yep. She's a nurse trained in a hospital. Some people prefer nurse midwives, some prefer lay midwives, so we make a good team." Cynthia turned off onto a narrow, gravel road.

"How did my aunt know you and Sandy?"

"Lucy has been active in the women's movement for decades. She was a founding member of the Circle of Sisters and always a staunch supporter of midwives. I met her at the Starglade Festival in New York about ten years ago. She was conducting seminars on the relationship between nuclear physics and Wicca."

"What?"

"Yeah, that's what I thought. Nuclear physics and Wicca!" Cynthia laughed.

"I mean, what's Wicca?"

"Oh! You've never heard of Wicca?"

"No."

"Gee. You're greener than I thought. You've never heard of *Wicca*?"

"Never."

"Okay, well," she furrowed her brow, searching for a way to explain. "Well, Wicca is what some people call witchcraft."

"Oh great," I whispered under my breath, covering my eyes with my hand and realizing that maybe the witch rumors I had heard in Montana were true, that Lucy *was* involved in this stuff.

"I heard that," Cynthia said. "Most people don't understand Wicca, and you're obviously one of them."

"I *know* what a witch is."

"Really? Did you know that 'witchcraft' means 'craft of the wise'? In the not so distant past, so-called 'witches' were the wise ones of their village. They knew about natural healing; they handled legal matters, and spiritual ones. They were the doctors, the lawyers, and the priests!"

Even in the darkness I could see that Cynthia's face was flushed. "I'm sorry if I sound defensive, but people are generally so ignorant about this sort of thing and they keep perpetuating the same old myths. Wiccans aren't ugly women on broomsticks with black, pointed hats and warts on their noses cackling over cauldrons of boiling bat lungs. We've been unfairly portrayed that way by religious and medical zealots for centuries. Actually, Wiccans are both women *and* men. They're intelligent and kind people who believe in a spirituality that's inextricably connected to nature. And it's the spiritual connection to nature that puts off the religious fanatics. They want to call us heathens, pagans, and satanic because we don't believe in *their* god. But they're just boneheads. Most people don't know that, and I have to spend a lot of my time setting them straight."

I realized I opened a Pandora's Box when I asked Cynthia about witchcraft. She was getting a little too worked up and since I wanted her to keep her hands on the wheel and her eyes on the road, I attempted to steer the conversation in a different direction. "So let me get this straight, my Aunt Lucy was teaching seminars on the relationship between nuclear physics and witchcraft? I can't say that I'm too surprised about the witchcraft part anymore, but I didn't know she had an interest in nuclear physics."

"Your Aunt Lucy was a nuclear physicist."

"Excuse me?"

"You didn't know that?"

"Of course not."

"How could you *not* know *that*? She was your aunt!"

"I didn't know *anything* about Lucy. She was the black sheep of the family. The only time I saw her was at a funeral, twenty years ago."

"Lucy had a Ph.D. in nuclear physics and she taught at the University of Montana in Missoula."

"And she was a witch, too?"

"We don't call ourselves witches," Cynthia replied curtly.

"Oh, so you're one, too?"

"Lucy was deeply involved in Wicca, and so am I. We dabble in what you might call 'white magic.' I think you could really benefit from a short history lesson. It might help you understand where I'm coming from."

"Okay. I'm all ears."

"Midwives and herbalists have traditionally been in direct competition with the medical establishment, mainly because we provide health care services without drugs or invasive procedures," she explained. "Some people in the medical establishment consider this a threat to their ability to make money. Historically, those types of people played a big role in branding us as witches, attempting to eradicate us. Even today, midwives are sometimes persecuted by unethical people in the medical establishment. Whether you realize it or not, childbirth is a big business, and they don't like us cutting into it. It's pretty disgusting, especially when you consider that midwife-attended births are statistically far safer than hospital births, and a heck of a lot cheaper, too."

Cynthia's passion was a little overwhelming. I searched for the right words to reply, but decided again to try to change the subject. My nagging doubts about this whole trip persisted, and it seemed like we had been on a dirt road for an awful long time. "So exactly where are we going?"

"Our coven is meeting tonight, strictly for your benefit, and that's where we're headed. We'll be there in about five minutes."

I started to feel a little nervous. "What do you mean 'strictly for my benefit'?"

"Look, Joe, I don't know what Lucille had in mind when she chose you to carry her torch, because I don't see — well, I don't know how to say this, but you seem a bit naive about all this. For chrissakes, I know more about your own aunt than you do. Lucille was a genius; besides that, she was very psychic and sensitive. As I understand it, she was working on a very important project with a group of scientists and lay-people scattered all over the world. I can't quite fathom it, but I think that's where you come in. I guess we're going to try to find that out tonight."

"Do you know what her project was called?"

"If I remember right, she called it the *Balance Point*." I recalled Lucy's letter that I had found in the lockbox. She had mentioned something about me finding what she called my "personal Balance Point." She hadn't mentioned it had anything to do with an international research project. I was beginning to feel like an involuntary guinea pig, and not sure whether I wanted to resent it, or to accept the challenge.

"I know this sounds strange, but I can't explain what the project is exactly. According to your aunt, it was extremely important. At least that's how she explained it to me, and I believe her." Cynthia turned her head and looked straight at me. "Did you fast today as I requested?"

I was pondering what she had just said, the balance point and all, and I didn't hear her question.

"Well, did you *fast*?"

"Huh? Yeah. And I could really go for a big chunk of food right about now, like some ribs or something. My stomach is doing cartwheels. Will there be any food where we're going?"

"There'll be food, but no meat. They're mostly vegetarians. In the Coven, that is. But we'll have some food after the ceremony."

"And what ceremony would that be?" I asked tentatively.

"The one our Coven is doing tonight — just for you. The divination ceremony. Looks like you're going to experience witches firsthand," she chuckled.

We turned down a tree-lined lane.

"We're here."

6

Sacred Circle

THE VAN'S HIGH BEAMS LIT UP A HOUSE AT THE END OF the lane. As we got closer, I was surprised to see a red brick ranch style home with a neatly trimmed lawn and square hedges hugging the house. A huge, beige and brown motor home sat in the driveway. Several cars filled a small parking area off to one side of the lane.

"Where are we?"

"This is Rhonda's house. She's hosting the gathering tonight."

Cynthia killed the engine and opened her door, throwing her keys on the dashboard. I got out, deciding to keep my mouth shut for a while and absorb as much as I could. I followed her up concrete steps to the front walk. A motion sensitive light blinked on as we neared the front door. A dog barked a repetitive, lonely howl behind the house, while a huge Luna moth fluttered at the glass on the front door, as if desperately trying to warn anyone inside of our arrival. When we knocked on the door, the moth disappeared into the darkness like a silk scarf whisked away by the wind. The door suddenly opened and a portly, ruddy complexioned blonde, apparently in her late fifties, stood before us, a toothy grin on her face.

"Cynthia! We've been waiting," she said smiling, as the creaking screen door swung open. "C'mon in. This must be Joseph. I'm Rhonda."

"Hi," I said, extending my hand as I walked in. "Call me Joe."

Four women sat silently in the living room, staring at me with concerned looks on their faces. It seemed like I was attending someone's funeral. "This is Sandy," Cynthia said, gesturing to a forty-something woman of medium height and heavy build, with shoulder length brown hair and glasses. Sandy rose to shake my hand. "Sandy's the nurse midwife we talked about — my partner. And this is Doris." A younger woman with straight, long blond hair nodded and smiled. "Doris is a librarian at an elementary school in Youngstown. And this is Linda," she pointed to a short woman whose young face belied her age; her cropped hair was lightly salted with gray. She wore a row of earrings up both ear lobes. "Linda's an artist."

"Actually, I'm a gardener. But I'm an artist too!"

"What sort of art?" I asked, trying to be cordial as I shook her hand.

"Watercolors mostly, but I also make jewelry, do some batik, you know, that kind of thing."

"I'm Deb," the fourth woman said. "And I don't know what I am!" They all chuckled at Deb's comment, effectively warming the icy atmosphere that gripped the room. Deb was dark complexioned, perhaps Latin American or Middle Eastern. She was the youngest of the bunch, maybe twenty-seven. I thought she was attractive, but I also saw something vaguely attractive about all of them. I no longer suspected that they wanted to boil me in a cauldron of witch's brew. They had a sincerity about them, maybe a sense of maturity or something I couldn't quite put my finger on, but I felt fairly comfortable among them. Most of the women were dressed in long, flowing skirts, and had an artsy gypsy look about them, except the younger, dark-skinned Deb, who wore blue jeans and a tank top.

"I know who I am," I said. "But exactly what I'm doing

here I don't know. Maybe you all can fill me in."

They looked at each other as if they didn't understand what I had just said, then Cynthia blurted, "Joe doesn't know as much as I thought he did!"

"What exactly *does* he know?" asked Sandy.

"Not very damn much," replied Cynthia, whose Pippi Longstocking braids flapped behind her as she laughed. "He doesn't even know anything about his own Aunt!"

"Lucille?" one of the women asked.

"Yeah, my Aunt Lucy. She died and now I'm here. Go figure."

"Well, why *are* you here?" asked Doris. Someone chuckled, and she said, "No, I mean, how did you happen to come *here*? How did you know to contact *Cynthia*?"

I sat down on the couch, made myself comfortable, and proceeded to tell them of Lucille's original letter, my subsequent trip to Montana, and of the tin box with the business card inside and "Sisters of the Sacred Circle" written on the back. I also told them about the money, although I had a lot of reservations about doing so, since I didn't really know these people. And I confessed of my persistent skepticism and how Annie was the one who actually talked me into following the mysterious trail. When I was done recounting my story, they all wanted to see the letter, so I pulled it out of my pocket, relieved that I had remembered to bring it with me.

"Incredible!" exclaimed Linda, passing the letter.

"Really!" Rhonda muttered, her ruddy complexion turning even redder. "This is unfuckingbelievable." She glanced up self-consciously, and grinned. "Pardon the French."

"So what are you saying? This is something serious?" I asked.

"What did you do with the money?" asked Sandy.

"I put it in my bank account. I spent some on the trip to Montana."

"Thirty thousand dollars?"

"No. I still have the twenty grand check at home. I'm

just going to hang onto that one. I don't want to get too deep into this if I don't have to."

"Good."

"Why good? What do you mean 'good'?!"

"Good that you're hanging onto the money and not squandering it."

Doris emerged from the kitchen, carefully balancing a large ceramic teapot and cups on a wicker tray. She went from person to person, handing them each a delicate china cup filled with an aromatic greenish tea. The women took small sips from their cups and passed the letter back and forth. I raised my cup to my nose and noticed the unusual odor of the steam rising from the tea. "What is this?" I asked, gesturing toward my cup, trying not to look repulsed.

"That's a cleansing tea. It will prepare us for the sweat tonight and the divination. Drink it all, if you can," Doris instructed.

"Sweat?" I asked.

"Sweat lodge ceremony. We're going to do a sweat to prepare for the divination," replied Rhonda rather matter-of-factly. "The sweat will purify us." She offered no further explanation, but told me to drink my tea and bring the letter. She seemed to be somehow "in charge" here. She was built like a tank, too, and I wasn't going to argue with her.

"C'mon everyone. It's time. The fire should be ready by now."

I decided to go with the flow and reminded myself to keep an open mind. Besides, I was outnumbered. Me versus six women. I chugged the bitter tea as a shiver went down my spine. Everyone stood up. Someone threw me a towel and a thin wool blanket.

"What're these for?" I asked.

"The sweat."

Of course. Silly of me to ask. The tea I drank had sunk to the pit of my empty stomach; I fought a wave of nausea. Everyone grabbed their towel and blanket, and we all filed out the back door into the darkness. Rhonda led the way, I was second in line, and the rest followed along behind. The moonless sky was strewn with stars, and a chorus of tree frogs and crickets serenaded us as we walked on a dark path behind the house, directly into the woods. When the going got too dark, someone behind lit a flashlight to keep us on the path. Our shadows cast eerily in front of us, dancing up the tree trunks and across the trail as we marched along. Foliage crowded us on both sides, and an occasional thorny bramble tugged at my pants.

"Don't worry," Rhonda whispered over her shoulder as we walked, "There's no poison ivy in here."

Ha! I thought, that's not exactly what I was worrying about. "You don't sacrifice virgins or anything like that, do you?" I asked.

"Why, are you a virgin?" someone behind asked. The rest of the group chuckled.

"No."

"Then you have nothing to worry about."

But I was hardly reassured. We walked a hundred yards or so until the woods opened into a small clearing. The trees arched overhead, but the center remained open. Smoke from a fire in the middle of the clearing snaked its way through the opening in the trees and disappeared into the pitch black sky above. A fire had burned down to a large bed of red coals and a number of softball-sized rocks sat in their midst. Off to one side, about fifteen feet from the fire, sat a small, dome-like structure. In the darkness, it looked like an igloo covered with blankets. Several plastic gallon milk jugs sat on the ground beside it.

The women set their towels down on a log and gathered around the fire. They gestured for me to join them. The firelight danced on the front of our bodies as we reached out and joined hands in a circle around the low flames. I didn't know what they were doing, but I did my best to follow along. We stood quietly for a few minutes, hand in hand, arms outstretched in order for our circle to reach completely around the fire. Some of the women had their eyes closed, some cast their eyes heavenward, some stared at the glowing coals. They looked deep in thought. I kept my eyes wide open to make sure I didn't miss anything. The mood became somber. Then Doris started to sing in a soft, melodious voice. The rest of the women joined in, one at a time. They repeated a few words over and over, harmonically combining their voices into a haunting melody.

Earth my body,
water my blood,
air my breath and
fire my spirit.

Their voices reached a crescendo each time they sang the last three words, as if defiantly announcing their spiritual nature. I self-consciously stared at the fire. Just when I thought the song was going to go on forever, they suddenly stopped singing. Then we let go of our hands and the women began unbuttoning their shirts and removing their shoes.

"I hope you're not uncomfortable with nudity," young Deb whispered as she yanked off her jeans. "Because you

The lodge of the Sisters of the Sacred Circle
prior to the sweat ceremony.

need to get naked. We're going into the lodge now, and our contact with the ground helps us to connect with the Earth."

I watched, with some embarrassment, as all of the women completely undressed and slowly crawled on their hands and knees into a small hole in the side of the igloo-lodge. Each carried a towel; one-by-one they disappeared into the semi-spherical black abyss.

"C'mon Joe! Bring your towel," someone whispered from inside.

Well, it was dark enough, and I'd always considered myself willing to try anything once. I figured there were worse fates than sitting around a fire with naked women on a Monday night in an igloo, so off came the clothes and into the lodge I went, stark naked on my hands and knees like the rest of them. Rhonda sat beside the entrance and guided me past her as I crawled in. Someone shut the door behind me. The ground was damp and chilly. "Sit here," she whispered, patting a layer of straw beside her. It was so dark I couldn't see a damn thing and had to be guided by sound and touch. As soon as I was seated, Rhonda crawled out through the doorway, leaving it slightly ajar. Through the small gap I caught a glimpse of her large naked body poking through the fire with a pitchfork. She was back at the door in seconds.

"Hot one coming in!" she warned.

Doris, who was on the other side of the door, held the flap back and grabbed the pitchfork handle with one hand. She very carefully guided the red hot rock that was balanced on the tines into the lodge. Rhonda, bent over and peering through the door hole, held firmly to the pitch fork. The two of them directed the glowing stone over a breadbox-sized hole, about a foot deep, in the middle of the earth floor. Doris yelled, "Okay, let 'er go!" and Rhonda tilted the fork, dropping the brick-sized rock deftly into the depression. The ground sizzled as the intensely hot stone cooked the moist earth. Although I couldn't see smoke, I could feel it burning my eyes. Rhonda went back to the fire and got another rock, then another, and another, and, with Doris's help, dropped each one into the hole in the lodge floor until it overflowed. An intense heat radiated from the stones. Rhonda crawled back in and shut the door tightly behind her, leaving us with only the faint glow of red stones in the center of an inky blackness. Sweat almost immediately began beading on my skin.

I couldn't hear anything except heavy breathing. Then Rhonda began to speak. "This is the womb of the Earth Mother. We ask her for purification. We rejoice as we feel her strength and power under our bodies, as our ancestors have since the beginning of time. I hold this cup of water, the water of life, the blood of the Earth Mother, and I pray for the guidance we need for our brother Joseph. I pray for our beloved sister, Lucille, who has passed into the universe. I pray that her spirit will join us now and guide us tonight." Rhonda emptied the cup's contents on the stones and a great hissing sound preceded a rapidly rising cloud of steam. The hot cloud, although invisible in the darkness, billowed to the top of the hut and rolled down along the outside walls and over our backs, enveloping us in a sweltering heat. Sweat poured profusely from my body. I could feel a hand reach for me in the dark as it groped my right knee. I took it in my own hand, then I reached out to the left and took Rhonda's hand.

We were all presumably joined hand-in-hand, some breathing deeply, almost gasping, when another melodious chant began, this time by Rhonda.

> *Where I sit is holy,*
> *holy is the ground.*
> *Forest, mountain, river,*
> *listen to the sound.*
> *Great spirit circles all around me.*

Everyone joined in the chant, which was repeated over and over. I eventually joined in, quietly at first, then louder as my deeper voice balanced the tone of the six female voices in the lodge. The chanting continued, developing into what seemed to be a trance-like atmosphere. Then suddenly, our voices merged into a single voice. For a brief moment, no separation existed between them, there was only one voice and it was no one's voice and everyone's voice at the same time. At that point, we abruptly ended the chant together, on the same note, as if by magic. I was stupefied and exhilarated at the same time by this phenomenon. I had never experienced anything like it.

"I will pass the cup," Rhonda announced quietly. The cool glugging of water could be heard being poured from a plastic milk jug. In the hazy glow, I could just barely see the cup being passed between shadowy silhouettes, traveling clockwise. When the cup reached Doris's hands, she began voicing aloud her life's hopes and concerns. When she finished, she poured the water onto the hissing stones and began another chant. We soon joined her and chanted together until our voices merged again into that single, incredible voice. This procedure continued around the circle from person to person until the lodge dripped in hot steam and our bodies issued sweat from every pore. At one point the heat was so unbearable I had to put my face to the ground where a tiny bit of coolness remained.

Finally, the cup came full circle to me. Whoever had the cup obviously had the "floor," so to speak, and the others simply listened, or allowed the cup holder to be silent if she so chose. With the cup of water in hand, I took a sip, as I had heard others do, and thanked everyone for including me in this experience. I confessed that I had never been in a sweat lodge before and didn't usually hang around (no pun intended) in the company of naked women. I jokingly added that it was something I could get used to and maybe even learn to enjoy — the naked part, that is — I wasn't sure about the sweat lodge. I said I would prefer a hottub next time. Nobody laughed. I admitted that I never did much singing, but that the chanting experience in the lodge had been satisfying in some inexplicable way. In jest, I couldn't resist telling them that the whole experience was my idea of a tea party in hell. I voiced some doubts about whether this experience is what my aunt had intended for me, and I hoped out loud that there would be a cooling off period at some point. Then I poured my share of the water on the stones, and waited. After only a few minutes of silence, Rhonda crawled out the door. Everyone followed, one at a time. I was the last one out.

In the cool night air, steam rose from our bodies like smoke from chimneys. Little was spoken, the mood was quiet and serious as we stood around the fire. Rhonda picked up a jug of water and poured it over Cynthia's shoulders and down her back. Cynthia gasped in relief, took another jug, and rinsed the sweat off her legs. Each of us rinsed in this manner, one by one. I reached for my clothes.

"We don't need to dress yet, Joseph. We need to do the divination now, and clothes would just impede our connection," Rhonda whispered.

"Connection to what? What divination?"

"Now that we've purified ourselves in the sweat, we're going to consult the Cards. They always reveal the truth. They'll answer your questions."

7

Divination

THE SIX WOMEN FORMED A CIRCLE ON THE GROUND TO
one side of the fire, sitting cross-legged on their towels and
facing each other. They sat close enough for their knees to
touch, and their blankets were wrapped over their shoulders. My towel was placed in the center of the circle. "Sit
here, Joseph," I was instructed.

I carefully stepped through the circle of women and
started to sit down, wrapping my towel around my waist.
"Face me," whispered Rhonda. I turned to face her; she
seemed to be sitting at the head of the circle, if there was
one, and I sat cross-legged like the rest of them with the
fire at my back. My blanket was handed to me and I
wrapped it around my shoulders like everyone else. The
evening air was beginning to feel cool on my bare skin.

I seemed to be in an altered state of consciousness. My
brain felt very elastic and passive and I didn't feel like
talking. I was hungry and tired and I didn't know what was
in that tea they gave me earlier, but now I was feeling very
strange. My intellectual processes seemed to have gone
into neutral. Although I could still think very clearly, I was
no longer dwelling on my thoughts. I was going with the
flow of things, watching images gently pass through my
mind like leaves floating on the surface of a stream. It was

an extraordinary state of mind, one completely unfamiliar to me.

The women joined hands. Rhonda took my hands in hers. The women on either side of her put their free hand on Rhonda's knee. In this way, we were all physically connected, all touching each other. The circle of women bowed their heads and became totally silent except for their deep breathing. The only sound other than the crackling fire behind me was the constant, piercing call of tree frogs hidden in the surrounding trees.

Rhonda closed her eyes momentarily. Then she looked at me and said, "Joseph, we're going to do a reading now. We'll ask the powers that can't be seen to come to us and reveal information about your situation." She placed my hands on her knees. Reaching into a canvas bag behind her, she pulled out a small black velvet pouch and untied its drawstring, removing what appeared to be a deck of thick, oversized playing cards. Handing the cards to Sandy, who sat on her left, she placed her hands upon mine, which were still resting on her knees. I tried as best I could to hold my gaze onto her eyes. I felt like I was looking through her, rather than at her.

Sandy held the cards for a moment, closed her eyes, then passed the deck clockwise, to Deb. This was repeated until the cards had been passed, full circle. Rhonda again took the cards and held them between her breasts, to her heart, eyes closed. After shuffling through the deck, she chose one card, all the while holding me with her piercing gaze. She laid the selected card face up on the ground in front of me, between my knees.

"The King of Rods is your personal card, Joseph. This card represents you specifically. It signifies a gentleman of noble character, usually married, just, and honest. A countryman."

Leaving the card on the ground, she held the deck to her breast again and closed her eyes, breathing deeply. She opened her eyes, stared into mine, and drew another card from the deck. "This is your character card," she said, laying it on her right knee. "It's the Ace of Swords. This card represents a personal triumph, one of great force." She stared at it curiously, then returned it to the deck. "However, it may represent a negative or a positive force that you vanquish. That remains to be seen. Take this deck in your own hands and hold it to your heart."

I did as she instructed.

Then she spoke in a low, earnest voice. "Close your eyes. Focus your thoughts on your situation. Think of your aunt and her instructions, and ask for her guidance. Try to be single-minded. Concentrate." At this point, all the women began to hum in a manner reminiscent of the chanting they had done earlier. The sound was soothing and caused me to go deep within myself, almost into a trance. I concentrated as best I could. The sweat lodge had left me feeling like a rung-out washrag, relaxed and limp. Holding the cards against my chest in both hands, head bowed, I thought about Lucy and everything that had happened so far. After these thoughts passed, all thoughts then left me, and I was filled with only a question: "What should I do now?"

"Shuffle the cards, please."

I slowly shuffled them until I thought they were thoroughly mixed. "Cut the deck into three piles and set the three piles face down on the ground in front of you."

I did so, placing the three piles of cards in the narrow space between our legs. Rhonda picked up the three piles and put them back together into a single deck. The other women continued holding hands and quietly chanting. One by one, Rhonda removed cards from the top of the deck and laid them in the space between us. She set my "personal" card, the King of Rods, in the center. The first card she drew off the deck was laid on top of my personal card. She laid the second card on top of that one, turning it sideways. The third was laid above the personal card, the fourth below it, the fifth to the left, the sixth to the right; the seventh, eighth, ninth, and tenth cards were placed in a vertical row to the right of all the cards. After drawing the ten cards, she set the remaining deck behind her, out of sight.

Rhonda stared at the cards, wide-eyed at first, then, after quite some time, her eyes narrowed. The women, as if on cue, abruptly ceased chanting.

Finally, she broke the silence in a whisper. "This is what the cards say about you and your situation, Joseph. Listen carefully," she instructed. "Your personal card is covered by the Judgement card. That is the first card I drew. The Judgement card covers you completely. It signifies that you are growing in awareness, that you will have a shift in personal consciousness toward a union with the Universal. It is a very significant card to be covering you, and it means that you're being watched over by angels in regard to this situation. It also may mean something more ominous. The card shows the archangel Gabriel, and thereby signifies the Last Judgement. That may mean he is heralding either souls to the heavens, or ushering in a cosmic shift of some sort. Somehow this will overshadow everything you do in regard to this situation."

"You are being crossed by the Eight of Rods. That is the second card I drew. It represents forces of either good or evil, and signifies great expectations, and a powerful momentum toward a desired end. It speaks of a rapid movement toward a goal, and of a spiritual journey. It's a traveling card. Your journeying is not over — you must travel again."

"You are crowned by the Nine of Cups. That is the third card, the one above you. It represents what you aim for, but what has not yet happened. It is your card for the future. The Nine of Cups signifies victory, well-being, and happiness. It is the ideal which you yearn for."

"The fourth card, the one beneath you, represents what has already happened. It is the Seven of Cups. This is your foundation card. You are building upon this now. The Seven of Cups signifies earnest seeking, but it suggests that you lack a tenacity to translate ideas into reality."

"The fifth card represents an influence that has just

passed or is now passing. It is The Fool. For you this card is not reversed or upside down, so it's a positive card. It represents both nothingness and unlimited potential. It says that you must make an important choice, and it's telling you that you should not try to do it alone, that you should seek guidance."

"Your sixth card represents what will happen in the near future. It is the Eight of Swords, and it signifies an inability to extricate yourself from a difficult situation. Although you must go on with your endeavor, you will feel bound and trapped."

"Your own attitude toward this situation is indicated by the seventh card. It is the Ace of Swords. It is the card of triumph."

"The eighth card represents the attitude of your friends and family. It is the environment that surrounds you in this situation. It is the Seven of Swords, and it says that those in your environment believe that you're not doing your task well or properly. They think your planning is bad and will fail, although they may not be thinking clearly on this issue. You may become dispirited by others."

"The Sun has appeared as your ninth card. It indicates your desire for contentment, liberation, and attainment of personal goals."

"The last card, the tenth, is a culmination of all the preceding cards. It is the Moon." At this, Rhonda stared at the cards and shook her head, almost imperceptibly. "The moon is a reflector. It may reflect your subconscious, or something else," she spoke quietly. "The Moon signifies disillusionment and fear. You will have a deep yearning for security and fulfillment. You may be faced with a harsh and perilous period, including deception. You and your loved ones may be exposed to threatening situations."

Rhonda fell silent. After a moment, I asked, "What does that mean?"

"What does it all mean, Joseph? If I must interpret this for you, then let me say this," She closed her eyes, took my hands in hers, paused a moment, then said, "It seems obvious that you are destined to pursue a journey of some sort. You have become embroiled in something greater than you can understand at this moment and you cannot extricate yourself from this situation. You have felt trapped and reluctant to continue, but you *must* continue. It is your destiny. You believe in yourself, and have a strong confidence that you can achieve your goals, but others around you do not see you in this way; you may become disheartened by them. You have blundered your way so far with doubts and skepticism, and now you must earnestly and with utmost seriousness seek out the guidance of others. You must physically travel yet again, and at times you may be faced with difficult, even perilous, situations. However, you will be watched over by an Angel or Angels, perhaps even the Archangel Gabriel, the one who is prophesied to rule over Armageddon. The cards know all and would tell us more if we were clear enough to ask the right questions."

"So, where do I go from here?"

"We don't know."

"Well, how do I find out?"

"We can consult a crystal."

"What crystal?"

"A sacred crystal. In my house. On the windowsill."

8

The Crystal

WE DRESSED QUIETLY BY THE LAST LIGHT OF THE FIRE'S dying embers and slowly shuffled back toward the house through the wooded darkness. I was dead tired, starving, and had some leaves stuck in my underwear. Furthermore, a nagging specter of skepticism continued to lurk in a corner of my mind. I wondered how much accuracy I could assign to a deck of cards. There *had* been a ring of truth to what Rhonda had said, and the Fool card kept haunting me. Was I a fool for *doing* this, or a fool for being so *skeptical* about it? The card showed a person looking away as he was about to step off a cliff to a sure death. Did that mean I should be looking forward? Or should I stop all progress before I get myself killed? Needless to say, I was more confused than ever.

"Let's consult the crystal before we eat," suggested Cynthia. All the women seemed to agree, although I didn't know what they were talking about. I tried to ask them about this crystal thing as we walked back through the woods, but they just told me to wait and see. Back inside the house, Rhonda drew open the curtain on the picture window in her living room to reveal a row of quartz crystals and other stones arranged carefully on the window sill.

"The crystals sit in the sunlight during the day for recharging," she said, picking out a large, clear quartz point about six inches long. She inspected the crystal closely, and put it back.

"What's that supposed to mean?" I asked.
"Recharging? How does a rock 'charge'?"

"By the sun. That's not the right one, anyway. Here, let's use this one," she said, offering no further explanation. She picked up a smaller pointed crystal, pencil-thin and about three inches long, and cradled it in the palm of her hand.

Rhonda tied a short, thin hemp cord around the blunt end of the crystal, then laid the contraption on the edge of the circular coffee table in the living room. Unrolling a large world map, she spread it out on the table, securing its upturned corners with four ceramic coasters, then placed the crystal on top of the map, near its center.

Deb struck a match and lit one end of what appeared to be a small, tight bundle of straw, about the size of a large cucumber, which began smoking profusely. She carefully waved the smoking bundle around each of us, one at a time, directing the smoke onto our bodies with her hand. "This is a smudge stick of sweet grass and sage," she said. "The smoke purifies us before we consult the crystal."

All six women knelt around the coffee table, insisting that I join them. Rhonda held the free end of the foot long cord with her right hand, allowing the crystal to dangle a couple of inches over the map's center. Each of us placed our right hand on Rhonda's, one at a time, clockwise; we did the same with our left hands. Rhonda's large hands seemed like iron, and the entire mass of hands was very solid and surprisingly motionless. The crystal point remained suspended at the end of the hemp cord, fractions of an inch above the map.

"Let's close our eyes tightly," she said, "Very tightly. Concentrate on the pressure behind your eyelids. Concentrate." A gentle "om" chant began, and I quietly joined in. The kneeling women began to lean back and forth in a slow sideways rhythm, moving me with them, our hips, arms, and shoulders touching. "Concentrate on the pressure behind your eyelids," I heard Deb's voice whisper. The quiet chanting continued, as we moved like seaweed coaxed by gentle waves, leaning slightly one way, then another, back and forth, chanting, concentrating on our eyelids, gracefully weaving and undulating, chanting hypnotically, focusing. The clump of hands suspended in mid-air in front of us became very warm. This went on for quite some time, perhaps for hours. I was soon in some sort of trance, it seemed, and time became unnoticeable and irrelevant. I could feel my knees on the carpet beneath me, and the warm pressure on my hips and arms from the women on either side, first pressing against my right side, then my left, over and over again, pushing me ever so gently back and forth, back and forth. My eyes remained closed.

Eventually, I became completely oblivious to everything, as if I had fallen fast asleep. My mind became totally blank, and although I was physically present, I was not there in any other way. Strange visions tumbled through my head uncontrollably, as if I was drifting into a dream world, sinking deeper and deeper. Suddenly, the chanting and movement stopped. I impulsively snapped opened my eyes. The women were staring at me, smiling. The crystal lay on the map, utterly still. "Don't move," Rhonda whispered. "Remove your hands very slowly and carefully, one at a time," We did as she said. She set the hemp cord on the map, careful not to disturb the crystal.

"There you have it, Joseph," she said, with a nod of her head toward the map and a pleased look on her face. I looked down at the table. The sharp point of the crystal lay directly on St. John's, Newfoundland.

9

Newfoundland

I WAS WEARY ON THE RIDE BACK TO CYNTHIA'S, FIGHTING the urge to sleep in the car. It was two a.m. and she was rattling on about the Sisters and their uncanny abilities. I was half listening to her and half lost in thoughts of my own, having undergone a steep learning curve regarding altered states of consciousness, witchcraft, divination, groups of naked women, and other things which I had previously known little about.

"Why Newfoundland?" I finally asked.

"How should I know?"

"Well, how should I know, either? What's in Newfoundland?"

"I have no idea, Joe. It's a long way out there, isn't it? The map showed it to be the farthest point east on the North American continent. Do you think the direction 'east' has something to do with it?"

"Hell if I know, but I can't imagine actually *going* there. Where would I go, anyway? St. John's? What's there?"

"Don't ask me."

"Well, who do I ask? A goddam crystal? What's with this crystal thing anyway?"

"The crystal is simply a tool, Joe. It is, to a diviner, or

---

group like the Sisters, as a hammer is to a carpenter. If you know how to use it, it gets something done."

"I'm not following you."

"The crystal has no power of it's own, in the same way a hammer is useless without the carpenter. The people who *use* the tool have the power. Practice makes perfect. A good carpenter can wield a hammer rather deftly, don't you think?"

"Yes, *and* ...?"

"We Sisters can use crystals as tools to focus our *own* energy. It was the focus and concentration of *our* power that has pointed you to Newfoundland. It wasn't the crystal. That was just the tool we happened to use. People have used ritual practices and sacred tools for eons to reach into the subconscious and do seemingly supernatural things. But it's totally natural and anyone can do it — it just takes practice. And it works. I've never been to Newfoundland myself. I bet it's an interesting place."

We bantered back and forth about Newfoundland, a subject neither of us knew anything about, and finally dropped the topic entirely and talked about our kids instead. Before we knew it, we had arrived back at Cynthia's. I quickly offered a short good-bye, explaining that I was tired and had more than an hour's drive ahead of me. Although Cynthia offered me the couch at her place, I politely declined and was soon fighting the late-night truck traffic on Interstate 80. I made it home to a dark and quiet house, and stumbled upstairs to bed. Annie was sound asleep. I glanced at the clock; it was 3:30 a.m.

I slept late into the morning, dragging myself out of bed around noon. "I didn't even hear you come in last night," Annie commented when I stumbled downstairs looking for a cup of coffee. "Where were you? Why did you come in so late? What happened?" After a few minutes of interrogation, I managed to explain the events that had transpired the evening before as best I could. A lot had happened during the night and I had to skip over some of the details. The one event of the evening that most interested Annie was the crystal, and the fact that it pointed to Newfoundland. When she heard that part of the story her face first drew a blank expression, and she stared at the wall of the dining room as if lost in a daydream. "Newfoundland?" she finally asked. "For heaven's sake, *why?*"

We got out a map and looked up Newfoundland. From our home in western Pennsylvania, the distance to Newfoundland was equal to the distance to the Yucatan Peninsula of Mexico. Not exactly a weekend getaway.

"I think we may have reached a dead end with this Newfoundland thing," I told Annie. "I'm drawing a complete blank. There's no way I would actually go all the way the hell up there. I don't know a soul anywhere near that place. This is looking like it may become the world's biggest wild goose chase!"

"Wild moose chase, I think," Annie joked. "Maybe you don't need to go there, anyway. Just because a crystal pointed to Newfoundland doesn't mean you have to *go* there. Maybe something *from* there will provide a clue."

"Such as? Last night's cards said I had more traveling to do. That's why it seemed to me that the message was for me to *go* to Newfoundland." I realized what I'd just said and shook my head in utter disbelief. "I can't believe I'm even considering for a second that a damn dumb deck of cards should tell me what to do. Or a crystal for that matter."

"Now don't be so skeptical. What was that Fool card all about? I think it may have hit the nail on the head."

"Thanks a lot."

"Seriously, though, sometimes you just have to let go and allow things to happen. You know — *trust*. You're not always in control, and only a fool would think he was. We don't go through life always following an exact road map. Sometimes we have to wander off the beaten path and stumble through the bushes to find the real treasures."

"Okay, Ralph Waldo Emerson, I get the point."

Annie's eyes widened as if a profound thought had just

occurred to her. My brain wasn't quite working yet, but it seemed that hers was. "*You* don't know anyone in Newfoundland, but maybe *Lucy* did."

"What?"

"Didn't you get an address book out of her house?"

I jumped out of my chair, nearly knocking over my tea cup, and went to my office to find the address book. Back at the dining room table, I leafed through the small, black book, page by page, starting with the A's.

"Boy, I'm glad I thought of this," I said, as Annie made a face that would have turned a lesser man to stone. "Ah Ha! I'll be damned. Here's a listing in Nova Scotia!" I scanned down each page quickly. "And here's a listing in Newfoundland!" I marked the page, scanned the remainder of the book, and went back to what was the only name with a Newfoundland address: Professor Brian Gaulton, St John's. "There's a phone number." I said. I stared at Annie and she stared at me.

"Well?" she asked.

"Well what?"

"Call the number!"

"Well, I *will*. Give me some time, dammit." I hesitantly walked over to the phone hanging on the wall, and I dialed the number. It was busy.

"Maybe we should wait a minute and think about what we're going to say to this person before you call again," Annie advised.

"What's this '*we*' business? Maybe *you* should call him."

"You're doing just fine," she assured me.

"Well, I just want to get to the bottom of this. This is the only clue linking me to Newfoundland at this moment and I need to talk to this guy, whoever he is. Who knows, maybe he's expecting my call like Cynthia was." I hit the redial button. It rang.

"St. John's College," answered a receptionist's voice.

"I'd like to speak with Brian Gaulton, please."

"Sir Gaulton? One moment. I'll connect you."

(Pause) "Hello?"

"Is this Brian Gaulton?"

"Speaking," said an amiable voice.

"Hi. This is Joe Jenkins. I'm calling from Pennsylvania in the United States. I was wondering if you would have a few minutes right now to talk."

"Well sir, you're in for a bit of luck, aren't you? You caught me in my office, which is very unusual. Very unusual. I was just leaving for home. In two moments I would have been out the door. What can I do for you?"

"Well, I'm not really sure."

"Ah. Well, that's helpful," he laughed.

"What I mean is, I'm in the process of doing some work for my Aunt Lucille Boggs. I think you knew her."

"Dr. Boggs. Yes, I did. Of course."

"Well, part of my work has something to do with Newfoundland, but I'm not exactly sure what it is. I know this doesn't sound like it makes much sense, but I understand that you may have had some connection with Lucy."

"Of course I did. She was a great and trusted friend of mine and a colleague, and I admired her very much. Her death was a great loss to us all." He paused, as if considering what he should say next. "However, as far as your work is concerned, I will not discuss anything that has to do with her over the telephone."

"Did you work together?"

"Look, Mr. Jenkins. I don't know you or what you really want. Dr. Boggs *may* have been your aunt. Maybe she was, maybe she wasn't. If you *are* her nephew and you really want to talk with me about her, then you'll have to do it in person."

"Mr. Gaulton, I did say I was calling from Pennsylvania. How can I talk with you in person?"

"My formal title is Sir Gaulton. Most refer to me as Professor Gaulton. I'm at St. John's College. My office is in room 217. I have office hours every day from noon to 2 pm. Sorry to be this way, Mr. Jenkins, but I have little choice under the circumstances. Would you like to make an appointment?"

"Let's cut to the chase, Mr. Gaulton. Professor. Lucy requested of me, posthumously, to take on a project of hers. She wasn't very clear about the exact nature of the project and I'm trying to figure out what to do. Your name has come up, via quite extraordinary circumstances, as someone who may be able to help me. So far, I've been running from one place to another, covering great distances, at great expense, losing sleep over this, and, as far as I can tell, getting nowhere. I don't know whether this is all a colossal waste of my time and energy, or what. The thought of traveling yet another huge distance to talk to someone I don't know regarding an uncertain subject seems a little unrealistic to me. I *do* have the money and I could afford a plane ticket to St. John's, but how do I know it would be worthwhile?"

"I can't promise you anything, Mr. Jenkins. Whether your efforts would be worth anything would be entirely up to you. I am quite familiar with Dr. Boggs' interests. She was particularly enamored with an entomological theory of mine that she felt related quite closely to her own understanding of what she considered a dreadful human condition. I would be happy to talk with you about it — in person. I can even show you a real-life example if you have any luck at all. Remember that great things do not occur without some risk taking on the part of the participant, Mr. Jenkins. How about two weeks from tomorrow? Meet me in my office at noon? I really do need to be going now."

"Uh, noon, two weeks from tomorrow. Alright," I said resignedly. "I'll see what I can do. Do you have a fax number? I'll fax you a verification as soon as I book the flight."

"Sure thing."

I wrote down Professor Gaulton's fax number, said goodbye, and hung up the phone. "Well, how would you like to go on a wild moose chase with me? To Newfoundland?" I asked Annie, who was practically hanging on me, wanting to know what plans had been made on the phone. "In two weeks."

"See, I told you. I *knew* you were supposed to call that guy. I've always wanted to go to Newfoundland, too, moose chase or no moose chase."

"Really? I didn't know that."

"There are lots of things you don't know about me, dear," she said with a cryptic grin.

"Oh great, that's all I need right now — more mysteries to solve!"

10

Hive Animals

WE ARRANGED FOR PENELOPE TO STAY AT HER GRAND-mother's house for a few days, faxed our itinerary to Gaulton, and took a Thursday morning flight from Pittsburgh to St. John's. At the St. John's airport, we picked up a small rental car, a cherry red two-door compact — the cheapest car available. My meeting with Professor Gaulton was scheduled for the next day, and we decided to take advantage of our extra time by touring the area.

The day we arrived was blustery and overcast, but by late afternoon the sun had started to poke out from behind the thick clouds. We spent the afternoon driving along the sea coast and enjoying some of the beautiful ocean vistas on this rugged island, soaking up the sea air like sponges.

In St. John's, the local people were amazingly friendly; even the drivers were unbelievably courteous. If we stopped along a curb to cross a street while walking through the city, the traffic in both directions would stop to let us cross. In Pittsburgh, had we tried a stunt like that we would've been flattened like roadkill. We liked Newfoundland immediately, and we found St. John's to be a charming, progressive city with lots of quaint restaurants and pubs. We took advantage of this, and spent the evening strolling from pub to pub, trying out the local brews.

The following day, after getting directions at the hotel, we decided to walk the few short blocks to St. John's College. The grounds were strangely quiet; only a few students milled about the campus. I realized that the college

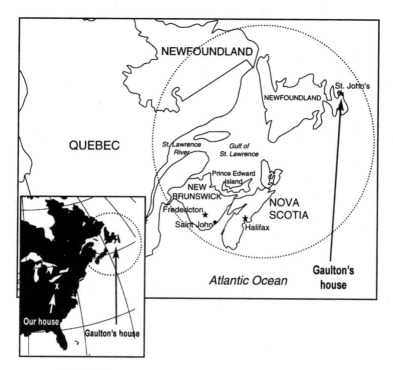

was probably between terms, and that the summer school student population was small.

We easily located the building that housed Professor Gaulton's office. Like most of the structures on campus, it had a faded brick facade and a green and purple slate roof. Hand in hand, Annie and I climbed the set of stone steps leading to the heavy front doors. After finding our way to room 217 on the second floor, I rapped loudly. The door swung wide, and a short, middle-aged, balding man with a dark ring of hair, impeccably dressed in a black suit and lavender tie, stood before us, wearing a blank expression. When I introduced the two of us, a broad smile flashed across his face. "Ah ha! Yes! Come in! Please do come in and make yourselves at home." Professor Gaulton gestured with a sweep of his arm, ushering us into his office. "Please, have a seat. Here, Mrs. Jenkins, please, sit," he said. "Make yourselves comfortable. Can I get you some coffee?"

What ensued was a seemingly interminable string of courtesies and hospitable gestures, and we soon had coffee and shortbread cookies in hand. Professor Gaulton's office was small, dim, and stuffy, reminding me of Lucy's abandoned cottage on the Indian reservation. Book cases crammed with books and plastic models of insects lined two walls from floor to ceiling. A small window opposite the door afforded only a limited view of the tiny campus. An enormous oak desk cluttered with papers, books, and framed photographs, dominated the middle of the room. Large posters of praying mantis life cycles and insect pests covered the wall around the door. A coffee-maker and a tin of cookies sat within arm's reach of the desk.

I surveyed the piles of books in every corner of the room. "How long have you been here, at this college, Professor Gaulton?"

"Nearly 30 years, sir. I'm now considering retiring, in fact. But what would I do if I retire? This has been my whole life. Maybe I could get a job flipping hamburgers?" The professor leaned back in his chair, threw his head back, placed his hands on his round belly and began to shake. A booming laugh erupted from his smiling face. After a bit of such jovial chit-chat we soon warmed up to each other enough to get to the meat of things, and at one point, Annie simply asked, "Do you know what we're doing here, Professor? Because we don't, and we've come a very long way. I sure hope you can help us."

"Yeah, you wouldn't believe how we got here," I added.

"If it had anything to do with Dr. Boggs, I would probably believe it," he replied.

"Well, at my aunt's suggestion—"

"And how did she make a suggestion to you while dead, if you don't mind me asking?" he interrupted, raising an eyebrow.

"She left me a note."

"Oh. Okay. Whatever works. What kind of note?"

"After Lucy died, her lawyers sent me a letter that

she'd written. Her letter requested for me to go to her house in Montana where she had left some things for me." Professor Gaulton listened intently. "One of those things was a business card that led me to a group of women who call themselves the Sisters of the Sacred Circle."

"Were these women nuns?" he asked, obviously unfamiliar with the Sisters.

"Not by any stretch of the imagination. They're Wiccans."

"Oh yes. I'm familiar with that. Neowitchcraft."

"Well, it was certainly new to me. Anyway, at the meeting I had with these sisters, they suggested that there was a good reason for me to go to Newfoundland. Trouble is, they didn't say what that reason was."

"How did they decide upon Newfoundland, if I may be so bold as to ask?"

"They consulted a quartz crystal."

The professor leaned back and let out another of his earthquake laughs. "That sounds just like something Dr. Boggs would do! I fear you've bitten off more than you can chew! Yes sir, Dr. Boggs, she was like that. Ha!"

"Yes, I know it sounds bizarre. It's a long story, but believe me, it's been interesting. Basically, the Sisters used a crystal to point to a place on a map. They said I had a journey to take and the crystal would show me where to go. It pointed exactly to St. John's, Newfoundland. I couldn't figure out any connection until I looked through the address book I'd found in Lucy's house. You were the only contact I could find in Newfoundland, and you were even in St. John's. That's why I called *you*. So here we are, and feeling rather foolish to have come so far on such scant information. I hope we're not wasting our time or yours by being here."

"We don't usually have crystals make our decisions for us, professor. We're not that kind of people," Annie said.

"Under normal circumstances," I added. "But these aren't normal circumstances. You see, my aunt left us some money and asked us to finish a project of hers. Trouble is, she didn't say what the project was. So we're kind of groping through the dark with this thing, trying to figure it out. We're hoping you can help us."

The professor looked a bit startled. "Incredible. So the crystal sent you to me, did it?" He strummed his thick fingers on the desktop. "Well, I think that maybe I can help you."

Annie and I looked at each other, relieved.

"I believe you are who you say you are. And I think I can give you a piece of Dr. Boggs' puzzle. But only a piece. I don't know what the project is that you speak of, but I may be able to provide some information that could prove useful. You see, your Aunt Lucy, as you call her, was very interested in my entomological work. She was a scientist in every respect, and she had a keen understanding of interrelationships. A couple of years ago, she attended one of my presentations at a conference. She hounded me ever since."

"What sort of presentation was it?"

"Hive insects. I did a honeybee presentation. What I refer to as their 'Robbing Frenzy.' It's a behavioral aberration that has thus far been exhibited only by honeybees, as far as anyone knows. We've been aware of this behavior for quite some time and find it to be very interesting. Perplexing, in fact. Extraordinary."

"Why would Lucy be interested in honeybees?"

"Oh, she wasn't, actually. Her species of interest was *Homo sapiens*."

"What do you mean? You're an entomologist, a specialist in insects, not an anthropologist, aren't you?"

"Precisely. It's quite simple, Mr. Jenkins. Dr. Boggs considered humans to be herd animals in small groups, and hive animals in large groups, such as in cities. An interesting theory, I must say. She thought that the Robbing Frenzy anomaly was possibly not limited to honeybees, afterall. It was her belief that this perplexing psychological behavior is also being exhibited by one species of mammal. And that this behavior, if it continues, may lead, in effect, to the demise of our entire planetary ecosystem and destroy the delicate ecological balance of the Earth itself. All indications are that such destruction is already underway."

"What mammal, Professor Gaulton?" asked Annie.

"Why, *Homo sapiens*, human beings, of course." The Professor gathered up some papers on his desk, placed them in his briefcase, and snapped the latches shut. He rose from his chair and brushed a piece of lint off his tie. "Look, why don't you two come with me to my home? I live outside the city on about forty acres, right on the seashore. I have the rest of the day off, and I noticed this morning that the damned bees were up to no good. I need to go deal with that right away. It would provide you with a perfect opportunity to see *exactly* what I'm talking about. Besides, my wife makes the best apple pie you've ever eaten, and I would *insist* that you join us for dinner. Just watch out for moose on the road. We don't see them very often this close to the city anymore, but if you hit one with your car, you may as well drive into a stone wall."

11

Robbing Frenzy

WE FOLLOWED THE PROFESSOR'S SMALL, WELL-WORN
pickup truck out of the city, winding through pine forests
and rocky shorelines dotted with peat bogs. The gray sky
had opened up and fingers of sunlight reached through the
scattered, cottony clouds. The constant, stiff wind that had
buffeted us since our arrival was finally dying down and it
looked like the day was going to turn out nice afterall.

Twenty miles later, we arrived at a modest, white,
wood-frame house sitting about a hundred yards off the
road. The gravel driveway was hedged on the left by high,
prickly gorse-like bushes sprinkled with small, pale-yellow
flowers. To our right sat an old, freshly painted, white,
wood-framed garage, which leaned slightly, as if surrender-
ing to the constant ocean breeze. On a small patch of lawn
beside the garage, a woman sat in a collapsible lawn chair,
spinning wool with a drop spindle. As we drove past, she
looked up and smiled. Professor Gaulton swung his little
pickup into the garage, and we stopped on the grassy edge
of the lane beside it.

Gaulton greeted his wife as he emerged from the
garage and then introduced us. Judy was in her late fifties
and was rather nice looking. The sunlight splashing on the
last remnants of auburn in her graying hair brought out
the hazel color in her eyes, while her rosy cheeks gave her

---

a healthy, vibrant glow. She remained seated on the chair and continued to spin from a woven reed basket full of black wool as she welcomed us. The afternoon weather had become glorious.

"Nice place you have here," I said, admiring the neatly kept homestead. A small orchard laden with pink and white blossoms could be seen behind the house, and a newly planted vegetable and flower garden practically wrapped itself around the screened porch on one side of the building. Freshly washed tea towels looking like colored prayer flags stirring in the gentle breeze, hung out to dry on a rope strung between two trees in the yard. The blue sea could be seen beyond them in the distance, stretching past small, craggy islands and extending to the horizon. Crimson wildflowers blazed along a fence line that led toward the sea, and white sheep dotted a grassy meadow as if in a Wyeth painting. The smell of salt and sea wafted in the breeze, while the shrill call of sea birds shattered the otherwise quiet sky. The property lay on an inlet protected from the rough seas that pounded the shore further out. Tiny, rocky islands pierced the water in the bay.

"This is gorgeous!" exclaimed Annie, looking toward the verdant meadow and the endless blue sea beyond.

"We've been here a long time," Judy replied, "and we wouldn't want to be anywhere else. Places like this are hard to find nowadays."

"You can say that again! How long have you been here?"

Judy glanced at the professor. "How long, Brian? Maybe twenty-five years, don't you think?"

"About that," the professor said absentmindedly. "Listen honey, these fine folks are related to Doctor Boggs. You remember her, don't you? She taught at the University of Montana."

"Yes, of course I remember. We all had lunch together the last time she was here, a year ago, I think it was."

"Oh, right. Well, Joe and Annie have come all the way

from Pennsylvania just to visit us and find out about one of Dr. Boggs' pet interests — the robbing frenzy of hive insects. I have to attend to one of my hives right away because it is, in fact, being robbed even as we speak. This is a perfect opportunity for them to witness this unusual behavior. Perfect!" he said, rubbing his hands together excitedly.

Judy paid him little mind, and continued her spinning. "Don't mind him," she said to us. "He gets excited about that sort of thing."

"You folks came at exactly the right time," the professor said. "The chances of coming during an actual robbing frenzy are almost nil. Maybe there's more to that crystal stuff than we realize. So we need to get suited up and over to the apiary immediately. You folks aren't allergic to bee stings, are you?"

"I don't think so," I shrugged.

"Why? Are we going to get stung?" asked Annie.

"Not necessarily. It *is* possible, but we're going to get suited up in coveralls and bee veils, just in case. I keep extra suits around for my students. Luckily, the weather is perfect. Bees are much friendlier when the skies are clear and the humidity is low. If it was cloudy and humid today, they wouldn't want us to be messing with their hives. They'd be afraid of impending rain, which would be a disaster if their hive was open and the inside got wet. In any case, all we have to do is plug some holes, which won't take long. Come along, I'll show you."

"I'll start dinner. You are staying, aren't you?" asked Judy.

"Of course they are!" the professor answered for us.

We followed him to a shed attachment on the back of the garage, and he fitted us with white coveralls, bee veils, and long gloves that went nearly up to our elbows. He pulled a bee smoker off a shelf, which looked like a cross between a beverage pitcher and a small bellows, and stuffed some burlap inside it. He wadded up a piece of newspaper and stuffed it in the smoker, too, right beside the burlap. Then he grabbed a pack of matches from a drawer and lit the paper, all the while gently squeezing on the bellows. Soon, a thick white smoke spewed out of the pitcher spout.

"Good, good," he said. "Perfect! Let's go before this damn fire goes out." He grabbed a few more pieces of burlap and stuffed them into a pocket in his coveralls. "Just in case," he said. "We don't want to run out of smoke."

"What's the smoke for?" I asked.

"It pacifies the bees. They instinctively gorge themselves on honey when exposed to smoke. They must have evolved that behavior over eons as a result of fire in or near their trees, but I don't know why exactly. It's good for bee-keepers because honeybees can't sting when gorged on honey. For one thing, they're not thinking about stinging when they have their little faces buried in a honey cell, and for another, their abdomen becomes so distended they can't bend it enough to get their stinger into anyone. So I smoke them a little whenever I work with them. All we need now is some duct tape. Where is that damn duct tape?" The professor glanced around the ceiling. "Ah, here it is! Right where it's supposed to be." He grabbed the roll of silver tape that was hanging on a nail in a ceiling joist.

We walked, somewhat awkwardly with the bee suits on, through the tall grass behind the house and toward the orchard. A line of white, wooden bee hives stood sentry-like on the edge of the pasture. As we trudged stiffly along in single file, lifting our feet high to get through the hay-field, our bee veils and white garb made us look like astronauts walking on the surface of the moon. Three paces ahead of us, the professor trailed a thin stream of smoke, adding to the strangeness of our parade. As we neared the hives Professor Gaulton suddenly stopped.

"Look. Over there. The hive on the right. Far right. See it?" He pointed a gloved hand in the direction of the hives.

Annie and I stood in awe at the sight. Each of the five hives had a steady stream of honeybees pouring in and out of what appeared to be a slot on one side of the hive body. The sweet aroma of honey hung thickly in the air. Bees flew out of these slots in droves, rising straight into the air in individual, thick, cloud-like columns, then turning and dissipating. Except something odd was happening at the hive on the far right. It was enveloped in a dense cloud of bees flying every which way.

"That's the hive being robbed." The professor pointed. "Those bees aren't friendly when they're in the middle of a robbing frenzy like that. Smoke won't help a whole lot."

"Won't they gorge themselves?"

"Not when they're robbing. Their entire psychology changes. They lose touch with their natural instincts. They become unfriendly, aggressive. The smoke will only keep the non-robbing *resident* bees away from us. On the other hand, the *robbing* bees, which don't live in the hive being robbed, are so caught up in their pillaging that they won't want to have much to do with us, anyway. Normal bees would come after us if they thought we were threatening their hive. Robbing bees don't care about the hive. Afterall, they're stealing from it."

"Why don't the resident bees defend the hive? Can't they chase away the robber bees?" I asked him. "What are these robber bees, anyway? Are they honey bees? And why are they robbing only that one hive?"

"That's what makes this behavior so extraordinary," explained the professor. "The robber bees *are* honey bees, just like the ones in all of the other hives. They're robbing *that* particular hive because it has a *hole* in it."

"What do you mean, a hole?"

"There's a hole, a back door, so to speak, in the hive. See that opening in the front, that wide slot on the bottom that the bees are going in and out of? That's the hive door, which is guarded by the resident bees. It should be the *only* door into the hive. There should be no *back* door. The resident bees aren't naturally programmed to defend an entry hole that isn't supposed to be there. Yet, sometimes the wooden frame of the hive will rot a bit over time and a hole will work its way through on the back side of the hive body. When a bee from another hive discovers this unguarded hole, that bee can enter the hive and take honey, sneaking it out the back door. Soon, bees from all over find out about the unguarded hole, and they begin stealing the honey, too. Then a full-scale robbing frenzy begins. The bees go crazy. That's why there's an agitated cloud of bees surrounding that hive. It's the robbing frenzy I was telling you about in my office."

"How often does this happen?"

"Not very. That's why I said you're damn lucky to be seeing this. It only happens when a hole accidentally appears in a hive. If you're a really good beekeeper, you'll never see a robbing frenzy. If you're more relaxed about it, like I am, then this kind of thing can happen once in a while."

"Once a year?"

"I've been keeping bees for fifteen years and this is the third time I've seen a robbing frenzy on one of my hives. Every time for the same reason — an old hive with wood starts to rot and a hole develops in the back of the hive."

"So what do you do about it?"

"That's what I'm going to show you right now. There are only two things that will stop it."

"Which are?"

"Obviously, it will stop when all the honey is gone. That happens much sooner than you may think. An entire hive can be depleted of its honey by the robbing bees in about one week. That's fifty or sixty pounds of honey gone forever. Then the hive will, unfortunately, die because the resident bees will starve during the winter months. For some reason, honeybees, which are normally very organized, efficient creatures, and which have evolved almost a perfectly sustainable lifestyle, will abandon their natural predilections toward sustainability and destroy each other when free honey becomes available. It's like people looting department stores during a riot. This is the perplexing bee psychology, if you will, of the robbing frenzy phenomenon."

"How else can it be stopped besides all of the honey being stolen?"

Professor Gaulton reached into his deep coveralls and pulled out the duct tape. Holding it in the air, he answered triumphantly, "Plug the hole."

The professor walked over to the hive on the right, all the while squeezing away at the bee smoker, which gushed clouds of white smoke in front of him as he moved closer. We stood still. Soon, the entire hive was enveloped in smoke as if a forest fire was blazing nearby. The bee cloud visibly thinned, but did not dissipate completely. Bees bounced off Gaulton's veil like tiny kamikaze pilots. We decided it was a good idea to keep our distance. Gaulton set the smoker on top of the hive, and then, with some difficulty due to his gloved hands, ripped off a piece of duct tape. He plastered it over the dime-sized hole, the unguarded "back door" to the hive, rubbing it good and hard to be certain it wouldn't come off.

"That's all it takes!" he shouted through his bee veil as he picked up the smoker and turned toward us, waving at the bees diving in front of his face. "I hope they didn't take too much honey, the little bastards. Let's go. Job done."

The professor trudged off through the meadow toward the house, and with the buzz of bees behind us, we followed in close pursuit, a little puzzled by what we had just seen. The solution to this potentially self-lethal bee behavior seemed too simple — a piece of duct tape.

"Ah, Brian —," I began to ask.

The professor sensed that he was about to be inundated with a barrage of questions. "Let's get these outfits off and we can discuss what you saw in the meadow over a cup of tea in the house. Or better yet, you should try my homemade beer."

"Sounds good to me!" said Annie. "I make beer, too!"

"She's a brewmistress," I explained.

Annie and the professor chatted amicably about their brew-making experiences as we removed our bee suits and stowed the equipment. Soon we were in the house sampling a black, rich, double stout, the professor's specialty. He gave us a short walking tour of the house and garden, beers in hand, as the sun began to set in a blaze of red across the road. Back inside, we were greeted with the smell of bread fresh out of the oven, and seafood boiling on the stove in a large cast iron pot. Judy bustled around the kitchen, putting the finishing touches on what appeared to be a first class dinner. The professor ushered us into their cozy living room and brought another round of drinks, much to our pleasure. He settled into an overstuffed easy chair, propping his feet up on a matching ottoman. I could see a smile sparkling in his eyes; he already knew what I was dying to ask him.

12

Ancient Heat

I TOOK A LONG DRAW FROM MY FROTHY BEER MUG AND rested the glass on the coffee table in front of me, licking the foam off my moustache. "Brian, I'm still not quite sure how the bee behavior we witnessed out there in your pasture has anything to do with my Aunt Lucy. I just don't get the connection. And if I have too many more of these beers, I'm not gonna understand anything."

"Ha! Yes, sir, these stouts will do that to ya!" The professor's cheeks were flushed with color. Judy entered the room carrying a plate full of small, peeled carrots. "Here's some finger food from our garden to hold you until dinner's ready, which will be in about a half hour."

"Thank you very much," Annie said, taking a few carrots from the tray and passing it over to me. She turned to Professor Gaulton. "Professor, what *do* those bees have to do with Aunt Lucy?"

"It's quite simple. Your Dr. Boggs was rather brilliant in many ways. When she heard my lectures on how bees abandoned their natural inclinations for order, efficiency, cooperation, and sustainability, and instead robbed honey until a hive was destroyed, she had a flash of insight. If such aberrant behavior can be triggered in *honeybees*, can *other* species also exhibit anything like this?" The professor leaned over and took a carrot from the tray, shrugging his shoulders. He munched on the carrot as he continued. "She was horrified to realize that yes, not only can another species be subject to such dreadful behavior, but that species was *us*, for god's sake. You see, it occurred to her that humans are right now, as we speak, in the midst of a huge robbing frenzy."

"What?!" we both said in unison.

"It makes complete sense when you think about it. A honeybee robbing frenzy only lasts until the honey is gone, maybe a week or two at the most. Humans, on the other hand, are on a different time scale. That means that a human-species robbing frenzy could last much longer, perhaps centuries. Lucille's theory is that we've been in the midst of such a frenzy for generations, that's why no one is noticing it. Everyone alive today was born into it and simply takes it for granted as normal behavior."

"What are we humans robbing? Where is the back door to the hive, so to speak? I don't get it." Annie asked.

"We're robbing the Earth's resources, particularly the non-renewable ones. The frenzy really took off when oil was discovered. That was in, ah, Pennsylvania, I believe. That's where you're from, right? Quite a coincidence."

"Yeah, oil was discovered at Drake's well. That's actually not very far from where we live," I explained.

"You don't say? Well, the world changed when Mr. Drake drilled his well and discovered oil. Because, at that time, according to Dr. Boggs, he discovered that there was a back door to the hive, and no one was guarding it. The non-renewable resources that had taken nature millions and millions of years to create, and which had laid in storage in the ground, kind of like honey in a hive, except this had been around for eons, could now be extracted by anyone with the means to do so. People could claim the resources for themselves and thereby get fabulously rich overnight. A colossal robbing frenzy began in earnest in the late 1800s, and continues to this day, unimpeded. No one has a roll of duct tape big enough to plug the holes. It could be done politically, but the politicians have their fingers in the honey pot, too. And there are thousands of these holes, all being sucked dry by people who are now very rich and powerful."

"So, you're saying an oil well is like a hole in the back of a bee hive. It makes people crazy?" I asked.

"No, that's not quite it. When our ancestors first came over to this continent, they found an immense storehouse of natural resources from coast to coast. They also found that the native Americans, the people who already lived here, were incapable of defending those resources. The Europeans could easily take the resources for themselves — land, forests, slaves, game, minerals, gold — and they did just that. So, in effect, a robbing frenzy probably started with the Spaniards and their quest for gold in the late 1400s. The pilfering of resources continued through the 19th century, when oil was discovered. It was the oil that really made people rich. People became millionaires overnight. This added a new and earnest momentum to the robbing frenzy that was already underway. Essentially we still believed, psychologically, that we were stealing from the native Americans. What we didn't understand was that the country was now ours and we were simply robbing ourselves. According to Dr. Boggs, the robbing frenzy continues to this day, except we're robbing our own hive, so to speak, and don't realize it. She said that this was pathological behavior and insisted that something must be done to stop it."

"So what are you saying, that our hive's going to run out of honey and we're all going to die?" I asked in disbelief.

"Well, yes, and no. You may be missing the point. Honeybees are, by nature, very productive and rather sane creatures. They have a way of living that has evolved not only to perfection, but in complete harmony with their surrounding natural world. They can sustain themselves indefinitely, efficiently, and happily, while living in balance, cooperation, and mutual benefit with nature. Unless, that is, their behavior is triggered by some unknown pathological influence, call it greed, perhaps, which sparks a disastrous robbing frenzy. They don't have the means to stop the frenzy themselves, so it has to either be stopped by a higher power, which is perhaps an egotistical way to refer to a beekeeper, or it has to run itself out, continuing until the honey is gone and a hive has been destroyed."

"And humans?"

"The human species is essentially in an identical situation. For all we know, we're also by nature efficient, cooperative, and sustainable creatures. We humans can also live in harmony with the planet, and perhaps play a mutually beneficial role in the web of life, just like bees do as pollinators. In fact, we might very well do so naturally and effortlessly, like honeybees, if we weren't caught up in a robbing frenzy, which is totally distorting our view of reality, and draining the hive, so to speak. Perhaps humans, like honeybees, suffer from a psychological weakness called avarice, triggered by the availability of unguarded resources. Like alcoholics, we can't control this illness. According to Dr. Boggs, this is leading to world wide disaster. And we can't see it because our awareness and understanding is clouded by our culture's collective pathological behavior. We're taught from a young age that the excessive accumulation of material wealth is a good thing. Therefore, according to Dr. Boggs, we can't gain a proper perspective on our behavior."

"What do you mean, disaster? You mean we're going to run out of oil? That doesn't sound like a disaster. It's not like we need oil to survive; we don't eat it, for chrissakes. As the supplies drop, our use of it will drop, too, don't you think? It seems to me that it's simply a self-regulating process."

"I wish it were that simple, Joe. There are a few problems, however, with that argument. You're right, we don't *eat* oil, but we've developed global agricultural systems which are totally dependent on oil to synthesize fertilizers, power the tractors, ship the goods around the world." I nodded, suddenly beginning to understand what he was saying. "We're increasing our population exponentially, a population now dependent on the availability of oil for food production. As our population increases, our species becomes top-heavy in numbers, so to speak, while the non-renewable resource base supporting it is slowly being whittled away. Eventually our entire support system could topple. That's an impending disaster scenario, like the bees finding they don't have enough honey to survive the winter. By the time they've figured this out, it's too late. Humans are setting themselves up for a similar fate. And that's not the worst of it. Not by a long shot."

"What do you mean?"

"According to your aunt, we've become so blinded by our robbing frenzy mentality, a behavior that we've learned to take completely for granted, that we've lost touch with the natural balance of the Earth. A balance that we, in our blind race for more 'honey,' are pushing farther and farther off kilter. As a species, we're now burning up so much oil, gas, and coal and releasing so much ancient heat into the atmosphere, that we've begun a shift in the Earth's climate that appears to be making the planet sick, if you will, and is quite likely to yield deleterious effects of untold proportions, for all of life, for centuries to come."

"Ancient heat?" asked Annie.

"Plants collected energy from the sun for many millions of years," the professor explained. "That energy became stored in the Earth in the form of fossil fuels. We release ancient heat when we burn those fuels. So the heat energy that's taken plants eons to collect on this planet is being released back into the atmosphere in a split-second of Earth time, by humans. We're also releasing an incredible amount of carbon dioxide into the atmosphere when we do this, and the carbon dioxide helps to hold heat near the surface of the planet. Our robbing frenzy is heating the planet unnaturally, creating a rapidly descending spiral toward planetary imbalance."

"Okay, Brian. Now hold on a second. We're just country people from small town America. We should be home feeding our animals right now. I have firewood to split, and a garden to tend. By the time we get home it'll be a 4,000 mile round trip for us. You're saying that we've traveled all this way just to find out that my Aunt Lucy thought that the human race is like a bunch of psychotic bees? That information's about as useful to me as tits on a chicken," I said sarcastically.

"Joe!" Annie scolded. "Maybe if you pay attention, you might learn something!"

Professor Gaulton looked at the floor and shook his head ruefully. "*Neurotic* honeybees would be a more appropriate way of stating it. Dr. Boggs had concluded that certain subcultures of the human species, including ours, by the way, are indeed like neurotic bees. But she also was forced to speculate on the theory that humans, like honeybees, are also perhaps quite sane under normal conditions, and could perhaps be a thing of beauty on this planet, rather than the plague we seem to be becoming. She thought that if we could cure our alcoholism, so to speak, our avarice, we'd do just fine on this planet. That may be her greater discovery, her more profound theory. In any case, I think that your aunt's bee theory is just one piece to a puzzle. She never revealed the other pieces or the entire picture to me, because she was still finding and putting the parts together herself the last time I saw her, a year ago. Apparently, she was well on her way toward piecing together a puzzle of a profound nature. Why else would she have made preparations to have someone carry on in her footsteps in the event of an untimely death?"

"So what're we supposed to do now, Professor? Joe's aunt had an epiphany somehow linked to the behavior of honeybees. Where does that leave us? If we're to pick up where she left off, she did a lousy job of preparing us. We are, to be honest, quite clueless about all of this. My husband's a roofer, not a researcher. I'm a housewife and a mother. Is it really worth it for us to be running around on what may be nothing more than a wild goose chase?"

"I assume Joe's aunt gave you some kind of instructions, Annie. If so, did she say anything about the end of the world?"

"Well, she said that a terrible battle is upon us —"

"At hand, those were her words. A battle is at hand," I interjected.

"Whatever. Please don't interrupt me," Annie said with obvious irritation. "And Lucy said the future of the planet is in question."

"Can I talk now?" I asked impatiently. "She said the future of our species and the world is *at stake*. Believe me, I've read her letter fifty times."

"Then I must pose the obvious question to both of you," the professor interjected. "Is the future of our planet, our world, and our species, worth what may appear to you to be a wild goose chase? Does the end of the world mean anything to you? What if your aunt is correct in her assumptions? Maybe she was on to something. Maybe you'd be abandoning an opportunity of a lifetime by going home and forgetting about all this. Or maybe going home and tending to your garden is the right thing to do. I don't know. I just can't tell you what the answer is. You have to feel it in your own hearts."

"What's with the long faces, here?" asked Judy, walking into the room untying her apron. "Whatever Brian told you, I really am an okay cook! And it's time to eat!"

"You're a wonderful cook, dear. We'll be right there."

Judy wiped her hands on her apron and shook a finger at the professor as she left the room, "You have five minutes!"

"One final thing, Joe. Did Lucille ever talk to you about a Dr. Tomasso? Cecilia Tomasso? She's a pathologist in Nova Scotia."

"I never talked to Lucille about anything, actually. I didn't even know her personally."

"That's odd. Why would she have entrusted you to take on a project of hers, then? Quite strange. In any case, Dr. Tomasso was a friend of Dr. Boggs. She may have some further insight into Lucille's theories. My guess is that you'll be stopping in Halifax on your flight back. Is that so?"

"Yes," Annie said. "Our plane does stop over in Halifax. But only for a couple hours."

"It may be worth your while to extend your stop-over for a day and look up this Dr. Tomasso. It's just a suggestion. Obviously, you can do what you want to do. But, I have her phone number and can give her a call for you. It's up to you."

I looked at Annie. She just shrugged her shoulders. I shrugged mine back and concentrated on draining the rest of my beer.

"C'mon, everyone," a voice impatiently called from the kitchen. "What do you want, a handwritten invitation? Dinner's getting cold!"

Halifax

Dr. Tomasso was a medical doctor who worked in Halifax, Nova Scotia. After dinner that evening, Professor Gaulton had telephoned her and made arrangements for us to meet her on Monday.

We caught a flight into Halifax on Sunday afternoon and checked into a hotel near the airport. We had to pay an extra $50 per plane ticket in order to alter our flight schedule and extend our layover for a day, but it seemed like a small price to pay under the circumstances, and besides, Lucy was covering it. We were to meet with Dr. Tomasso at noon the next day.

We spent that Sunday afternoon and evening walking about downtown Halifax, trying the microbrewed beers and doing a little shopping, mostly for souvenirs for the kids back home. Like St. John's, the people were extremely congenial and the city, the capital seat of this eastern Canadian province, had a homey, small town atmosphere, especially in the city center. Although the weather was a bit drier than in Newfoundland, the sea, as in St. John's, was everpresent. Halifax Harbor was having some water pollution problems at the time, however, and the issue seemed to be popular on the local news media. Apparently, sewage was collecting in the harbor and ruining the water quality; no one quite seemed to know what to do about it.

We made our way to an old pub in the city center. Its darkened wood interior was decorated with antique harpoons, while fishing nets and a wooden row boat hung from the ceiling. The place, reeking of briny marine memories, was filled with crusty-looking patrons, many of whom probably made their livings from the sea. Annie managed to strike up a conversation with a gentleman sitting beside her at the bar. After critiquing the pub's selection of lagers and ales, their discussion quickly turned to homebrewing, one of Annie's favorite topics of conversation, since she's the "brewmistress" of our household. I was left to pick at the popcorn in the basket in front of me. I listened to their chitchat with little interest, until, quite unexpectedly, the subject shifted to Newfoundland.

"So you just came from Newfoundland?" I heard the bearded man say. "Lots of unemployment up there, ay?"

"What do you mean?" asked Annie.

"Everyone's out of work up there, don't you know? The fisheries collapsed."

"What fisheries?"

"So you weren't there long, huh? Tourists, no doubt."

"No, actually, we were there on business," I heard Annie explain.

"Oh? What business is that? Not the fishing business, I'd say."

"No, just some research. It's hard to explain. My husband's doing some research on, ah, honeybees. That's why we went up there."

"Well, if he'd been doing research on fish, he'd know that the Newfies fished the hell out of the Atlantic cod. Depleted the entire stock. Used to be so many cod up there you could practically walk across the ocean on their backs! Now you're lucky to find two to rub together." He shook his head in dismay and took a long swig from his mug. "The government had to step in and ban cod fishing after the collapse of the fishery. Too bad they didn't do it sooner. Yep, used to have the biggest cod schools in the world. All gone now. Everyone made their income from the cod. Now they're all out of work. The world's just going to hell in a handbasket."

It was the first I had heard of any collapsing fisheries, and, remembering the news about Halifax Harbor's pollution problems, I leaned over the bar in front of Annie and asked, "What did you say killed the cod off Newfoundland? Pollution?"

"Nah. Overfishing. People just don't know when to stop, ay? They see a good thing and then the buggers exploit the hell out of it, like they don't have a brain in'r head. Like there's no tomorrow. Like their grandkids won't want fish to eat. Bloody hell!" The man shook his head and took another long draw on his draught. "My grandfather was a fisherman," he continued, wiping his beard with his shirt sleeve. "My father fished for a while, too. I got fishing in me blood. We'd all be eating fresh Atlantic cod today if the Newfies had protected their fisheries. I don't know what gets into people. I think the Japs took a lot of the fish. And the Russkies too. Goddam..."

Our new-found friend began grumbling under his breath; he'd worked himself into quite a mood. Annie and I downed the last few drops of our beer and decided it was a good time for us to exit.

Back in our hotel room, we felt like vegetating in front of the television for a while, a novelty, since we didn't, by choice, have a TV back home. We ordered room service, and found ourselves sitting on the bed, side by side, eating pizza, the flickering blue light of the TV dancing on our faces. I held the TV's remote control in my hand and was flipping from channel to channel, which was driving Annie crazy.

"Why don't you just put it on *one* channel and *leave* it there!?"

"I do," I said, clicking a button.

"You just changed it again!" she protested. "You're giving me a headache!"

"I leave it on one channel until there's a commercial.

Then I look for something else. I'm not watching any goddam commercials."

"Just *mute* it when there's a commercial, dammit! Give me that remote control!"

"Like hell!" I fought Annie back with one arm and kept surfing through the channels, finally hitting a public broadcasting station. Then I stopped. "There. No commercials."

"Finally!" She rolled her eyes at me and sank back into the pillows we'd propped up behind us. "Thank god. I was going blind!"

"Shocking developments in the world's climate are now unfolding before our eyes around the world," the TV announcer intoned. *"Scientists are attributing the developments to global warming. Over a thousand square miles of Antarctic ice shelves collapsed into the sea from March 1998 to March 1999. Glaciers are also melting at unprecedented rates in Peru, Russia, and India. The resulting rising seas are killing coastal mangrove forests in Bermuda, destroying beaches in Hawaii, and inundating shorelines in Fiji."*

"Listen to this," I said to Annie.

"The warmest June on record in Lhasa, Tibet, occurred in 1998, the warmest August in Cairo occurred in 1998, the warmest July in New York City occurred in 1999." The voiceovers were spoken in dramatic tones as deep drums boomed in the background. *"Malaria is spreading in Kenya and Indonesia to elevations where it has never existed before. Mosquito-borne dengue and yellow fever are climbing to record elevations in Colombia."*

"Look. This is really happening," I said incredulously. "These aren't predictions, they're *reports*. This is the *news*. I didn't see any of this on the other channels. Just a lot of hair spray commercials and crap that women buy," I said.

"Like hell. How would you know? You skipped over the commercials!" Annie said indignantly. "Besides, they were car commercials, mostly gas-hog pickup trucks for macho men."

"Trucks, hell. They were selling fur coats," I replied.

"Men don't wear fur coats."

"What about those viagra commercials?" she snapped back.

"I saw feminine hygiene spray commercials," I countered.

"They were selling crap to get rid of baldness," she said.

"They were selling panty hose."

"In England, migratory birds are now laying their eggs almost nine days earlier than in 1971. An unheard of 22 inches of rain fell on Santa Barbara, California, in February, 1998, the highest ever recorded. In a three-day period in 1998, over a foot of rain fell on Sydney, Australia, equivalent to an incredible three months rainfall. 1998 was the hottest year ever recorded, perhaps the hottest year in the last millennium, and exhibited the largest annual increase by a wide margin, according to alarmed NASA scientists."

"Shaving cream."

"Lipstick."

"Snowless days in Barrow, Alaska, have increased by more that 20% since the 1950s. Arctic sea ice has receded by six percent just since 1978. Severe widespread droughts and forest fires occurred in Spain in 1994, Mexico in 1998, and Indonesia in 1998."

"Look at this stuff," I exclaimed. "Didn't Professor Gaulton say something about global warming? The bees were robbing honey so fast that they were heating up, or something?"

"You *are* dense, aren't you? Don't you *ever* pay attention? Jeez!" she sighed, exasperated. "Humans are burning so many *fossil fuels* that the Earth's climate is heating up. Haven't you ever heard of the Greenhouse Effect? It's causing severe weather conditions around the world. Listen to what they're saying. It's the *result* of Lucy's robbing frenzy!"

"Global warming may disrupt the North Atlantic Current to such an extent that it actually drops the average temperature in Europe by 9 to 18 degrees Fahrenheit due to a stalled Gulf

Stream, creating a disastrous mini Ice Age there. Record-breaking 240 mile-per-hour winds were recorded in Guam in 1997. In 1998, at least 56 countries suffered severe floods, while another 45 cooked under the heat of severe droughts. Global warming, with all of its associated weather extremes, is now a scientific reality, and there is no end in sight. Scientists have no idea how hot things will get, or how long they will stay that way."

"Good pizza, huh?" I said, ignoring the TV. "Let's see what's on another channel. Maybe there's some sci-fi."

"You're hopeless!"

"Why? What did I say now?"

"How and why your aunt ever picked *you* to do her research is a mystery to me. I don't think she knew that your skull was solid clear through. Here's a program that's really worthwhile and perfectly suited to the research you're supposed to be doing. And you want to flip through the channels!?"

"I don't know what research I'm *supposed* to be doing. Okay, okay, I can see that maybe there is some global warming occurring. But what the hell am *I* supposed to do about it? What can one person do about something that's changing the entire world? What do you want me to do? Huh? Just tell me!"

"I don't know!" she said, punching down the pillows. "Let's just get some sleep and worry about it tomorrow. Maybe Dr. Tomato or whatever her name is will have some answers."

"Fine with me. Good night." And good riddance, I thought, biting my tongue. I flipped through the channels some more while Annie rolled over and pulled the blanket over her head. "Look! Star Trek!"

"Gimme a break. I'm trying to sleep," Annie murmured, burying her head in the pillow. I dimmed the lights and watched Captain Kirk battle aliens until my eyelids got too heavy to hold open.

14

Microhumans

WE ROSE EARLY, HAD COFFEE AND DONUTS IN THE HOTEL lobby, and then checked out. Our meeting with "Dr. Tomato," as Annie had referred to her, was not until lunchtime. That gave us some time to wander around the city. Eventually, we found the little café, a Middle Eastern restaurant, where I had agreed to meet Dr. Tomasso. Although we were a half hour early, we decided to rest our legs. We found a table by an open window.

"What is this Dr. Tomasso supposed to look like? How will we recognize her?" asked Annie.

"When I talked to her on the phone, she told me she was from India," I explained, "and has long black hair, dark skin, and would be wearing a red scarf."

"Well then, that must be her," she replied, nodding toward the sidewalk outside. A tall, slender woman with a bright red silk scarf paced outside the restaurant.

"Yep, you're probably right. Maybe she said she'd meet us out in front of this place. I don't remember now." Before I had finished my sentence, Annie had pushed back her chair and was headed toward the door. She stepped outside into the warm summer air and approached the lady.

"Dr. Tomasso?" Annie said tentatively.

"Yes?" the doctor spun around, surprised to find Annie beside her.

"I'm Annie Jenkins," I heard her say. "My husband, Joe, is inside. We have a table. Would you like to join us?"

Annie extended her hand in greeting and Dr. Tomasso took it with a smile.

"Oh yes, of course." The doctor accompanied Annie into the café and introduced herself to me. I stood to shake her hand.

"Please, sit down! No need to get up!"

"Do you have time for lunch, Dr. Tomasso? We were just thinking about trying some tabouli," I offered.

"Good choice. It's the best in Halifax," she commented. "Actually, I'd love a bite to eat. This is one of my favorite restaurants."

We all placed our orders over small talk about the city, Dr. Tomasso's job, the restaurant and pub scene in Halifax, and our families. Soon, heaping bowls of tabouli, fragrant with parsley and lemon, meticulously arranged plates of stuffed grape leaves, and a basket of steaming flat bread were set at the table. We hungrily filled our plates. Although the restaurant was tiny, I noticed a disproportionate number of middle eastern folks eating there; I took it to be a sign that we had indeed been served authentic ethnic food.

I helped myself to another piece of flatbread, and passed it on to Annie. "If you're from India originally, Dr. Tomasso, what brings you to Halifax?"

"Please call me Cecilia. Actually, Joe, I was raised in Canada, near Toronto. My parents left India when I was only a small child. After I got my master's degree in chemistry, though, I decided that I wanted to return to India, so I joined the Peace Corps. That's where I met my husband — in Delhi. He's Indian, too. After a couple years in the Peace Corps, my husband and I moved back here to Canada. I went back to school, got my medical degree, and we moved to Halifax. I've been here about twelve years now."

"And your husband? What does he do?" Annie scooped up a forkful of tabouli.

"He passed away three years ago. Cancer." Cecilia ran a finger down the side of her glass, drawing a line in the condensation on its surface.

"I'm sorry," Annie said quietly.

"Yes, he was a good man," Dr. Tomasso straightened up in her seat and turned to me, her eyes barely hiding her sadness. "So, you know Brian Gaulton?"

"We just met him and his wife a few days ago," I explained, glad to change the subject. "We're trying to take care of some unfinished business of my aunt's. Maybe you knew her? Dr. Lucille Boggs from the University of Montana. She passed away recently, too."

"Boggs is dead? Oh no, I'm sorry to hear that. She and I went way back." Cecilia paused and looked down at her plate, as if reminiscing. She had a doleful look on her face. "She was a very good friend of mine and a colleague. I hadn't heard from her in awhile, but that was typical — and with my schedule, I have a hard time keeping up with correspondence, too. I even get behind in my email," she admitted. "But, I didn't know she died. How awful! Brian didn't say anything."

"Well, frankly I wasn't close to my aunt at all. I hardly knew her. In fact, I only ever laid eyes on her once and we didn't even exchange two words then. After she died, her lawyers forwarded a letter she had written to me. The letter was basically a cryptic set of instructions for me to try to complete a project she was working on. Why she picked me is anybody's guess." I took a swallow of iced tea.

"I knew about some of Lucy's research. She was working on a project that many scientists would consider 'out in left field,' so to speak," she commented. "So, you're a nuclear physicist as well, Mr. Jenkins."

"Please call me Joe. Heck no, I'm no nuclear physicist. Do I look like a nuclear physicist? I'm a roofing contractor."

"Then why would Boggs — sorry, but that's what I called her, and she called me Tomasso, it's a long story — why would your aunt want you to complete a project for her? Was it a new roof?"

"Ha! If only it could have been that easy. No, it seems

my aunt had a penchant for puzzles. She sent me a very confusing letter with a very skimpy clue, and instructed me to follow it. It has led me to you at this point. Annie has been coming along for the ride. She keeps me out of trouble." I tapped Annie's leg under the table with my foot and looked at her out of the corner of my eye with half a wink.

"I don't understand. What puzzle? What clue?"

"In the letter she wrote, Aunt Lucy said that there was a battle brewing between the ego and the eco, and that the fate of the world was at stake. Sounds rather ominous, don't you think?" Cecilia just stared at me blankly. "I thought she was a crazy woman from day one," I continued, "but she left me a rather large chunk of money on the condition I do as she requested. The reason my wife and I are here with you today is because we don't understand what the hell Lucy wanted from us and we don't know what we're doing. I have to wonder if maybe we're just fools, allowing ourselves to be manipulated by the corpse of a woman who wasn't playing with a full deck, if you know what I mean." Cecilia stared at me without responding. "But Professor Gaulton seemed to think that Aunt Lucy was on the trail of something important. He suggested we stop and see you before we go back to Pennsylvania. Can you tell me why he would make that recommendation?"

"Probably because I knew your aunt quite well. She certainly did have a 'full deck,' by the way. We were undergrads together in Toronto many years ago. After college, we'd see each other maybe once every two years or so, but lately we kept in touch by email. She never married, you know. Never had children." Cecilia slowly shook her head. "I can't believe she's dead."

"When was the last time you saw her?" I asked.

"About four months ago. She was up in Toronto on business and I was there visiting my family. We got together and had dinner. She was really excited about a theory she was working on at that time. It had nothing to do with nuclear physics, which wasn't unusual for her. She had a lot of other interests. She indicated that she was intending to work with a team of scientists around the world on this new theory, but she had to put some finishing touches on it first."

"What theory?"

"Actually, it was rather intriguing. She said that nuclear physicists sometimes imagine the universe as a macrocosm and atoms as a microcosm, both domains ruled by essentially the same forces. The forces of electricity, gravity, and magnetism among the planets and stars are like the forces among electrons, protons, and neutrons. She referred to such viewpoints as 'quantum levels of perspective.'"

"Quantum levels of perspective?" Annie repeated.

"Yes. She said that if you look at something from the next quantum level of perspective, you can see it in an entirely new manner. She thought that was why scientists have so much trouble understanding the 'whole picture,' as she called it. They don't know how to adjust their perspective. It's the ones who can look at things in new ways that make the exciting new discoveries. If you were to look at solar systems from the next quantum level *up*, for example, celestial bodies might appear as atoms. Understand?"

"I think so. And if you were to look at atoms from the next quantum level *down*, they might appear as celestial bodies. Right?"

"Exactly. You got it."

"But I don't see where you're going with this," Annie replied.

"Well, Boggs thought we could look at biological systems from other quantum levels of perspective, too," Tomasso answered.

"In what way?" I asked.

"She said that if you view the Earth from a distance, say from outer space, which would be the next quantum level up, then the planet appears to be a single, relatively tiny organism, and all of the life forms on the earth appear to be microorganisms."

"Yes? And?"

"Well, she was intrigued with the idea that the human species could legitimately be considered microorganisms when viewed from this scale."

"We're microorganisms now, according to Lucy?"

"Yes, it sounds crazy at first. She said that people would tend to immediately discount this idea because of their egos. No person wants to admit that they're as insignificant as a germ in the overall scheme of things."

"Ego? That's the first time we've heard that word used by anyone so far. It's one that Lucy used in the letter she sent to Joe," Annie added.

"Well, yes. According to Boggs, the ego is the sense of the human 'self'; it acts as a barrier between humans and the rest of nature. Having an ego is a natural thing, but it can cause people to feel unduly separate and removed from the greater scheme of things, from the natural world around them. Anyway, Boggs insisted that I meet with her in Toronto to discuss this. She said she needed to run it all past me since I'm a pathologist. She was very excited about it."

"Why you? Why a pathologist?"

"Well, if you think about it, it does make sense. If, in fact, the human species can legitimately be viewed as microorganisms, then where would you go to find out about the behavioral patterns of the species?"

"To a microbiologist?"

"Exactly. Boggs thought that someone who was an expert on microorganisms could give her some clues about the behavior of the human race. She said that humans were relating to the Earth as microorganisms relate to a host organism. She was concerned because this perspective was not being noticed by the scientists of the world, who instead insist on seeing human behavior only in the context of large mammals, not as microorganisms."

"It does sound kinda crazy. Human microorganisms."

"It sounds crazy when examining human behavior in

relation to the other *life forms* on this planet. Humans don't relate to cows, for example, like microorganisms do. But it doesn't sound crazy at all when considering human behavior in relation to the planet as a *whole*."

"So, you're a microbiologist and Lucy thought you could give her some insight on all this? Is that what we're supposed to understand here?" I asked.

"Not exactly. It gets better. Or maybe I should say it gets worse."

"In what way?"

"I'm not a microbiologist. I'm a pathologist," she clarified.

"Meaning?"

"Meaning she's an expert on disease, Einstein," Annie so kindly offered.

"Yes, that's right. I study microorganisms of a particular type. The ones that cause disease."

My face must have looked completely blank.

"He's slow. Don't mind him. Give him a few hours. Have some more iced tea, dear," she said, patting my hand. "Maybe you can get another brain cell to start up."

"Ha! Your husband is smarter than that, I'm sure, Annie."

"Yeah. I'm not as dumb as I look!" I declared. "But what were you saying?"

"No one's that dumb, dear."

Cecilia shook her head and chuckled, amused with our bantering. "How long have you two been married?"

"Well, it *seems* a *lot* longer than it actually is," I earnestly replied.

"Thanks a lot! Twelve years. If we make it to twenty, I get a medal," Annie insisted.

"Let's get back to our original point of discussion," Cecilia said, laughing. "I have to get back to the clinic and I don't have much more time. Is there anything else you want to know about Boggs?"

"Yes," I said. "What were you just saying about diseases before we were so rudely interrupted?"

"Your aunt practically interrogated me about disease-causing microorganisms. We call them pathogens. The more information I gave her, the more startled and disconcerted she became. I explained to her that pathogens can often dwell within their host without causing harm and that, for example, we all probably have some disease-causing microorganisms in us — or on us — right now. Our system of antibodies keeps their population low enough that we never show any disease symptoms." Cecilia folded her arms on the table and leaned toward us, explaining, "When the population of pathogens rises to a certain level, though, they begin to suck the vitality out of their host, consuming and multiplying to such an extent that it taxes the host to a perilous degree. Pathogens seem to have no genetic ability for symbiosis. They don't *want* to live in harmony with their host organism. If anything, they act like they want to *kill* it. They secrete enough toxic waste to poison their host. If they keep multiplying without being checked, their host gets sick and dies."

"So it was Lucy's idea that people are like disease-organisms on the Earth. Isn't that right?" asked Annie.

"Exactly. Whenever I described a particular behavior of a pathogen to Lucy, she translated that behavior to her next quantum level of perspective. She said the behavior of the human species in relation to the Earth parallels the behavior of a pathogen in relation to a host organism. She said that humans dwelled on the planet for eons and never did much perceivable long-term damage. Then they multiplied to a certain population level and their toxic discharges began harming the planet. Just like disease-organisms, humans began consuming and multiplying and polluting, showing little regard for their host. Since this is the typical behavior of pathogens, Lucy wondered if the human species was, in fact, a planetary disease. I know she did a lot of soul-searching, trying to figure out if that is our destiny as a species, or if it is a choice for us to make. She thought that if it was a choice, then people needed to know what was going on before it was too late to change anything. Before we reached the point of no return, as she called it. People needed to know what we were doing, collectively, as a species, before the disease became incurable."

"She thought the human species was a sort of pathogen, then?" I asked.

"Actually, no. Let me clarify that. She thought that *some* human *cultures* were exhibiting pathogenic behavior, but not the species as a whole. In fact, she made it very clear that some human cultures appeared to be able to live quite harmoniously with our planet and its ecosystems. Most indigenous cultures, for example, have lived for millennia in a sustainable manner. It's the *American* culture in particular, and others with similar economic systems, such as Japan, that she was worried about. She was also concerned that China would be next to become obsessed with an environmentally destructive form of material consumption. If that happens, she said, we'd be in a very sorry state of affairs."

"Do you think we'll kill the Earth?" Annie said quietly.

"According to Boggs, our disease-like behavior will either kill the Earth, or maybe just make it sick enough that many of the more vulnerable life forms on it will die, or, and this is one of her theories that seemed a bit dire, the Earth will kill us in its own defense."

"What?! How would it do that?"

"Well, pathogens don't exist in a vacuum," Cecilia patiently explained. "Lucy really grilled me on this issue. Wherever there are disease organisms, there are things that fight the disease in defense of the host. I explained to Boggs that when a person gets sick, the body temperature rises as a defense mechanism against the disease. People think that diseases cause fevers, but the body boosts its *own* temperature in response to a disease."

"Why?"

"Because, when the body's temperature is higher, it can generate many, many more antibodies, T-cells, and the like. It needs these things in order to fight the disease.

Boggs said that the Earth's temperature is beginning to rise now, and that it's rising at an unprecedented rate. Skyrocketing, in fact. From the next quantum level of perspective, it looks like the Earth is getting a fever. Your aunt suspected that the warmer global climate might allow the proliferation of organisms that would make life miserable for humans, and maybe even exterminate us."

"What kind of organisms?" I asked.

"A very simple example would be mosquitoes. Mosquitoes have killed more people than all wars combined. A warmer planet would mean a vastly expanded range for disease-carrying mosquitoes. And that's just a simple example. We actually have no idea what new, mutated, or evolving life forms, viruses, or bacteria may be sparked into existence by a warmer planet," she folded her napkin in her lap. "This is my own personal area of interest. You know in the past fifty years, at least fifty new human diseases have emerged?" She began listing them, ticking them off on her fingers. "Ebola. AIDS. Hantaviruses. Lyme's Disease. Pretty scary stuff."

"Let me see if I can get this all straight," I said. "It was Aunt Lucy's theory that some human cultures may be exhibiting the behavior of pathogens in relation to the planet as a whole."

"Precisely."

"And that we're behaving in such a manner without realizing it," I continued.

"That's correct."

"But if we realize it, we may be able to change our behavior so that we're no longer a disease."

"If it's not too late," added Cecilia.

"And if we don't," added Annie, "the you-know-what will hit the fan."

"According to Boggs, my friends, it's already hitting the fan. I think that may be what she meant when she said the fate of the world may be at stake."

"But Lucy also said a battle was brewing between the ego and the eco," I interjected. "What did she mean by that?"

"Well, if I may hazard a wild guess, I'd say that, to Lucy, the ego is what blinds humans to the destruction they're inflicting on their host planet. The ego is what allows the individual human to feel more important than anything else on the Earth, or in the universe, for that matter."

"And the ego is pumped up by things like material wealth and social status," remarked Annie. We turned to each other, then stated in unison, "The robbing frenzy!"

"What's that?" Cecilia looked at us in confusion.

"It's a long story, Cecilia. Another of Lucy's grand theories," I explained. "Lucy seemed to think that we're in a sort of robbing frenzy, stealing all of our planet's natural resources. Like alcoholics, we're in denial that we have a problem with consumption."

"She's probably right about that. It wouldn't surprise me at all. But Lucy did have some questionable ideas, I must warn you. I did have some doubts about her."

"Oh? What, specifically, do you mean?" Annie asked, glancing at me out of the corner of her eye.

"She was a bit paranoid. She thought that if she could identify the roots of our disease behavior and make that information public, to try to change our course on this planet from..."

"From destructive parasite to symbiotic organism," I interrupted.

"Yes." Cecilia smiled gracefully and continued. "Anyway, she was sure that if she tried to make this information public, the powers that are benefitting the most from our destructive behavior would try to stop her. Maybe even kill her."

"You're kidding, right? Who would've wanted to kill Lucy?"

"She said that a few people were making a lot of money at the expense of the environment. She believed that their egos had become so utterly bloated and pathogenic that they would stop at nothing to prevent anyone from getting in their way. She told me that sometimes she had a feeling she was being followed. She was afraid that her phone was tapped. She was afraid for her life. She confided in me about these fears of hers, and she made me promise that I'd tell no one. She even stated with tears in her eyes that she didn't know if she would ever see me again. Now that she's dead, I feel it's important for you to have this information. It's possible she may have been delusional, but how *did* she die?"

"I'm not sure how she died, actually," I said. "I thought that maybe it was from a heart attack, because I saw blood pressure pills on the desk in her house."

"Maybe you should get a copy of her death certificate. Even an autopsy report. Tell you what, I'll look into that for you. I may be able to get that information easier than you can. Give me your address and phone number and if I find out anything, I'll call or send the information to you."

"Now just hold on a minute," I said, feigning seriousness. "How do I know you're not a spy?"

"You have to trust me, Joe. Who else are you going to trust?"

I handed Cecilia one of my business cards. "It's all there, Cecilia. Thanks for doing this. We need all the help we can get."

"I think so."

"See dear, she's got you pegged already."

"I'm late for work. It was a real pleasure meeting you two. If you're ever in Halifax again, please do look me up. And do keep in touch." Cecilia stood up to leave. "You'll be hearing from me."

"The pleasure was all mine, Cecilia," I said as I stood to shake her hand.

Annie and I remained in the restaurant a while longer, finishing our lunch and discussing the salient points of our discussions with Dr. Tomasso and Professor Gaulton. If the Sisters and their crystal had been correct, which was a giant leap of faith in the first place, as far as I was concerned, and we had been steered in the right direction, we had now, presumably, come to the right place with regard to my aunt. Apparently, Aunt Lucy had been on the trail of a theory about humans inadvertently damaging our planet, perhaps irreversibly. She had somehow been able to imagine humans as microorganisms on Earth, and had seen that we were treating the planet like a disease organism treats its host. She seemed to believe that humans were unknowingly and psychologically locked in the grip of a consumption frenzy, one that could have disastrous results. It all sounded incredible and a lot like doomsday. We didn't know *what* to think. What did this have to do with *us*? What were we supposed to do next? The fact that our knowledge of this was based almost entirely on a group of witches and their magical stones left us extremely skeptical. We both decided there was only one sure thing for us to do now: get to the airport, catch our flight, go home, and worry about it all later. Little did we know that we had set foot on a very slippery slope, and whether we wanted to or not, there was no turning back.

15

Ecocide

BACK HOME, WE BECAME DISTRACTED FROM LUCY'S quest as Annie and I quickly fell back into our mundane routines. There was plenty of homestead work to deal with. Seventeen acres of rural land in Pennsylvania is an opportunity in itself. After twenty years of cultivation, we had established an orchard and a large garden, and grew a lot of our own food, including grapes, berries, and vegetables. We kept ducks and chickens, grew mushrooms on logs, fermented and even distilled our own beverages, designed and built our own buildings, heated with wood, homeschooled Penelope, and preserved food in our root cellar, or by canning or drying. Yet Annie still managed to find time to spin, weave, knit, tutor, and play the fiddle, and sometimes I accompanied her on the guitar. With a steady supply of friends, neighbors, and visitors, our days were full — without having to volunteer for bizarre adventures on behalf of dead relatives.

What remained of the $10,000 Lucy had originally given us sat in our bank account; the other check sat, uncashed, in my desk drawer. Both served as constant reminders that we had been lured into doing her work by the prospects of easy money. However, the farther we ventured down Lucy's path, the more convoluted it had become. The money she gave us looked more and more like money we were going to have to earn with considerable hard work. And although my "inheritance" was certainly interesting, it took a lot of time and energy; I wasn't even remotely sure our efforts would lead to any constructive outcome.

Nevertheless, we spent quite a few evenings and many mornings over tea discussing our improbable situation. Our conversations reviewed the events in Newfoundland and Halifax, then we translated what we saw and heard there into terms that we could communicate to others. I started keeping a journal. We began to do research of our own in order to verify or discredit Lucy's theories. Was our culture really in a robbing frenzy? Were humans really acting like disease organisms on the planet? Is environmental degradation as pervasive and ominous as Lucy would have liked us to believe? Or was she an environmental extremist whose theories and warnings were simply to be discounted? We needed to find out the truth.

One nice thing about roofing work in Pennsylvania is that it rains a lot. Not only does this force people to really value a solid roof over their heads (and value competent roofers), but it gives me plenty of time off to do other things — like go to the library and do research.

Annie, Penny, and I spent an entire rainy day at the local university library searching the computer database for information about global warming. We even brought home an armful of books and research journals and spent a few evenings leafing through them. To my surprise, report after report pointed to the same conclusion: the scientists of the world were in agreement that the global climate is actually changing as a result of human activity; we were to blame for the Earth's "fever." As Lucy had warned Cecilia, though, there were powerful business people with deep pockets that loudly condemned this prevailing opinion by saying it was not based on valid science. Various industries had even banded together under the guise of the "Global Climate Coalition" for the apparent purpose of discrediting scientific climate change theories.

Researching further, I learned that the only thing that makes the Earth different from our cold, lifeless moon is the atmosphere that envelopes our planet. Although the atmosphere holds in heat, creates rain and snow, gives us air to breathe, and enables life to exist, it is actually little more than a gossamer veil draped tightly over the Earth, an extremely thin, protective membrane enclosing the planet. If the Earth were the size of a chicken egg, for example, the entire atmosphere would condense down only to the volume of 1/40th of a water droplet. I had never before considered the delicate nature of the atmosphere; the sky had always looked amazingly broad and immensely powerful. But when I tried one of Lucy's quantum leaps and looked at it from a different perspective, I began to understand that, looking down at the Earth from afar, the sky is only the thinnest of skins. Like humans without *their* skin, the Earth would soon die without its protective covering.

I also found it interesting that the composition of the atmosphere was created by Earth's evolving lifeforms over a period of about six billion years, finally culminating into an intricate, and delicately balanced masterpiece of nature. Furthermore, although ninety-nine percent of the atmosphere is nitrogen and oxygen, I learned that these two gases don't hold in heat. "Greenhouse gases," which make up the leftover one percent, including carbon dioxide, are what help keep the Earth warm. Without them, the Earth would essentially be a cold, dead rock. Annie and I were both fascinated to learn that our atmosphere has maintained a steady temperature on the planet's surface for the past three million years. On the other hand, we found it alarming that too much greenhouse gas can throw the sensitive atmospheric balance off kilter, theoretically overheating the planet. In fact, the Earth's temperature is now rapidly increasing, apparently due to the sudden and excessive release of "ancient heat," as Professor Gaulton had called fossil fuels. And the finger on the thermostat apparently belongs to *Homo sapiens*.

Although Earth-warming greenhouse gases come from natural sources, they're also emitted from smokestacks, auto exhausts, burning rainforests, furnaces, electrical generators, and many other human activities. Because we've chosen to use mainly fossil fuels, like coal, oil, and gas, to power many of our activities, we've inadvertently increased the amount of greenhouse gases in the atmosphere. With every mile we drive, with every turn of the thermostat, little by little, drop by drop, we've raised the amount of carbon dioxide in the atmosphere to a level significantly higher than it has been in the last 420,000 years, and it's steadily increasing, with no end in sight.

Annie was just as diligent in digging up information at the library as I was. She found it interesting that the industries primarily responsible for our excessive greenhouse gases were in denial about global warming. The people profiting from the extraction, sale, and use of fossil fuels, she discovered, argue that small increases won't do any harm, that plant life will absorb the excess. Although their argument sounded reasonable to Annie, I mulled it around in my mind. I thought about cycles, like water, for instance, moving from ocean to atmosphere to land, and back to the ocean. Carbon just seems to be a slower, less obvious kind of cycle; we breathe it out, plants breathe it in. We're a source; they're a sink. I wondered if it was possible to release so much carbon that we could actually overflow this sink? To use an analogy, I considered our own kitchen sink. When we run water into the sink at the same rate in which it goes out the drain, there's nothing to be concerned about. But when the tap is opened just slightly more, the sink begins to slowly fill up. Eventually, it overflows. According to our research, the scientists of the world were telling us that our atmospheric sink is now filling up and we have to do something before it overflows. Annie agreed that the data we were collecting was corroborating my aunt — Lucy's theories were beginning to ring true.

Still skeptical, however, I contacted my father and his siblings, who were scattered in various cities across the states, and asked them what *they* knew about their sister, Lucy. Maybe they could splash some cold water on my face by telling me something like Lucy was in and out of psychiatric hospitals all her life. According to them, however, Lucy was sane, although she didn't associate with her siblings much, and they didn't have anything much to say about her. They thought her remains had been cremated and there had been no funeral to attend that they were aware of. Their collectively held opinion seemed to be that she was a recluse; they all seemed a bit put off by the fact that she had never attended family reunions and had only very rarely posted an appearance at any other family events.

I went through Lucy's address book several times, trying to find information about her that her own family couldn't give me. I spoke to a few of her colleagues at the University of Montana. They didn't know anything about extracurricular research Lucy was doing regarding the environment. I talked with her auto mechanic (he didn't have much to offer, except that she was diligent in maintaining her little truck). I inquired, through the university, about her estate, and verified that she did, in fact, have a half million dollars worth of retirement benefits due her. I also talked to her lawyers at length. Although cordial and cooperative over the phone, they weren't much help. They reiterated the information I had read on Lucy's lockbox note. I had one year from the date of her death to find my personal "balance point" and claim her estate for myself. In the meantime, they were to hold the estate in escrow. Not only could they not tell me what a balance point was, but they sounded surprised that I seemed to not know myself. I racked up quite a large phone bill those few weeks, although Lucy paid for it. In the end, it all seemed to get me nowhere.

"Now what?" I asked Annie one morning as I was packing my lunch for a long day of roof repair. "What do you think we should do with Lucy's Goose Chase now?"

"I've been thinking," Annie replied. "Why don't we go back to the beginning — or at least back to Ohio and visit that midwife over there? The one who told you to go to

Newfoundland in the first place. I'd like to meet her anyway."

"You mean Cynthia? She didn't tell me to go to Newfoundland, a crystal told me," I reminded her. "You're probably right, though. We *should* go see her, I certainly don't know what else to do."

When I finally got around to calling Cynthia, she was excited to hear that we had gone to Newfoundland and wanted to know everything that had transpired there. I told her that I could speak more clearly over a dinner table than over a telephone, and suggested that we would probably be available to come to their place for dinner. Cynthia readily took the hint, and invited us for dinner that weekend.

Annie and Cynthia became immediate friends, and, over dinner, chatted about their common interests in gardening and weaving. It was with a bit of effort that I finally steered the conversation toward Lucy and our associated escapades.

"So you think the crystal pointed you in the right direction then, Joe?" Cynthia asked.

"Well, we met a couple of interesting people up in Newfoundland and Nova Scotia and they certainly did have some interesting things to say about Lucy. But I have no idea what to do now. I'd be open to consulting the crystal again," I said, hoping for an easy answer.

"You only need to do that if you know you have to travel but you don't know where. Are you thinking you need to travel again?"

"I don't know *what* we need to do. That's the problem." I described the events that took place in Canada, telling Cynthia about the bees, about Gaulton and Tomasso, and about Lucy's reported paranoia.

"So what have you done since you got back? Have you heard from this Tomasso woman?"

"Nope. What we've done is return to life as normal. I'm swamped with roofing work; I can't just abandon my job for this. We have work to do around our place, too.

We're thinking we need to do more library research or book research or something on these theories of Lucy's to see if we can make more sense out of them."

"Well," Cynthia said, thinking for a moment. "I can probably help you with that. In fact, I know two people to talk to who live nearby. They're researchers at the University of Ohio in Youngstown doing computer modeling of environmental systems. They're both friends of mine. I attended their daughter's birth five years ago. That's how I met them. Anyway, they've come up with some interesting information that might be of use to you. According to them, if you enter current environmental data into a computer and then have the computer extrapolate the data into the future, it says we'll eventually reach a point of environmental collapse. Tom and Lana want very much to get this information published, but it's been discredited by a number of industry scientists. The university won't let them publish their findings until they've verified their data again and can do so without being discredited. The problem is that the industry scientists don't want Tom and Lana's research to become public, and the university gets a large share of its funding from those same industries. So Tom and Lana are between a rock and a hard place."

"I'm not following you," I told Cynthia. "Your friends have some sort of computer program that can predict the future?"

"Well, kind of," Cynthia replied. "It's not exactly that simple. Tom and Lana do systems theory research. . ."

"Wait a second. What is systems theory research?"

"Do you know what a system is?"

"I think so, but feel free to explain," I offered.

At that moment, Cynthia's teenage daughter entered the room carefully carrying a huge roasted chicken on a platter. She set it in the center of the table and stood for a moment admiring the bird, wiping her hands on her apron.

"That's one of ours," she proudly admitted. "I raised it

as a 4-H project. His name was Buddy." She stared another moment, then abruptly turned and left the room. Penny's eyes popped open as her jaw dropped. "We're going to eat *Buddy*?!" she mumbled to herself. We all heard her and chuckled.

"That's the life of a chicken, Penny. Consider this a chicken funeral," I suggested lamely, trying to make light of the situation, then added, "It sure looks good to me!"

"Smells *wonderful*, Penny. I'm sure it's quite delicious." Annie added, giving me a withering look out of the corner of her eye.

Cynthia stood and bent over the table to carve the bird. "What were we talking about?" she asked, digging in with the carving tools. "Oh yeah, systems theory. As I was saying, a system is a group of, ah, interconnected . . . well, *elements* that are organized around some purpose. A weather system, for example. Weather systems have elements of air movement, precipitation, and sun, among other things, all of which work together to make weather. Are you following me?"

"So far."

"OK. Do you want a drumstick?"

"Sure." I held out my plate and Cynthia loaded it with a the biggest drumstick I'd ever seen. I could hardly hold the plate with one hand. Annie doesn't usually eat meat, but Cynthia served her a slice of white meat anyway, then she served herself and the others and sat back down.

"As I was saying," Cynthia continued, "Lana and Tom developed a computer program where they can plug systems data from the past and present into the program. They can then tell the program to run the data into the future. Please help yourself to some mashed potatoes, by the way. They're from our garden. Sorry to interrupt. Say you keep track of the average temperatures at noon in Youngstown for the past hundred years. You enter this information into the computer and then ask it to tell you what the average temperature, based on that data, will be at noon in Youngstown fifty years from now. The computer will do its calculations and then come up with a temperature. If the average temperature has been slightly decreasing, for example, over a hundred years, then the computer will likely tell you that fifty years from now the temperature will be lower, get it?"

"Yes."

"OK. Lana and Tom's program is much, much, more complicated than that. They've entered thousands of sets of systems data related to the Earth's environment into their very sophisticated computer. It's taken them years to do this. Global temperature, population changes, soil erosion, atmospheric carbon dioxide, sea temperatures, water consumption, data like that. They've run the program over and over, trying all sorts of variations. Funny thing is, the computer always comes up with the same conclusion."

"Which is?" I asked, ladling gravy over my potatoes.

"The computer tells them that if things continue the way they're going, even if we fix a few of the problems, there will still be an inevitable collapse of the planet's ecosystems with regard to the human race."

"What do you mean, *collapse?*"

"I mean," Cynthia continued, chewing on a piece of chicken, "that, as far as the human race is concerned, the planet will no longer be able to support us. We'll have created too much pollution, squandered too much topsoil, contaminated too much atmosphere, depleted too much ozone, and used up too much drinkable water to be able to support what will be too many people. They call it 'Global Collapse,' which sounds both awful and appropriate to me. It's also called *Ecocide*, because it means that we'll have destroyed the Earth's ecology, as far as the human race is concerned."

"Ecocide? And in what century will this take place?"

"Global Collapse is the bad news, but it gets worse. According to the models, it'll take place within about forty years. 2040. All of the computer graphs show increases in things like population, pollution, and waste occurring today, with no let up in sight. The lines on the graphs go up and up. Until about 2040. Then they all take a plunge. Everything drops dramatically — food, resources, quality of life, industrial output, population. That's why they call it global *collapse*."

"Forty years ago I was in second grade!" Annie exclaimed. "You're telling me that kids in grade school today are going to see the collapse of life as we know it? My daughter Penny May has this to look forward to? That's hard to believe." Penny was poking at her slice of chicken with her fork as if it were still alive. She had a scowl on her face.

"Yes, it seems unbelievable," Cynthia continued. "There's one big problem with being a skeptic, however. The rate of change in the environment is increasing *exponentially*. That means it gets faster with each passing year. And it's hard for most people to grasp the concept of exponential growth."

"I guess I'm one of those people," I admitted.

Cynthia looked at me warily out of the corner of her eye as if she couldn't believe I didn't know what exponential growth was. "Did you ever hear the story about the wise man who agreed to work for a grain of wheat?"

"No."

"Well, then, I'll just tell it to you. It illustrates how exponential growth works." Cynthia took a long drink of white wine, settled back in her chair and began, "It seems a wise man was forcibly taken before a King and told that he was henceforth to work for the kingdom. The King agreed to pay a fair wage for the man's time, however, and offered him a standard monthly payment. The man replied that he was honored to work for such a fair and just King, but he would only accept one grain of wheat for his first day's work. A single *grain*." She took another sip of wine and dabbed her mouth with her napkin. "The King burst into laughter at this apparent act of charity," Cynthia continued, "and insisted that the man agree to a standard rate of pay. The man refused, but suggested that the number of wheat grains should be *doubled* each day. At the end of thirty days, he told the King, he would no longer accept *any* payment at all. The King laughed again at the man, thinking him a fool, but agreed to the pay scale. One grain of wheat the first day, two the second, four the third day, eight the fourth, 16 the fifth, 32 grains the sixth day, and so on. Now tell me Joe, at this rate of pay, how much wheat would you expect the man to have acquired at the end of thirty days?"

"Probably a large bag or two," I guessed.

"Nope. That's what most people think. Exponential rates of increase don't work like that. In thirty days, the wise man would be due a half *billion* grains of wheat. More than all the wheat in the kingdom. Enough to bankrupt the king. You see, exponential growth rises slowly at first, almost imperceptibly, then it increases more and more rapidly until it's totally out of control. That's what's happening to the environmental problems facing our planet. Problems like population growth, resource consumption, waste production. They increase at exponential rates. It seems unlikely that one man can obtain all of the wheat in a kingdom in 30 days by starting with one grain and doubling it each day. And it seems equally unlikely that ecocide can occur in forty years. But only a fool, like the arrogant King, would risk ignoring the math. And that's what Tom and Lana's computer is doing. The math. My friends are like lemmings that can climb trees."

"What the hell are lemmings?" I asked, setting my fork on my plate.

"Lemmings. You know — little rodent-like creatures. They're known for the peculiar behavior of banding together in great hordes and running off the edge of cliffs. Mass suicide."

"Weird."

"Yeah. Imagine a hoard of lemmings racing toward a cliff overlooking the sea. As the great rodent herd gets closer to the edge, one or two lemmings break off from the rest of the group and climb up the trunk of a tree, maybe by accident. In any case, the tree-climbing lemmings now have the extraordinary ability to look ahead, and, to their horror, realize that their hundreds of thousands of lemming friends are all rushing off to a sudden, needless, and gruesome death over the edge of a cliff. The lemmings with the newly acquired foresight also then realize that a simple change of direction would prevent a catastrophe. And so they begin squeaking to the scrambling masses underneath them to change course. No one hears them. Tom and Lana are like that. Their computer enables them to foresee things to come, but no one will listen."

"Why, for heaven's sake, aren't your friends getting this information out to the media?" asked Annie.

"They've tried. But the media, which is controlled by big business, says it's inflammatory, frivolous, and not newsworthy. And Tom and Lana can't publish it independently either without risking their jobs at the university. The industries that help fund the university are putting pressure on the university to keep the information quiet."

"Can we talk to these folks? Your friends?" Annie asked.

"I don't see why not. I'll get you their phone numbers. I'm sure they'd love to talk with you."

By this time we had all finished eating. Penny's plate was completely empty except for her piece of chicken, which was untouched. As Cynthia's daughters were clearing the table, I called the scientist friends, told them of our interest, and made arrangements to meet with them. It sounded like they were on the same track as Lucy had been, and we needed to find out what else they knew.

16

Warning to Humanity

FOUR DAYS LATER, I KNOCKED ON TOM AND LANA'S
door at their second floor apartment near the university.
Lana opened the door, smiling, and ushered us in. She
appeared to be in her early forties, with straight brown
hair down to her shoulders, and bangs cut across her fore-
head to give her a school-girl look. She was slightly plump,
wore glasses, and looked the intellectual type. Her bespec-
tacled husband Tom stood behind her as we entered. He
was tall, lanky, and nervous, and vigorously shook my hand
in greeting. Their five year-old daughter was at daycare.

Annie accompanied me to this meeting, not wanting to
miss anything. The whole Lucy affair was getting more
and more interesting to her, and she was increasingly
intrigued at the new concepts she was being exposed to.
Ecocide, no less. Secretly, despite the global warming
homework I had done, I remained skeptical, but I wasn't
about to stop moving forward on this if it seemed like we
were actually making progress.

Lana welcomed us into their cramped apartment,
quickly clearing the dining room table of papers and
books. "You'll have to excuse this place," she said.
"Juggling our teaching loads, research, and a five year-old
leaves little time for housework."

"I know you're a busy person, Lana," I replied, "and we don't want to waste your time. We're here because we're interested in learning more about that computer program you developed. Your friend Cynthia told me the program predicts the end of the world. My Aunt Lucy, who died recently, was a professor at the University of Montana and she was apparently doing similar research. Nothing personal, but we're just here to see if there's really anything to this."

"Have a seat. Here, make yourselves comfortable." Lana gestured for us to sit at the dining room table. She pulled out a chair for herself and sat down too. "First of all, Joe, our computer modeling program doesn't necessarily predict the *end* of the world, but the end of the world *as we know it*," Lana corrected, placing her elbows on the table and clasping her hands in front of her chin. "The world will probably carry on after a global collapse. It just won't be able to support the human race in a manner we're accustomed to. It's more likely that our computer is pointing to the eventual *extinction* of the human species rather than to the end of the natural world."

"If not a total extinction, then huge numbers of people will probably die," added Tom, who remained standing behind Lana.

"Why's that?"

"Starvation. Water pollution. Disease. Extreme weather and other natural disasters. War," he replied.

"Your computer is telling you these things?" Annie asked.

"In a roundabout way, yes," replied Lana. "Look, if we continue eroding our topsoil at the current rates, depleting our fossil fuel reserves, pumping our aquifers dry, while dramatically increasing the human population, how will we provide the food needed by the larger and larger numbers of people? Where will the soil fertility come from? Where will the wastes from these people go when nature's ability to absorb them has been pushed beyond the limits?"

"It becomes pollution," interjected Tom. "And

unchecked, excessive pollution fosters disease. Add a polluted environment to a hungry, over-populated, over-heated world and you're setting the stage for epidemics to sweep across the globe." Tom walked over to a nearby window and pushed it open, then sat down at the table opposite Lana.

"How would pollution lead to epidemics?" Annie asked.

"Take water pollution, for example," offered Lana, folding her arms on the table in front of her. "The human population on our planet has been increasing exponentially since the early 1900s. In 1999, our numbers climbed to six billion, the highest human population this planet has ever seen. Although it took humans hundreds of thousands of years to reach these numbers, because of exponential growth, we're going to double that within the next forty years." Lana peered at us over the top of her thick glasses. "So what does that have to do with pollution or disease?" she continued. "Well, every human body emits solid and liquid by-products on a daily basis. Because humanity is the only organism on the planet that insists on excreting directly into water, we're fouling our own water supplies. In fact, half of the world's major rivers are already polluted by human waste of various types, that is, if they're not already going dry due to human overuse. If we look ahead, in forty years there will be twice as much waste going into the same amount of water, or, more likely, *less* water. This is a recipe for disaster. Sources of safe drinking water are already becoming scarcer and scarcer, while diseases associated with water pollution are already epidemic in some parts of the world. And that's just one form of deadly pollution that's inevitable if we don't think ahead and find ways to live that won't force us to drown in our own excretions. Another is air pollution. Then, of course, there's body pollution."

"What's that?"

"What?"

"Body pollution. Sounds like something I'd have after

a long day at work," I laughed.

"Body pollution won't go away with a little soap and water," Lana said ruefully. "Body pollution is the accumulation of toxins *inside* your body. It's also called the body *burden*. Mammals worldwide, humans included, have been exhibiting a constant accumulation of toxic chemicals in their body fat since about 1950, no matter where they live, even in the arctic. The average human can now expect to have at least 250 toxic industrial chemicals lodged in his or her fat tissue."

"Most of these chemicals cause cancer," added Tom, who seemed to be tense, as if he drank too much coffee. He spoke rapidly, his wire rim glasses barely hanging on his nose. "Toxic chemical body pollutants accumulate in fat cells over time until they spark a reaction in the body, usually cancer. That's one reason why cancer is now the second leading cause of death in America, and the leading cause of death among us baby boomers. That's also one reason why so many women get breast cancer. There are lots of fat cells in the breast."

"This is depressing," said Annie.

"Sure it's depressing," agreed Lana, leaning toward us, her voice taking on an added tone of seriousness. "What's more depressing is that no one seems to care. Our population is being kept in the dark about these problems. The media gloss over the dire issues as if they're not important. And both the medical establishment and the media refuse to point the finger at industries that pollute the environment with cancer-causing chemicals."

"Yeah, it's unbelievable," interjected Tom. "Even cancer researchers refuse to place any blame for cancer on chemical pollution of the environment. Even when the pollutants are known carcinogens."

"Why, I have a friend who had testicular cancer," Lana explained, leaning back in her chair and crossing her arms. "He had it treated with chemo, and survived. Figuring he had a new lease on life, he decided to adopt a baby boy. The first thing he did was go out and buy a wooden picnic table soaked with cancer-causing chemicals, you know, 'pressure-treated.' I saw him feeding his toddler a peanut butter sandwich directly on the table. When I told him that the wood was soaked with carcinogens and that they could be absorbed into the food the baby was eating, or into the baby's skin, my friend said that he was not aware of any dangers associated with treated lumber. I explained to him that most cancers have a twenty year latency period."

"That means it could be twenty years later before the baby could develop cancer from his exposure to the carcinogens," Tom explained. "That's why most people don't make a connection between their cancer and its cause. They can't remember what cancer-causing chemicals they were exposed to two decades earlier. Then they die, and are silenced forever. And chemical pollution continues to spread throughout the environment. It's a sinister and insidious problem."

"After my warning," continued Lana, "my friend sealed the hell out of the table with an oil based varnish. He now seals it every year in the spring. He's the exception — most people don't care. They've become terribly passive and uninformed about environmental issues, issues that directly affect their health and lives. If this widespread complacency continues, or, god forbid, gets worse, all roads lead to ecocide. Global collapse. Things have to change." Lana insisted.

"That's the problem," added Tom. "Change is inevitable. Even a cold, heartless computer will tell you that. Nothing stays the same. Ever. The question is, will we continue to allow things to change for the worse, or will we look ahead at the impending doom that lies waiting in our future like a coiled rattlesnake, and change course before we're within striking distance?"

"Which will be soon," concluded Lana.

"If it isn't already upon us," Tom said.

"OK. With all due respect, what do you say to those people who simply brand you two as environmental extremists? Wackos? How does anyone know that any of what you're saying is true? Maybe you're just making it all up. Or exaggerating," I argued.

"It's all documented. Scientifically. Everything we've told you, plus a lot more, is common knowledge among ecologists and environmental scientists around the world."

"Oh yeah? Then why haven't we heard it before?"

"That's a good question, Joe. Have you been living in a cave?" asked Lana.

"Or just watching TV a lot, which is about the same as living in a cave," added Tom. "Either way, you won't keep a finger on the pulse of the Earth if you're constantly inundated with messages from commercial media. They're trying to sell you something. They're trying to make money. There's no money to be made in warning people about ecocide. In fact, the commercial sector of our economy fears that if people knew what was coming down, it would hurt business. That's probably why you haven't been exposed to the concept of global collapse."

"Did you ever hear of the World Scientist's Warning to Humanity?" asked Lana, looking at Annie.

"No," we both answered. "What's that?"

"It's just one example of how the media controls what information the public gets," said Tom. "No less than 1600 senior scientists from 71 countries, including half of all Nobel Laureates, issued a world proclamation in 1992. You didn't hear about it because, incredibly, it was deemed 'unnewsworthy.'"

"What was it?" Annie asked.

"It was a proclamation that, well here, let me find it. I have it in a file right over here." Tom jumped out of his chair and jogged into another room.

Lana glanced around the dining room as if searching for something. "I'm a lousy hostess, folks. I haven't offered you *anything*. You get me talking about these issues and I forget about everything else. How about some tea?"

"That would be lovely," agreed Annie.

Lana got up from the table and ambled into the

kitchen. "With or without caffeine?" she shouted from the other room.

"Without!" shouted Annie as I yelled, "With!"

In a few moments she was back with a pot of hot water, four cups, tea bags, and a bowl of blue tortilla chips. Tom soon came rushing back with a file folder in his hand. "Sorry, I had trouble locating the file. It wasn't where I thought I put it. But I can't believe you never heard of this warning."

"Hardly anyone's heard of it, Tom," insisted Lana. "No one's heard of *our* research, either. We scientists aren't a wealthy bunch. We live in frustrating times. We do what we can, but it's not enough."

"*The World Scientists' Warning to Humanity*," began Tom, reading from a sheet of paper he had pulled from the file folder. "Listen to this: *Human beings and the natural world are on a collision course. Human activities inflict harsh and often irreversible damage on the environment and on critical resources. If not checked, many of our current practices put at serious risk the future that we wish for human society and the plant and animal kingdoms, and may so alter the living world that it will be unable to sustain life in the manner that we know. Fundamental changes are urgent if we are to avoid the collision our present course will bring about.*" Tom looked up. "That was in 1992!"

He began reading again, skipping through the proclamation, picking out the salient points: "*The environment is suffering critical stress,* yada, yada, yada, *ozone depletion, exploitation of ground water, pollution, destructive pressure on the oceans, loss of soil productivity, forests are being destroyed rapidly, irreversible loss of species* . . . Listen to this: *Much of this damage is irreversible on a scale of centuries or permanent... Our massive tampering with the world's interdependent web of life — coupled with the environmental damage inflicted by deforestation, species loss, and climate change — could trigger widespread adverse effects, including unpredictable collapses of critical biological systems whose interactions and dynamics we only imperfectly understand.* See what we mean about collapse? And our computer modeling is predicting this stuff too!"

"That's not all. There's more: *We are fast approaching many of the Earth's limits. Current economic practices which damage the environment, in both developed and underdeveloped nations, cannot be continued without the risk that vital global systems will be damaged beyond repair. Uncertainty over the extent of these effects cannot excuse complacency or delay in facing the threat.* See! We don't have the luxury of being able to delay in responding to these threats — that's what they're saying!"

"Let me see that," retorted Annie. She snatched the paper out of Tom's hand and held it in front of her, reading down the page. "Damn," she whispered under her breath.

"What?!" I asked.

"Not only does this look legitimate — it has the names of the signatories attached —"

"Of *course* it's legitimate. And you can download it off the internet, if you want your own copy!" exclaimed Lana.

"Listen to the conclusion," continued Annie. "*No more than one or a few decades remain before the chance to avert the threats we now confront will be lost and the prospects for humanity immeasurably diminished.*"

"That's right," said Lana. "One or a few decades. That's how long the scientists of the world give us. That was a declaration from 1992. According to them, we now have about twenty years left to make it or break it. They give us until 2022. In comparison, our computer model is being very generous in giving us forty years before ecocide — 2040. Twenty years to do something, forty years until the point of no return."

"Point of no return?" I looked at Annie. "Didn't Lucy say something about a point of no return in the first letter we got from her lawyers?"

"Why are you asking me? I thought you read that letter fifty times."

"Well, she said *something* like that. Forty years proba-bly doesn't seem very soon to most people, especially people over fifty who assume they'll be dead by then anyway. Twenty years, though, is right around the corner. Do you think these 'world scientists' know what they're talking about, Tom? It still all sounds just a little bit far-fetched to me, I have to admit."

"They're scientists," replied Tom. "It's their job. That's what they study. That's their speciality. If *they* don't know what they're talking about, who does. Exxon? Monsanto? The Global Climate Coalition? They're just industry mouthpieces. They'll tell you what they want you to hear. And what they want you to hear is that everything is rosy, just keep buying their products and everything will be fine."

"Joe's Aunt Lucy had a theory that the gross consumption we humans are engaged in, especially in the United States, is actually pathological," said Annie excitedly. "She thought that we would normally live in harmony with the world, but that the sudden availability of unguarded resources in the late nineteenth century, or earlier, sparked a psychological pathology in us she called a 'robbing frenzy.' And we can't stop it because it's gone on so long now that we're no longer really aware of it. We're born into it and we think it's normal, so we keep it going."

"Yes. She also thought that humans might just be a disease organism on the planet and therefore we're *supposed* to be killing the Earth," I added.

"I don't believe that," retorted Lana. "We are *not* a disease. At least *most* of us aren't. We *choose* how we live on this planet. It's our choice. We aren't destined to be a disease. I don't believe that. No way."

"Well, it's just one of her theories . . ."

"I agree with Lana," interjected Tom. "What a defeatist attitude! If we're destined to be a disease, then what's the cure? Has anyone considered that? Presumably every disease has a cure."

I looked sharply at Tom. "Don't ask *me* if there's a cure. My aunt thought we might be a disease because we *act* like one. Humans act like pathogens on the planet, according to her and her pathologist friends. But she also thought that we may have a choice in the matter, too."

"If it's a matter of choice," mused Annie out loud, "then the key must lie *within* ourselves."

"Oh yeah, Einstein? What key is that?" I remarked.

"Quit being such a damned skeptic! Just because you don't have any answers doesn't mean some one else can't come up with anything. For heaven's sake!"

"Well, I was just trying to ask an intelligent question."

"For a change."

"Time out already," called Lana. "I think we're all a little overwhelmed by all this. Twenty to forty years to doomsday and no one gives a crap about anything except what's on TV."

"Sorry," I said. "You're right, Lana. Maybe aliens will come from outer space and inoculate the Earth with antibodies to wipe out us humans."

"That's really helpful, dear. Forgive my husband. He has an overactive imagination. We probably should be heading home anyway, don't you think, Captain Kirk? If we hurry, I think I can get us there before aliens inoculate *you*."

17

Witch Doctor

THE CAR RIDE HOME FROM TOM AND LANA'S SEEMED interminable; Annie and I were both in an introspective mood, and hardly spoke two words to each other the whole way back. This Lucy business was becoming depressing; neither of us liked what we were hearing. Although the doomsday scenarios we were being exposed to seemed unrealistic, I had to admit that the arguments supporting them were becoming more and more compelling. Even if there was some kernel of truth to all this, I wondered what we could do about it. Not a damned thing, as far as I was concerned. If 1600 senior scientists couldn't create a unified voice loud enough to be heard over the commercial hoopla, over the din of commerce that we were inundated with each and every day, then what the hell could a small-time, self-employed roofer and housewife do? Not very damned much. That was my opinion.

After our talk with Tom and Lana, it seemed apparent that there was now a time element to consider. Twenty to forty years to ecocide added an enormous sense of urgency to Lucy's affair, especially when we took into consideration the momentum that was building behind the ecological problems. If what the scientists were saying was true and things needed to change significantly, it was obvious they weren't going to change overnight. It could take decades with everyone working together to turn things around; to steer us away from the precipice. That much time appeared to be an unrealistic luxury as days disappeared into the past like lemmings slipping over the edge of a cliff. Furthermore, it seemed that the average American still had no idea what was going on. I wasn't the only clue-less one — I had lots of company. Or if people *did* know what was going on, for some strange reason they didn't seem to care.

Although I still remained somewhat skeptical, I was becoming affected enough by now that I dropped the "Lucy's Goose Chase" moniker and started to take things more seriously. Annie and I were both a little shaken up after our discussion with Tom and Lana. Things seemed to be snowballing. A couple months ago, we were minding our own business, planning our spring garden and worry-ing about little more than paying the bills on time. Now, suddenly, we were faced with the thought of the extinction of the human race in our lifetimes. Or in our children's lifetimes. Well, maybe not the extinction of the entire species, but ecocide? This whole thing was like some B-grade sci-fi movie, and Annie and I were the dupes who were accidentally caught in an intergalactic battle.

I had to review Lucy's first letter again. Sure enough, she did mention a point of no return. But she had also said, "You are not alone — there are many of us spanning the entire planet struggling to avert the upcoming critical time." Her circuitous directions had led me to some of the people engaged in the struggle she was obviously referring to. To Tom and Lana, for example — the tree-climbing lemmings. And Tom and Lana had introduced me, so to speak, to a worldwide group of scientists embroiled in the same battle.

It was not hard to locate the World Scientists' Warning to Humanity on the internet. I simply logged onto Altavista.com, an internet search engine, typed in "World Scientists' Warning to Humanity," parentheses and all, being careful to keep the apostrophe on the word "scientists'" in the correct place (outside the "s"), and 519 web pages were soon listed. I scrolled down to about the tenth page on the list and found the warning in its entirety, without any additional fluff. I printed out a copy for myself.

The warning, released on November 18, 1992, was sponsored by the Union of Concerned Scientists. Amazingly, both the Washington Post and the New York Times had rejected this worldwide edict as "not newsworthy." The front page of the New York Times on November 19th, the day that should have headlined the scientists' warning, instead featured articles about the Catholic Church rejecting the role of women, police officers shooting each other, and rock music, among other things all apparently more newsworthy than the impending destruction of the planet. It was becoming evident to me that we humans were in a sorry state of affairs, and that there was no obvious way out of the woods that I could see. In fact, it all seemed totally overwhelming, if not hopeless.

But what happened next was remarkable, to say the least. I don't usually believe in fate, but sometimes coincidences occur that defy all logic and explanation. First, there was a message on the telephone answering machine when we got home. It quickly diverted our attention from the defeatist mindset that I, at least, had sunk into, and forced us both to think in a different direction.

I pressed the playback button on the machine and immediately recognized the distinctive accent at the other end of the line. "Hello, Annie and Joe? This is Dr. Tomasso calling from Halifax. Are you in? If so, please pick up the phone. [pause] Hello? Anyone home? Well, I'm just getting back to you about that conversation we had a few weeks ago. I've requested some documents from the appropriate sources, and am still waiting for them. When I get something, I'll let you know. That's not why I'm calling, though. I remembered something about Lucy that I thought you should know. She used to do some traveling out of the United States. I don't want to discuss it on your answering machine, but maybe you could call me back. Hope to hear from you soon."

It was still early, only nine in the evening when we listened to the message, so I picked up the phone and called Dr. Tomasso right back. Luckily, she was in.

"Hello, Cecilia? This is Joe Jenkins. I'm returning your call."

"Yes, hi Joe. Nice to hear from you. I called you earlier because I have more information about your aunt. I remembered something the other day that I thought could be of some use to you. It could be a lead. Did you know that Lucy regularly visited a shaman in Peru?"

"A what?"

"A shaman." Cecilia answered. "You know, a person in an indigenous culture who's usually considered the healer of the community. Sometimes they're called medicine men or women."

"Like a doctor?"

"Yes and no. A shaman would probably be my equivalent in a native culture, but they often resort to the use of alchemy, parapsychology, and sometimes mind-altering plants as part of their healing regimen. They can be very accomplished in the use of herbs of all sorts. Nevertheless, they're often looked down upon and discredited by most allopathic doctors, which are standard American or Canadian doctors. Shamans are sometimes referred to as witch doctors, usually in a derogatory manner. I don't know a whole lot about them, but I remember your aunt being thrilled to be able to spend some time with a man called Eduardo. She said she was getting some training from him; she went down there, I think it was to Peru, several times. I started hearing about him maybe five years ago. Boggs never said much, though. So I don't have much to report. I think this fellow was a big influence on her, though. He may be someone to talk to."

"In Peru?"

"Well, it's just an idea."

"Do you have a phone number for him?"

"I don't think he has a phone."

"What about a mailing address?"

"I don't think he has one of those either. I think he lives in the jungle."

"I see. Yes, Cecilia. I appreciate the message, I really do. If you remember anything *else*, please do pass it along to me, too. At this point, I need all the information about Lucy I can get. I'll get back to you if we find out any more." I rolled my eyes in my head, thinking that this "lead" of Cecilia's was absurd, at best.

"One more thing, Joe," she added.

"What's that?"

"Lucy used to go to Peru with a woman I know of. She lives in Montana. I can give you her name and phone number. I got the number from directory assistance."

"Well, OK, why not? Shoot." I grabbed a pencil from the desk drawer, scratched the name and number on a piece of scrap paper, and bid Cecilia goodbye.

"Well, what did she say?" asked Annie, who was standing beside me, waiting for me to hang up.

"Not much, really. Just some hare-brained idea about a witch doctor in Peru. Nothing we can use," I assured her.

"Hare-brained? Dr. Tomasso is *hare-brained* now? What did she say?"

"Nothing, really. All she said was that Lucy used to go to Peru to visit some guy named Eduardo. He was supposed to be a shaman, which is a witch doctor."

"I know what a shaman is. It's a healer and a mystic."

"How do you know what a shaman is?"

"Didn't you read the Don Juan books back in the seventies? Don Juan was a shaman who could fly through the air and stuff like that. At least that's what Carlos Casteneda said."

"Well, what's that have to do with *us*? I am *not* going to fall for that sort of thing now. I don't believe in flying people. This is absurd."

"I didn't say I believed it, either. I'm just telling you where I heard about shamans. They can use hallucinogenic substances to escape the limitations of space and time.

That's how they find out things that you normally couldn't know. Like what's happening somewhere else at any given moment: past, present or future. Or in another country. Like with your mother, or a sick friend. They can tell you what's causing an illness that way. What else did Dr. Tomasso say?" she pressed.

"Not much."

"I saw you write something down. Why are you being such a pain in the ass?"

"Look. We need to maintain some vestige of reason with this Lucy stuff. It's hard enough to swallow what Tom and Lana told us. I don't even want to *think* about witch doctors."

"*What did you write down?*" she asked insistently.

"Here." I handed Annie the piece of paper with the name and phone number on it.

"Who's this?"

"The woman who, according to Cecilia, used to go to visit the witch doctor with Lucy."

"In Peru?"

"Yes. No. She lives in Montana, I guess. They *went* to Peru together."

"Well, call her," Annie insisted.

"No way."

"Why not?"

"Why should I?"

"Because you may find out something, that's why. What's one phone call?" she asked.

"It's a red herring," I replied defiantly.

"What do you mean, it's a *red herring?*"

"It's just one more thing that will take us off course. I think we're finally getting somewhere with this Lucy stuff. Tom and Lana have indicated to me what Lucy was all about. Ecocide. It's *scientific*. She was a scientist, Tom and Lana are scientists, the warning to humanity was issued by scientists. They have some *credibility*. Witch doctors don't. I simply don't want to be side-tracked on another wild goose chase."

"*Another* wild goose chase? When have we been on a wild goose chase? You've always *thought* we were on a wild goose chase, but you were wrong all along. I'll call her myself, dammit."

"Go ahead. You're just wasting your time. She's probably just another fat hippy lady with beads waiting for a UFO to pick her up."

"You're a jerk."

Annie picked up the phone and began dialing. "You'll never get anywhere with a closed mind," she said to me as she listened to the phone ring at the other end.

"Hello? Is this Melissa Berger?" I heard her ask. And the ensuing conversation as she later described it to me went something like this:

"Yes. Who is this?"

"Oh, you don' t know me. My name is Annie Jenkins. I'm calling from Pennsylvania. Your name and number were given to me by Dr. Cecilia Tomasso, a pathologist in Halifax. In Canada."

"Yes? What do you want?"

"I'm calling in behalf of my aunt, Lucille Boggs."

[Silence]

"My husband, Joe, and I have been trying to complete a project for our Aunt Lucy since she died almost three months ago. I was wondering if you could help us."

"In what way?"

"Were you a friend of Lucy's?"

"I don't know who you are. Why should I answer any of your questions?"

"Dr. Tomasso said that you and Lucy made trips to Peru to visit a shaman named Eduardo. Can you tell me anything about that?"

[Click]

"Damn! She hung up on me!"

"Ha! See, I told you! Her UFO probably arrived."

"That is so irritating. Should I call her back?"

"I wouldn't. What's the use?"

"I know *you* wouldn't. Maybe I should write her a letter

instead. You can't hang up on a letter."

"That's true," I agreed, smugly. "But what's her address?"

"You've got a point there — Wait! The address book! Did you see a Melissa Berger in it?"

Once again, I went off to retrieve the trusty address book, which I kept in the top drawer of my desk. I handed it to Annie, who was soon paging to the B's. Sure enough, Berger, Melissa, was listed at the bottom of the page, with the same phone number Cecilia had given me. Earlier in this Lucy escapade, I had tried to call her, but no one had answered; I never tried again. Her mailing address and email were also listed in the little black book. "Here's her email address," Annie announced. I'll try sending her a message. She can't hang up on an email, and she's not worth the price of a stamp."

18

Letter to the Dead

AFTER HER RUDENESS TO ANNIE, I PROMPTLY FORGOT
about Melissa Berger. She was a lead I was not interested
in pursuing. If Annie wanted to follow the witch doctor
trail, she could knock herself out. I had plenty of reasonable things to keep myself busy with.

My apathy, however, was short-lived. The very next
day, I received a packet in the mail from Lucy's lawyers.
My aunt had apparently asked her attorneys to collect her
mail for her, pay her bills, and forward any personal corre-
spondences to me, for god's sake. I sorted through the pile,
tossing the junk mail aside, until a peculiar postmark
caught my eye.

"Well, guess what?" I said, waving an envelope at
Annie. "A letter from Peru, with no return address, of
course. Probably the witch doctor himself," I quipped. It
was postmarked four weeks earlier. Whoever sent it had
mailed it when we were in Canada. I opened it carefully.
The light blue paper envelope was tissue thin. Inside was a
single, fragile sheet of yellowed paper. On it was scrawled
in pencil, only two sentences:

"*Lucita,*" it began, "*Please come immediately. If you are
dead, send someone in your place. Eduardo.*"

I began laughing hysterically. "If you're dead, send
someone else! This is the stupidest thing I've ever read!
What kind of an idiot would send someone a letter like
that?! What is this guy, a moron?" I tossed the letter to
Annie, who was slicing apples at the kitchen counter.

She put the paring knife aside, wiped her hands on her

apron, and stared at the letter lying on the counter as if she had just seen a ghost. Then she slowly lifted a nervous finger and pointed at the scrawled lines on the yellowed paper. "That means you."

"What? What the hell are you talking about?"

"He means you. He's referring to you. You have to go there. You have to see him."

"Don't be ridiculous. Only an idiot would take something like this seriously. The guy probably has the IQ of a chicken!"

"Sometimes you fit that description," Annie mumbled under her breath.

"What? What did you say?"

"Nothing, dear. I'm going to call this Berger lady in Montana back right now and tell her we just got a letter from her friend, Eduardo. Let's see if she hangs up on me *this* time." Annie went straight to the phone, dialed the number, and resolutely stood there waiting for the other end to pick up.

"Hello?"

"Hello, Melissa Berger?"

"Yes. Who is this?"

"Annie Jenkins. I talked to you yesterday. You hung up on me, remember?"

[Silence]

"But don't hang up on me now!" Annie blurted. "We received a letter from Eduardo today. From Peru. He wants someone to go down there to see him."

[Silence]

"Hello, are you there?"

"Yes. What did he say?"

"He said he wanted someone to go there."

"*Exactly* what did he say?"

Annie read from the letter. "He said, quote, Lucita, Please come immediately. If you are dead, send someone else. Eduardo. That's it. That's all he said."

"Oh my god."

"What?"

Melissa's voice was quite deep and matronly. She sounded older, maybe in her sixties. She had an urgent tone. "Someone must go. Lucille would have made arrangements for someone to go in her place. Death would not have been a barrier between her and don Eduardo."

"Yeah? Well, I think the person who Lucy arranged to take her place happens to be my husband."

"I am sure. You would not be calling me otherwise." [Silence].

"Well, my husband doesn't know this Eduardo person. He doesn't know where he lives. Doesn't know his phone number. Can he email him? Or fax him for directions? Peru's a long way off, you know. Can't he just call him?"

"Don Eduardo doesn't have a phone. Or a mailing address. He can only be reached by boat, and by foot."

"Can you tell us how to get there? What if we go there and no one's home?"

"Give me your mailing address. I'll send you a map. Don Eduardo will be there when you arrive. That's for sure."

Annie gave our mailing address to the Berger woman over the phone. Then the woman said, "He must go as soon as possible. I will send the directions today." And she hung up. Just like that.

"Hello? Hello? *Damn!* That's irritating! I *hate* it when that happens!"

"Did she hang up on you again? The conehead. Call her back!"

"No, she's going to send us a map. I can wait."

"Map? What do you mean, a *map?*"

Annie didn't answer.

"What map, *dear?*"

"The map that will show *you* how to get to 'don' Eduardo's."

"Like *hell* it will! Are you crazy? Earth calling Annie, come in Annie! We're talking about *Peru* now, not Canada! This is *ridiculous*. Absolutely ridiculous! I can't believe you'd fall for this witch doctor crap!"

19

Vision

I TURNED MY BACK ON ANNIE AND WALKED AWAY. I
wasn't going to have anything more to do with this witch
doctor nonsense. Instead, I spent the rest of the day in my
shop fiddling around with some little woodworking projects I had intended to complete months ago, before this
Lucy fiasco had begun. A couple of our dining room chairs
were falling apart and I was gluing them back together,
and I had some bird houses to rebuild, too. Although these
little projects kept me busy, I thought about the witch doctor issue throughout the day, and it kept me in a bad
mood. We didn't discuss the topic that evening over dinner
either. Annie could sense that it was potentially an explo-
sive one, and she was hesitant to light my short fuse. We
went to bed that night with an uncomfortable feeling
between us, and slept with our backs toward each other.

In the middle of the night, I awoke with a strange sen-
sation. The room was peculiarly dark; I could barely see
Annie's outline lying next to me. It was almost as if our
bed was floating in a black ocean. I lay on the bed with my
eyes open looking at what should have been the ceiling
above me, but I saw nothing. A strange feeling overtook
me, as if my cranium was expanding very slowly, giving me
a mild vertigo. The slightest motion, even of my eyelids,
sent the bed into a slow spin. I froze, gripping the sheet

underneath me with clenched fists.

Suddenly, the blackness above me appeared slightly cloudy. I thought I could see a tiny light spot in the darkness overhead, but I couldn't focus on it, no matter how hard I tried. It was a wisp of cobwebs floating above me, a fist-sized cloud turning inside-out. I closed my eyes, but could still see it. All the while, a warmth, a comfort, permeated me.

I felt utterly compelled to examine the odd glow above me. I focused and concentrated. Suddenly, I recognized a human form within the fog, appearing very distant. I focused on it with all my attention. The figure appeared to grow larger and came closer, revealing more figures behind the first. As they approached, I counted five ephemeral forms: human shapes with no faces. I concentrated intently. If I looked directly at them, they blurred into unrecognizable apparitions. However, I found that if I looked slightly askance, as if I were looking at a distant star, details began to reveal themselves. The largest form had a human face, a man's face, dark-skinned and bearded. The warm feeling seemed to emanate from him. I looked to his side and was astonished to recognize some of the other four people, all of whom simply appeared to be floating in bliss, angels garbed in white robes.

One of them was Annie. She turned her head to face me and our eyes met. She smiled as soon as I recognized her. I saw my eldest daughter Sarah, then another face, that of a young man whom I didn't recognize. The fourth face was my own, peering back at me through the blackness. When I saw myself, I suddenly jerked bolt upright and found myself sitting on my bed with daylight streaming in through the windows. Annie was not beside me. The warm feeling that had filled me in the black void lingered.

I laid back down and tried to rationalize what I was experiencing, telling myself that it was just a dream. But I couldn't deny the feeling that lingered inside me; I had never felt anything like this before. It was a good feeling, a sense of well being, almost palpable, vibrating within me and upon me as if I were basking under an invisible heat lamp.

The unusual feeling remained with me even as I made my morning tea. It would not go away; I felt utterly and unexplainably different. I could feel it when I ate breakfast, when I loaded my roofing truck, when I climbed on roofs that day, even when I ate dinner that night. Although I was fully aware that my unusual condition had originated from the encounter in the black void, I could imagine no reason for it that made sense.

Somehow, it occurred to me that the man I had seen in the dream was Eduardo, the witch doctor. I also realized that the other faces I had recognized were of people who would be accompanying me on my journey to see him. And yes, I knew without any shadow of a doubt that not only would I go, but that I *must* go. I couldn't offer any explanation for how I understood these things; I just *knew*.

I didn't mention anything about it to Annie until dinner that night. The experience had been too abnormal for me and I wanted to let it sink in for a while before I talked to anyone. I didn't know what to say anyway. How do you tell someone you saw a vision in your sleep and woke up with an odd feeling inside you that's stayed with you ever since? It's not that simple. It's like telling someone you saw a UFO. People think you're crazy. Yet, by dinner time I was utterly convinced that I had had some sort of paranormal experience that portended a future occurrence, and I needed to talk about it.

"Did you have any unusual dreams last night?" I asked Annie, nonchalantly.

"Nope." She was moodily picking at her broccoli with chopsticks.

"Well, I did."

"Oh really?"

"Yes. Really unusual."

"Like what?" she asked, impatiently.

"Well, I met that Eduardo fellow in a dream last night, believe it or not. I actually *saw* him. I know what he *looks* like. He has a black beard. You were in the dream too. It was more like a vision, actually. It left me with a certain feeling. I woke up with the feeling, and I haven't been able to shake it all day; in fact, I can still feel it now."

"What do you mean a 'feeling'?" She stopped eating and looked at me out of the corner of her eye.

"I can't describe it. I've never felt anything like it. Imagine tasting a really exotic fruit for the first time, a totally unusual, incredibly delicious fruit, and then having the memory of that taste stay with you all day long. Strongly. As if you're tasting it again and again, even though you aren't."

"Like a mango, you mean?"

"No, actually, fruit's not a very good example. It's hard to explain. It's more like a hangover. You know, you wake up and feel fuzzy all morning after drinking too much the night before. Well, that's how I've felt all day, except it feels good. And it won't go away."

"Maybe it was the pizza you ate. Maybe you just ate too much."

"No, no. I saw this witch doctor guy. I *saw* him in a dream. Last night! I saw Eduardo!"

"What makes you so sure you saw *him*?"

"I don't *think* I saw him. I *know* it. I can't explain that either. And guess what, I know now that we have to go and find him. You, me, and Sarah."

"Sarah?"

"Yes. I saw her in the vision too. And you. And another person who I didn't recognize, a guy. You were all there last night. I know that we'll all be in Peru together, with Eduardo. See, I told you it was weird."

"What makes you think Sarah can even go to Peru? She's up in Chicago, working in that greenhouse for the summer. You haven't seen her in six months, either."

"I don't care. She's going. I just know it."

"And what about Penny? Was she in your dream too?"

"No. She's not going."

"Where's she going to be then, if we go to Peru?"

"She can probably stay with your mother, don't you think?"

This was the straw that broke the camel's back. Annie had put up with just about enough from me by this time, and the strain of our bizarre inheritance coupled with the stress of our travels and now the possibility of a trip to Peru pushed Annie over the edge.

"My *mother*? Wait a second. What kind of hare-brained idea is this, to use one of your *own* expressions? You jump all over *me* because I make *one* phone call to a lady in Montana, one *reasonable* phone call, I thought, and now you have a crazy dream and you want us to rush off to *Peru*? *I* can talk to a living person in the real world and get concrete information about your aunt and you make me feel like a *fool*. But *you* have what was probably a pepperoni induced nightmare, and you expect me to go along with it like it's the gospel itself?"

"I know it sounds crazy."

"Crazy?! It's more than crazy..." Annie proceeded to give me an earful, ranting and venting built-up frustrations that had accumulated inside her since the beginning of this Lucy affair. I had not been very diplomatic with her a lot of the time and now she was giving me a big dose of what was coming to me — my own medicine. I guess I deserved it. Nevertheless, her withering diatribe went in one of my ears and out the other. I was absolutely convinced that I would be going to Peru and that I would have three companions, so I patiently let her get it all out. Eventually, she calmed down and I picked up the conversation where I left off, trying very hard to be patient and understanding with her. By the time we went to bed that night, Annie realized that my resolve was unshakable, and, by the next day, she became resigned to my premonition — we would go to Peru.

20

Berger's Map

I<small>T WAS ONLY A FEW DAYS LATER THAT THE FINAL</small>
elements of this strange set of coincidences took place. Just
three days after my dream, I got both a map in the mail
from the mysterious Melissa Berger, and a totally unexpected phone call from my daughter Sarah.

Although the envelope had no return address, I knew
the letter was from my aunt's somewhat malevolent friend
in Montana. Not surprisingly, the envelope contained only
a single sheet of paper with a crudely sketched map in
heavy black ink. The map was sparse in detail and included no signature, no note, not even the name "Eduardo."

I pulled an atlas off a bookshelf and looked up Peru.
About two-thirds of the way down the country's Pacific
coast, lay Lima, the capital. The small village of Puerto
Maldenado lay further inland near the jungle border of
Bolivia, and had no principal road access. The village lay
at the foothills of the Andes, nestled in the Amazonian
rainforest on the banks of the Rio Madre de Dios, or
Mother of God River, which flowed directly east into the
Bolivian jungle on its way to the Amazon River. Berger's
map led us toward a remote and uninhabited section of
Amazonian jungle, an uncharted region straddling the bor-
der between Peru and Bolivia.

I had just set the map down, and was massaging my
temples, wondering what the hell I was supposed to do
with it, when the phone rang. I answered, joking to myself

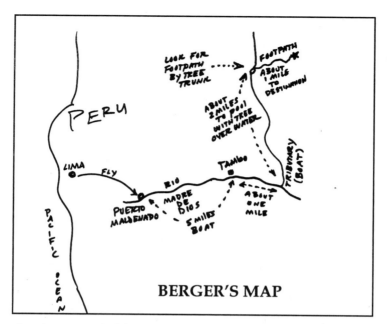

BERGER'S MAP

that it was probably a collect call from the Peruvian witch
doctor. I was almost as surprised, nevertheless, when I recognized the voice on the other end as Sarah's. A phone call
from her was unusual enough. A senior ecology major at
the University of Minnesota, it seemed she didn't have a
whole lot of time for others outside her immediate circle of
college friends, especially for her father. And, when school
dismissed each summer, she returned to her seasonal
employment in a Chicago greenhouse, or to her mother
and stepfather's house nearby. So, my visits with Sarah,
despite my urgings, were infrequent and usually limited.

Sarah had grown into a smart, capable woman. She
maintained an "A" average in school and had earned a near
perfect score on her college SATs. The previous year, she
had taken the opportunity to study abroad, and had spent
the winter in Madagascar. Although she was an adventurer,
I wasn't sure how to broach the subject of South America
to her, and I was certainly not expecting a phone call from
her. I was still processing everything myself, and I needed
it all to sink in before I approached her with the idea of

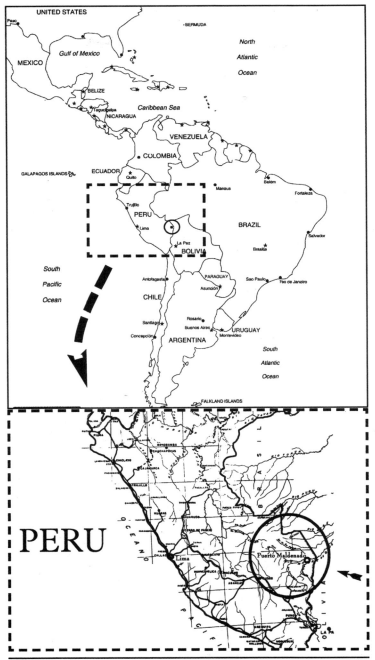

going to Peru with me. But I would not have the luxury of waiting.

"Hello?"

"Hi. Dad? It's me, Sarah."

"Sarah! I was just thinking about calling you. How've you been?"

"Well, for one thing, I quit my job at the greenhouse."

I was surprised at this news, as she'd been working there for years. "Why?"

"The new guy who started managing the place was completely ignorant. He wanted us to spray toxic pesticides on the plants and use all kinds of synthetic chemicals, but I refused. I didn't want to breathe that stuff, or even get it on my skin. We got into a rather heated argument over it and I quit."

"Good for you. I'm sure you can get a better job than that."

"Well, I was wanting to take some time off work anyway. And I was thinking..."

"Thinking what?"

"Well," she asked hesitantly, "do you think I could come and stay with you guys for a while?"

"Sure. When?"

"I was thinking in a few days. I was going to bring my friend Michael with me when I came down. We've been spending a lot of time together lately. He's really nice. I think you'll like him."

"Does he have dreadlocks?"

"Yes. How did you know he had dreads?"

"Just a wild guess."

"A pretty good one, Dad."

"Yeah. See you two in a few days. Don't forget to bring your passports."

"What on earth for?!"

"Just in case. I'll tell you about it when you get here."

Peru

ON THE MORNING BEFORE SARAH'S ARRIVAL, ANNIE
readied the guest room, fitting the bed with freshly laun-
dered sheets. The last of the irises were blooming and she
filled a Mason jar with their leggy stems and placed it on
the old oak dresser to welcome Sarah home. In the meantime, I quietly pondered the logistics of a trip to Peru, por-
ing over maps and calculating costs and timetables. When
I discussed the proposed trip with Annie, however, I was
surprised by her reaction, which could hardly have been
described as positive. Because of my dream, I was quite
convinced that we had to go; Annie, on the other hand, was
still searching for any reason not to.

"Don't they have dictators down there?" she wondered
out loud. "What about terrorists? Can't you get malaria
and yellow fever in the Amazon? What if we got lost? Who
would ever find us? How do we know Berger's map is accurate? Maybe it leads to nowhere! Where will we sleep in
the jungle? Aren't there boa constrictors, poisonous snakes,
piranhas, scorpions, tarantulas, stuff like that down there?
Isn't there a lot of poverty? Don't they resent Americans?
What if we get robbed, or kidnapped, or held hostage?"

Well aware of her reservations, I told her, rather
offhandedly, that I was planning on going to the travel
agency tomorrow to check ticket prices. She stood in front
of the dresser, arranging and rearranging the purple irises,
her back to me. "Do you want to come with me?" I offered.

"No," she answered abruptly. "I have things to do

tomorrow." After the outburst at the dinner table, I decided it best to leave her alone with her thoughts.

Despite her misgivings, I couldn't shake the feeling that the four of us were supposed to go. So I stopped by the travel agency and booked four tickets from Pittsburgh to Lima, Peru. Sarah hadn't mentioned that she needed to get back to Chicago right away. Annie had two weeks to change her mind, I rationalized, and Sarah's friend, Michael, would probably come along for the free ride. If nobody wanted to go with me, it was Aunt Lucy's money wasted, not mine. She's the one who got me into this anyway, I reasoned.

On the way home, I swung by the local bookstore and picked up a copy of the South American Handbook, a book the travel agent had highly recommended. It listed nearly every town in South America, and provided useful information about hotels, restaurants, bus and train stations, markets, rates, fares, customs, warnings, and just about anything else we could have wanted to know.

The Handbook described Lima, Peru's capital and airport hub, as very dirty and smoggy, and issued lots of warnings about pickpockets, thieves, and guerrilla activity. Puerto Maldenado, a jungle town of 10,000 at the confluence of two rivers, the Madre de Dios and the Tambopata, was described as a gold mining and timbering center around which much of the jungle had been destroyed. However, it's location at the base of the Andes allowed for an unusual microclimate harboring unique plant and animal life; several of the best jungle reserves in the world are still located there.

How we were to go from the gold-mining town down river into the jungle was a complete mystery to me. Not to mention how to get back. The thought that we would be attempting to do this in only two weeks was so overwhelming that it seemed best, although perhaps foolhardy, to just wait and cross those bridges when we came to them.

Sarah and her friend, Michael, arrived the next day. I immediately recognized him as the one I saw in my dream, and I couldn't help but stare at him when we were introduced. It was disconcerting enough to see someone that I had met in a dream, but when I gawked at him, I realized that I was probably giving him the same look Lucy had given me in the funeral home two decades earlier. Maybe Lucy had met *me* in a dream before we met physically. Maybe *that's* why she looked at me the way she did. Maybe that's why she decided to choose *me* as her successor in this ego-eco thing. Because of my dream, I knew that Michael was supposed to go to Peru with me. Maybe Lucy knew I was supposed to take up her cause after she died because of a similar premonition.

Luckily, they had done as I had asked and brought their passports. Michael, like Sarah, was also a senior ecology major at the University of Minnesota. Of average height and build, with thick, brown dreadlocks, his loose fitting hemp clothing and sandals gave him the appearance of a vagabond. He had traveled in Mexico extensively, and had done a sustainable agriculture internship in El Salvador the year before, so his Spanish was quite good. He seemed like a nice enough guy, and I thought he would probably be an asset to the crew. He seemed the type who said what was on his mind. Sarah, on the other hand, was quiet and spent most of her time writing poetry. She was unusually sensitive and soft-spoken, but her quietness belied a razor sharp intelligence and an uncanny perceptiveness. The two of them made an interesting addition to our little Lucy escapade.

They both were fascinated to hear the details about aunt Lucy and the "inheritance" she left me. The uncanny coincidence that they were both ecology majors who had been summoned, in essence, to investigate Lucy's "ecocide" theory did not escape me. They were mesmerized by the entire story, especially by Lucy's initial letter, and by the yellowed, cryptic note from Eduardo. They stared at them as if they were viewing the Holy Grail. The hand-drawn map of Peru also fascinated them; they acted at times like they couldn't believe this was all actually happening and that they were about to become involved. At night, Annie and I could hear their whispers in the dark, passing through the thin walls of their room.

In the evenings prior to our departure, the four of us sat by candlelight on the patio drinking homemade wine and talking at length about ecological and environmental issues. Sarah and Michael both knew a lot more than I did; they both agreed that the global environment was in a sorry state of affairs. They admitted, in frustration, that they hadn't learned about the grave nature of the issue through their coursework. In fact, they said that the concepts of ecocide and global collapse were not being addressed at all in their college ecology curriculum. If not for their own personal interest, they pointed out, they would have never been exposed to such concepts. Their classes at the university focused primarily on the pure sciences — how to identify plants and animals, rattle off genus and species names, test water for pollutants, estimate the number of board feet in a stand of trees, and write paper after paper after paper. Never once were they taught how to incorporate basic ecological practices into their personal lives. So they were excited to be involved in real-life environmental sleuthing, especially with so many bizarre twists.

None of us knew what to expect from a trip to the Peruvian jungle, and Annie was still having second thoughts. She insisted that we make out a will as well as put into writing our wishes for Penny, should we die. We decided to leave Penny with her grandmother for the two weeks we'd be gone, so we wrote out a declaration that if we should not return, Grandma would have custody. I suppose it was this notarized document more than anything that forced us to face the seriousness of our proposed undertaking. I secretly wondered if the trip would just be a waste of five thousand dollars, and I silently decided I would be satisfied if we simply got there and back again in one piece.

We did all we could to prepare ourselves for the journey into the unknown. We packed compasses, purchased solar flashlights, filled canisters with waterproof matches, checked and rechecked our emergency first aid kits, counted our water purification tablets, sharpened Swiss Army knives, rationed the freeze dried food, and waltzed around the house in our net bug hats, which delighted Penny, and took her mind off the fact that she would not be accompanying us. None of us had the slightest notion what dangers this trip might bear, and we didn't want to put our ten year-old daughter in harm's way.

WITH PENNY SAFELY TUCKED AWAY IN HER GRANDMA'S house, the four of us headed south. While the others made futile attempts at getting some sleep on the long overnight flight to Peru, I paged through my Spanish-English dictionary and tried to memorize some helpful words and phrases. I also looked through the Handbook knowing that we would be spending the first night in Lima. The Handbook listed numerous hotels, some of which were described as "Gringo-friendly and English-speaking." I underlined and bookmarked the name of the hotel that looked most appealing.

After a stop in Mexico City, and another in Panama, we landed at the Lima airport as the first rays of light crept over the mountains. Sleep-deprived and stiff, we were grateful to be on solid ground and were longing for hot showers and some decent food. Instead, we were herded between ropes down a long corridor like cattle and forced to stand in a long line to wait for customs clearance. We hoped this ordeal would soon end, not realizing that once we passed beyond the sanctuary of the customs gates, we would be thrust into the airport lobby where a throng of thieves, pickpockets and con artists waited to prey on naive Gringos like us.

I stood in line with Annie, shifting my weight from foot to foot; Sarah and Michael stood close behind us. We had filled out our visa forms, paid the fees, and now were waiting — for what, we didn't know. Behind a glass partition, a stern-faced customs officer spread all four of our passports in front of him on the countertop. He looked at me and, in an impatient and unfriendly tone, spoke a few words in Spanish through the hole in the glass. I stared at him blankly, not comprehending a word he was saying. He repeated himself even more loudly, almost shouting at me. I turned to Michael in desperation.

"He wants to know where we'll be staying," Michael explained.

"Tell him I don't know. I have no idea."

Michael exchanged a few words with the officer and then looked at me. "He said he can't let us into the country unless we have an address where we'll be staying."

"Damn! I didn't know that. Tell him OK. Stall him for a minute. I have an address."

While Michael pacified the customs guard, I rooted through my bag and pulled out the trusty Handbook. I opened it to the page I had marked, and handed it to the guard, pointing to the underlined hotel address. He hastily transcribed the information onto the customs forms, stamped our passports and dismissed us with a frown and a curt wave of his arm.

The waiting throng descended upon us like blood-thirsty mosquitoes. People were shouting and shoving, grabbing at our bags, offering to be our guides, pulling us every which way. We yanked our bags back and shoved our way through the swarm, trying our best to ignore them without being pickpocketed or robbed. At the front door of the airport, we all breathed a sigh of relief, thinking that we had successfully escaped the frenzy. But at the curb's edge, another horde, this time of shouting taxi drivers, jockeyed for position and bargained for the privilege of chauffeuring us to Lima.

"*Cuanto cuesta?* How much?" I asked.

"Ten dollars!" they clamored, all scrambling to be in front, some trying to take our bags to load in their idling cabs.

"Five dollars!" I shouted back.

"No, no. Ten dollars!"

"*Cinco*! Five! *No mas*! No more!" I insisted.

My bargaining worked. All of the cab drivers turned their backs to us and walked away, disgusted. We were now free from the maddening mob, but had no ride into Lima. The four of us stood on the sidewalk outside the airport as taxi after taxi left with passengers. We dare not set our bags down. Here we were in Peru, finally, and apparently I was so cheap that even the cab drivers wouldn't have anything to do with us. Soon, only one battle-scarred cab remained at the curb's edge. Its owner, a skinny man with wavy black hair shook his arm out the driver's side window. "Six dollars!"he shouted.

"Six dollars, okay!" I replied. Sighing with relief, we threw our bags into the trunk of the cab and piled in. Sarah tried to roll her window down, but the crank turned freely and the window didn't move. My window was already down and I tried to roll it up a little. Mine didn't move either. What did we expect for six dollars? Windows that worked? The driver climbed into his seat, turned and asked, in Spanish, where we were headed. Once again, the Handbook saved the day. I handed it to him, he recognized the name of the hotel, and a half hour later we were at its front door.

The driver pulled up to the front of the hotel, blocking traffic on the narrow street, got out and wrestled our bags from the trunk. He carried them into the narrow, three-story stuccoed building. We were greeted by Nellie, a friendly, English speaking, middle-aged Peruvian lady. As she guided us down a dim hallway, she explained that the rates were four dollars per night, per room. I told her that we would only be staying one night, and would need transportation back to the airport early the following morning.

"Where are you heading?" she asked, in heavily accented English, twisting the key in the doorlock. She pushed open the door with her hip, and stepped aside to let us enter.

I set my luggage down on the floor, and took out my wallet to pay her for the rooms. "A place called Puerto Maldenado," I explained.

"Puerto Maldenado? Are you going to visit the rainforest? Do you need a guide? I have a friend who may be able to help you. But, you get settled first. I'll see if she's around."

Sarah and Michael dragged their bags into their small room and collapsed on the narrow bed, after propping their door open with a clay pot they had scavenged from the breezeway. Annie stripped off her socks and hiking boots and stretched out on our double bed. In an instant, her eyes closed, and she was fast asleep. I busied myself, sorting through our luggage, and rearranging our gear. I found the map, safely tucked away in the side pocket of my pack, and smoothed it out on the floor to examine it more closely.

A knock on the door broke my concentration. A young woman in blue jeans and a white shirt stood in the doorway. As I stood with the map in hand, I pointed to Annie, asleep in the bed, and put a finger to my lips, stepping out into the hall.

"Do you speak English?" I asked the young woman.

"*Si*," she replied. "My name is Rosa, I'm a friend of Nellie's. She told me that you need a guide for Puerto Maldenado."

I showed her the crude map and she immediately assured me that she could get us there the next day, for a "small fee." We bargained back and forth until we finally arrived at a price. I agreed to pay her fifty percent down, gave her the money, and signed a handwritten contract with her. I'd pay the rest when we arrived at our destination. Rosa assured me that she would arrange for a guide to be waiting for us at the airport in Puerto Maldenado. She didn't ask me for any additional information, and I didn't offer her anything beyond Berger's map.

I tried to rest after Rosa left, but my mind kept wandering through the events that had led us here. Besides, I was too tired and too famished to think very clearly. Before long, Michael and Sarah appeared at the doorway, wiping their bleary eyes. "We're starving," Sarah said, patting her stomach. "Are you up for something to eat?" Annie easily roused at the suggestion of food, and we all stumbled down the hall together in search of Nellie. Surely she could suggest a suitable restaurant within walking distance. Nellie pulled a small map of Lima out of the drawer at the check-in desk and circled a spot on it.

"This restaurant is very nice, and not too far to walk. I think you will like it. The food is very good. Here is where you are now." She circled the spot on the map where her hotel was located. "Keep the map with you and you won't get lost."

We stepped out into the crowded, dirty, dry streets of Lima and soon walked past a ten foot high pile of garbage, choking on its awful stench. In twenty minutes, we arrived at the main square, a haven, according to the Handbook, for thieves and pickpockets. It was now mid-afternoon, we had been up all night with almost no sleep, and had eaten very little since we left home almost 24 hours earlier.

We walked along the streets at a fast pace, ignoring the stares of the locals, searching unsuccessfully for the restaurant Nellie had recommended. Finally, when we were about to give up, Annie exclaimed, "Look, there it is!" She gestured toward a stuccoed building squeezed between similar structures on a crowded stretch of sidewalk. An elegantly carved wooden sign hung over its entranceway. A man in a starchy purple uniform stood on the stone stairs by the door, greeting patrons. He beckoned us to come in.

"Let's go in," Annie urged.

"Yes, I'm starving," Sarah said.

"You've *got* to be kidding," I insisted. "A meal there would probably cost a small fortune. I don't think this was the place Nellie was talking about. Surely she could see we're not rich."

"Yep, this is it," confirmed Michael.

"OK, OK, whatever," I conceded.

A team of uniformed waiters, impeccably dressed in starched white shirts and fuchsia overcoats seated us at an ornately carved mahogany table covered with a crisp, white tablecloth. A crystal vase overflowing with fresh cut flowers graced the center of the table.

"We can't afford this place," I insisted to Annie. "Look at these prices. This is ridiculous. Twenty thousand Intis for a plate of seafood!"

"How much is that in dollars?" asked Sarah.

"I don't know and I don't want to know. This place is *way* beyond our means. Lucy may be paying our expenses, but there's no need to squander her money."

"Relax, dear, we're here," Annie cajoled. "Let's just order something and enjoy ourselves for once. We can splurge this one time. We don't need to order full course dinners."

A waiter approached and asked for our drink order. He recommended a "pisco sour," a popular local brandy drink, similar to a Mexican margarita.

"Oh hell, why not. Make that four," I replied, holding up four fingers. "*Quatro, por favor.*"

The waiter returned with four large frosty glasses filled with the iced pisco sour. They were delicious. Being famished, we drained them before the waiter came back to take our orders. "*Quatro* more pisco sours," I requested with a smile. I pointed to a menu item which we guessed was a seafood platter. "*Dos,*" I requested two of them, feeling financially brazen after such strong drink.

A new round of drinks and two huge platters of delicious shellfish were placed on the table. "Eat up," I urged. "We'll be broke after this." After two drinks on an empty stomach, I was almost beginning to slur my words. The other three couldn't finish their potent drinks, so I had to do it for them. Soon, I was feeling much better. Until the bill came.

The waiter approached gingerly, with a small silver tray in his hand. The bill was lying facedown on the tray.

He bowed forward, set the tray in front of me, and then turned curtly and quickly walked away. With a grimace, I flipped the bill over, praying that the fifty dollars worth of Intis in my wallet would cover it. I had exchanged some money during our stroll through the square, and still had the exchange slip in my pocket with the exchange rate printed on it. I pulled it out and began converting the restaurant bill into dollars.

"I don't believe this," I whispered to myself. "You guys won't believe this!" I announced to the other three.

"Oh no. How much is it?" asked Annie, a worried look crossing her face.

"Those sea food platters were one dollar each! The cocktails were twenty-five cents! Unfrigginbelievable! The total bill comes to four dollars!"

"See, I *told* you," Annie replied. "All that worry for nothing! Now you can afford to leave a tip."

I left a hefty twenty cent tip and we all stumbled out the front door into the sunlight, three sheets to the wind, but jubilant. The heat hit us like a slap in the face as we stepped out of the cool restaurant into the blistering afternoon. We only had to stagger two blocks to a marketplace to find more food being served at an outdoor café. Here, they offered a huge plate of rice and chicken, with a large bowl of turkey vegetable soup, and a tall fruit drink, for forty cents. Suddenly, our four dollar restaurant bill looked like highway robbery. Although I wasn't too sure about visiting a witch doctor in Peru, I was beginning to like it here, nonetheless. The prices, at least, were right.

22

Anaconda Neck Tie

WE HAD TO BE UP, BAGS PACKED, AND OUT OF THE HOTEL at five the next morning in order to catch our flight from Lima to Puerto Maldenado. Thanks to the miniature alarm clock Sarah had packed, we managed to drag ourselves out of bed and meet the taxi Nellie had arranged for us. It was dark and quiet in the streets of Lima when we threw our bags into the trunk of the aging black sedan, but we were thankful that the cab was there waiting in front of the hotel at such an ungodly hour. Nellie was obviously looking out for us, and for this we were immensely grateful.

By dawn, we were on a small jet flying east over the snow covered Peruvian Andes toward the steamy jungle at its distant foothills. The mountains underneath us stretched endlessly into the distance and were formidable in their rugged barrenness. Climbing to peaks of over 20,000 feet, it seemed like the belly of the jet almost scraped on their icy tops. As I looked down at the jagged, snow-covered terrain, I remembered the story of the soccer team whose plane had crashed in these very mountains. Incredibly, most of the passengers on the plane survived, a miracle in itself, I thought, as I scanned the impossibly vertical landscape. Yet, despite this miracle, their downed plane could not be located by the search and rescue teams, and the survivors had to stay alive by eating dead passengers. As I considered these things, I fervently hoped that Aeroperu had kept up the maintenance schedule on the jet we now occupied.

After a couple hours, the towering mountains gave way to hills, and the sterile white abruptly blended into a fecund green. The Amazon basin stretched out before us to the distant horizon as we began our descent. We landed at an airport that was little more than a patch of concrete carved out of a jungle clearing, with a small cinder block terminal building off to one side. Emerging from the plane into a wall of damp heat, we were greeted with the humid smell of rain and vegetation, which hung heavily in the air. Threatening black clouds sagged low in the sky, and puddles dotted the tarmac.

Outside the terminal building, a dark-skinned Peruvian teenager with Incan features, in a white tee shirt, leaned against the passenger side of a rusty old truck, holding up a sign with "Jenkins" crudely printed in thick black marker. This was apparently the guide Rosa had arranged for us. When he spotted us, he pointed to the wood-sided flatbed, and motioned for us to get onto the back of the truck with our luggage. The four of us looked at each other, shrugged our shoulders, and climbed in. The young man wandered around the parking lot and enlisted additional passengers until the truck was crammed with people standing shoulder to shoulder. Being the first ones on, we were crunched right up front, near the cab.

The last passenger, a wiry German man with a camera around his neck, stood at the back of the truck and gripped the wooden side with both hands for safety. As the truck lurched into gear, a Peruvian boy suddenly jumped out of the crowd, ripped the watch off the man's arm, and took off running. The truck was moving now and the startled tourist could only yell and watch in frustration as his wristwatch disappeared into the throng. He quickly tucked his camera into his bag. The sage advice of my traveler's handbook had instructed us to leave our watches and jewelry behind, and to keep all of our money and traveler's checks in a money belt strapped around our waists and tucked underneath our pants. Now we could see why.

The dilapidated truck bounced from pothole to pothole

on the unpaved road to Puerto Maldenado, its bald tires
splashing water out of each pit. We stood in the back of the
truck, hanging on for dear life, wind blowing through our
hair, absorbing the jungle aromas and the heavy, humid
air, while trying to cradle our bags between our legs for
safe keeping. A flock of gaudy, noisy parrots swooped low
overhead, an enthralling cacophony of sound and confusion — our first sight of tropical bird life. Before long, a
small village appeared over the crest of a hill. Tile-roofed
huts and pole shanties nestled between papaya and mango
trees dotted the landscape. A brown swollen river, the
Madre de Dios, wound its way around the village.

The truck came to a jarring halt in the middle of town.
Passengers scrambled off the back grateful to have arrived
at their destination in one piece. Michael jumped to the
ground and was offering Sarah a hand, when the young
driver came around the side of the truck and shouted
something at them. Michael nodded and climbed back on,

Annie overlooks Puerto Maldenado
(Río Madre de Dios in background)

informing us that the man was going to drive us down to the river's edge. Everyone got off but us.

We remained in the back of the truck, our bags still cradled between our legs, and breathed in the heavy tropical air. We were far from Pennsylvania now, and the strangeness of our surroundings drove the point home. We drove past huge piles of bananas stacked on the edge of the dirt street. Thatched roofed concrete buildings lined the roadway. Peasant women with black pigtails and brightly colored skirts haggled on street corners. A wide, lazy river approached ahead, overhung by lush tropical vegetation on its far bank. In minutes, our truck came to a stop only a few yards from the water's edge.

The driver tapped on the cab's back window and pointed to an oversized rowboat with a modest outboard motor, tethered to a clump of bushes. We threw our luggage off the truck and jumped to the ground. Our guide motioned for us to follow as he climbed into the boat. I handed him

Our river transportation

our packs and helped the other three aboard, where they took seats on the long wooden planks flanking each side of the boat. Stepping in, I handed Berger's map to our guide. He nodded and grunted something, started up the motor, and untied the rope that anchored us. The boat lurched ahead and the village rapidly disappeared behind us as we churned downstream.

The turbulent river water looked muddy, appearing remarkably like coffee with cream. The side tributaries flowing into the river were black. The abundance of organic matter leaching into the tributaries from the jungle darkened the water, in great contrast to the clear streams of Pennsylvania. Some timbering debris littered the river, mostly stray logs from upstream. Were we to hit one of these obstacles with our little boat we would be swimming to shore without our luggage. The young guide sitting in the back of the boat by the motor deftly steered around each log or stump as it approached. Nevertheless, we kept a close watch down river, yelling whenever we sighted

Tambo

something ahead — we all wanted to get where we were going, dry, and intact. Our attention was captivated by the impending disasters floating ahead of us, and time went quickly. Before long, we passed a group of thatched huts on the left bank of the river.

"Tambo," the guide said, pointing to the huts. He pointed to my shirt pocket where I had tucked the map away. I pulled it out and smoothed the wrinkles while he looked over my shoulder. He tapped on the place marked "Tambo," and again pointed back to the huts, which were already disappearing behind us.

"Keep your eyes on the river, dammit," yelled Michael. "There's a log up ahead!"

The guide was nonplussed; swerving sharply to the right, he narrowly missed a huge floating stump. We hung on for dear life. A mile further down river, we slowed, veered sharply to the left, and entered a narrow tributary almost completely enclosed by a green canopy of vegetation. Our young driver cut the engine and we slowly drifted into the narrow waterway. Large, stork-like birds took flight, while others of all shapes and sizes fluttered in the canopy overhead. Blazing exotic flowers tumbled in breathtaking bouquets of red and orange on the tributary's banks.

Our progress up the narrow tributary was exceedingly slow. The young Incan man stood on the boat's bow, hacking away at low hanging vines and branches with his machete while I steered the boat from behind. The waterway twisted and turned in and out of the thick greenery, sometimes doubling back on itself. Eventually, and after much time and effort, the tributary widened and we came to a shady pool. A dugout canoe was tied to a tree there, and a small stream entered the pool from the opposite side, splashing over large rocks to form a tiny waterfall before disappearing into the black water. Large, leafy trees arched over the idyllic scene, and a hundred foot long tree trunk, three feet in diameter, lay across the water ahead of us, blocking any further progress upstream. The pool was deep enough and wide enough, though, that the boat had little trouble maneuvering.

"I think we're here," I announced, looking again at the map and surveying the area. "In paradise."

"It's beautiful here!" agreed Annie.

Michael was deep in conversation with the guide, as he had been during most of the river journey. "He's going to tie the boat to this big tree," Michael said, "and wait for us. He said he thinks there's a path over there that will take us into the jungle, if that's what we want to do. If our map is correct and we only have one mile to walk, he thinks it will take us about a half hour to get there. If we want to go back to Puerto Maldenado today, though, we'll have to come back and let him know before he leaves. He'll only wait three hours."

"Well, we better get moving then," I decided, trying to find the sun in the sky to determine how late in the day it actually was. The overhead canopy blocked any view of the

Navigating up the tributary

sky.

"Can't we take a swim first?" Sarah asked.

Michael questioned the guide about swimming, then translated for us. "He says the fish are four feet long in this water, and the alligators eat *them*. He says you can swim here if you want, but he wouldn't."

"I think I just changed my mind," Sarah replied with a frown. "Let's go find that path."

The four of us climbed off the boat onto the huge horizontal log and walked it to the shore. The jungle looked impenetrable; you couldn't see beyond fifty feet in any direction. Our guide shouted something to us.

"He says he'll wait with the boat. We're on our own now. He's telling us to not go off the path. It's very easy to get lost. If we get lost, no one will be able to find us," Michael translated.

"Ok!" I shouted back to him, waving. "What path?"

"It's over here," yelled Sarah. "I see it. Here it is!"

A narrow, well-worn footpath disappeared into the thick jungle.

"Should we take our bags?" asked Sarah.

"I think we should leave them here," replied Annie. "We have no idea what's back on this path. We can always come back for the bags if we need them."

"Yeah, if they're still here," I added sarcastically, eyeing the guide with some distrust.

"I have my backpack," Annie said, unzipping her green satchel. "If you have anything you really want to take along right now, put it in here."

Michael and the guide yelled back and forth. "He says we can leave our bags. No problem. He says they'll be safe with him. He'll wait."

I led the way through the shady undergrowth, pushing past tall ferns as huge, vine-covered trees towered out of sight above us. The jungle was absolutely quiet. The only sound was the noise we made as we walked. No one dared speak. It was as if we were walking in an immense, silent cathedral. The sounds we were so familiar with — automobiles, sirens, roaring jets, barking dogs — were gone. Here in the thickest concentration of living beings imaginable — the most diverse population of flora and fauna on Earth — we experienced the most complete silence of our lives.

Sarah and Michael soon passed into the front of the caravan, forging ahead through the path's twists and turns, delighted when a bird would squawk in the upper canopy, or a brightly colored toucan, with its improbably huge beak, would fly past. The footpath wound around huge trees, their smooth, wide, flat trunks like gray walls defiantly standing in the jungle. Ant nests the size of basketballs hung low from tree branches. Fantastically huge fronds, bigger than a person, sprouted in the underbrush, and vines as thick as a man's leg wound themselves around trees as if to strangle them.

Our halting parade continued until Michael and Sarah doubled back to meet Annie and me on the trail. "There's something up there," they whispered, gesturing ahead. "It looks like some sort of dwelling."

"That must be the place," I said assuredly, assuming command with feigned bravado. "Better let me go first."

I walked up the path and stopped where Michael and Sarah had stood, squinting through the lush undergrowth. I could just barely make out the shape of a small thatched hut on stilts in the distance. I didn't see anyone around it, but when I got a little closer I called out "Hello? *Hola!* Hello?"

We all stood together on the footpath and waited in silence. I was beginning to think no one was home. Then, slowly, out of the shadows, stepped a dark-haired, bearded man in a long-sleeved white shirt. He slowly walked onto the path in front of us, turned, and faced us, not saying a word. His face, as best as I could tell from this distance, was expressionless. It looked like he was wearing a neck tie, which seemed bizarre under the circumstances. With a feeling of shock that sent a shiver up my spine, I recognized the man as the one I had seen in the dream. Black hair, full beard, angular features, dark eyes, wiry.

"Hello," I shouted, still fifty feet away. "We've come from the United States. We're looking for Eduardo."

Michael repeated my salutation in Spanish.

"I am Eduardo," the man replied with a heavy accent, walking toward us.

"You speak English?"

"*Si.* You are with Lucita, no?" he cocked his head and continued his slow, purposeful approach.

"We've come in behalf of my Aunt Lucille Boggs, if that's what you mean."

"What took you so long?" Eduardo stopped in his tracks, only ten paces away from me, unsmiling. I was unnerved to see that his "tie" was actually a live snake coiled around his neck. He held its head out in his left hand, as if to offer it to us. The snake's forked tongue darted in and out.

"You are afraid of the snake?" Eduardo questioned

Eduardo with his guardian snake.
Hut in background

with a raise of his eyebrows, a hint of a smile on his face.

"Is it poisonous?" asked Annie, recoiling, as Sarah asked, almost simultaneously, "Does it bite?" Michael stood back and stared with wide eyes.

"No. It is an anaconda, a baby. It will not hurt you," Eduardo assured us, straightfaced. "But you must meet him before you can come into my home. He is the guardian of my door and will tell me if you have come with good will."

"Well, hello snake," I said, not knowing what else to say, and trying to get the snake meeting formality out of the way. "Nice to meet you," I added, feeling like an idiot.

"Yes. Hello . . ." the rest of the gang murmured, equally uncertain about what to do.

"No. You must place him around your neck. That is how you meet a snake."

"I don't believe this," Annie whispered, apparently frightened. "Maybe we should go back."

"We are *not* going back," I insisted, whispering through my teeth, and wondering secretly what we had gotten ourselves into. We were far from home, standing in the middle of a deep jungle, and had no idea what to expect in this incredibly foreign land. I certainly didn't trust this stranger in front of me at this moment. He was creating an awkward situation, not exactly what I would have expected, considering how far we had traveled at his request. But, we *had* come this far and there was no turning back now. "When in Rome, Annie," I said. "Besides, we have to believe him. If he says the snake won't hurt us, then it won't hurt us. What do you want us to do, Eduardo? I'll be first."

"Take him by the neck with one hand and hold him firmly."

I reached for the snake. Eduardo stepped away, stroking the snake and mumbling something to it. "You are moving too fast," he said to me. "Move slowly." He carefully stepped forward again. "You must place him around your neck," he instructed. "That is how you introduce yourself to a snake. Take him by the neck with one hand and hold him firmly." I reached very slowly for the snake's neck, and wrapped my hand around it. It felt like a dry, squirming muscle. The snake twisted its head to look at me. "Now place the body of the snake around your neck. Slowly."

I held quite firmly onto the snake's neck with one hand, and, with the other, draped the snake's body over my shoulders. The snake coiled around me, but didn't squeeze. I was sweating bullets. Meanwhile, the snake comfortably settled on my shoulders.

Eduardo looked pleased. "It seems that he has found a friend," he told me. "Now pass him to her." He gestured toward Annie, whose eyes were as large as silver dollars. All the color had drained from her face. I assured her she would be fine and told her to just relax. Uncoiling the snake from my neck, never letting up on the firm grip I had on it, I handed the snake to Annie. We carefully

Author meets anaconda

exchanged grips on its neck. "Hold it firmly and don't let go," I recommended. "As long as you have hold of it here, it can't bite you."

Annie managed to take the snake and put it over her shoulders, almost tangling it in her net hat. The snake seemed satisfied with its new perch on Annie's shoulders, and Eduardo was again pleased. Smiling, he instructed Annie to pass the snake on. Sarah was also reluctant to touch the snake at first, but she overcame her fears, first stroking the snake's back with her fingers, then talking to it in a soothing voice. Finally, she took the snake's neck in her grip and placed its body over her shoulders. Eduardo watched the snake very closely, smiling as it slithered over Sarah's back.

"Good. *Bueno*! Now the *señor* with the hair."

Michael, who had busied himself snapping photos, set his camera down and gingerly took the anaconda in his own hands. With a firm grip on its neck, he lifted the snake over his head and draped it on his shoulders like a scarf. We all wore nervous grins by this time, and Michael looked particularly ridiculous with a snake wrapped around his dreadlocks. We broke out laughing.

"Cut it out, you guys!" Michael pleaded. "You don't want to get the snake riled up. *Dammit!*"

At this remark, we all doubled over in laughter. Michael continued to look uncomfortably impatient and refused to crack a smile. The snake seemed, if anything, to be bored by the whole event. Eduardo, smiling, examined the snake closely.

"He tells me that you all may pass into my home," he finally announced. At this declaration, Michael didn't waste another second returning the anaconda back to Eduardo. We all breathed a huge sigh of relief, hoping that this would be our first, and last, snake initiation.

"Come," Eduardo said, bending to the ground to release the snake. It quickly slithered off into the undergrowth. "Follow me. The snake tells me that you are friends. Come."

23

Eduardo

WE FOLLOWED EDUARDO TO THE THATCHED HUT, closely watching the ground out of the corner of our eyes for stray snakes. There were two other structures in a clearing behind the hut — another thatched hut on stilts, similar to the first, and a thatched lean-to, about ten feet long, between them. A smoldering campfire beside the lean-to snaked a thin curl of smoke into the air. Thick bunches of bananas hung upside-down from banana trees along the edge of the clearing. A small black monkey chattered from the top of one of the huts.

"You will sleep there," Eduardo said, pointing to the farthest hut. "And I stay here." He slapped one of the thick poles supporting his hut. "Lucita sent you. She has returned to the Great Mystery. How long can you stay here?"

"Well," I looked at Annie. "We're supposed to return to the States in twelve days."

"How long can you stay *here?* With *me?*"

"Well, this is the third of fourteen days," I replied, making some mental calculations. "We'll need at least three days to get back to Pennsylvania. We better make it four just to play it safe. That leaves us seven days. I suppose we could stay here a week, if we had to. What do you think, Annie?"

"Well, I guess we could stay that long, if we really needed to."

"Sarah, Michael, how about you two?"

They both shrugged noncommittally.

"Seven days is not enough," Eduardo insisted. "But if that is all you can stay this time, then we must make the most of it. I have already prepared four mosquiteras in your dwelling. I have been waiting."

"*This time?*" repeated Annie.

"What's a mosquitera?" Sarah interrupted.

"A mosquito net over a hammock," answered Michael. "You can't sleep without them in the tropics or the mosquitoes will eat you alive at night."

"How did you know there were four of us coming?" I asked Eduardo. "How did you know *anyone* was coming?"

"You already know the answer, *amigo*. Some things cannot be explained in words." He looked at me knowingly and turned toward our hut. "Come, I will show you your room."

We followed him up an eight foot ladder made of wooden poles lashed together with vines. Four woven hammocks, each with a mosquito net draped over it, hung closely together in the hut's interior. Crude seats fashioned from logs were positioned around the bamboo walls of the hut, and an oil lamp hung by a thin wire from the rafters. The filtered sunlight of the rainforest trickled in through the windows, which were merely openings in the walls without glass or screens.

Eduardo left us alone as we made ourselves comfortable in the small structure. We sat in a circle looking at each other, not quite sure whether to believe that we were actually at the lair of the infamous witch doctor. "If we're going to be here a week, we need to make some arrangements right away," I explained to everyone. "Michael, would you go back to the boat and put our luggage on the bank for us? Then take the boat back to Puerto Maldenado as quickly as possible and reserve our return flights?"

"No *problema*," Michael assured us.

"Would you mind picking up some food, too?" Annie asked. "As much as you can carry?"

"And come back as fast as you can?" Sarah added.

"It's only around noon, and if you hurry you'll be back before dark. Make sure you arrange for the boat to pick us up in seven days, too," I instructed.

"I better write this all down," Michael mumbled.

I handed Michael enough traveler's checks to pay for the plane tickets and food, and gave him an American ten dollar bill to tip the boat guide so he would remember to come back and get us in a week. We all climbed out of the hut and Michael took off at a slow jog down the jungle path. "We'll be right behind you to pick up the luggage!" I shouted to him.

Eduardo appeared again, seemingly out of nowhere, a disconcerting feat we would have to get used to. "What chance is there that our boat will actually come back in seven days to pick us up, Eduardo?" I asked. "Can we trust the guy with the boat? Is he reliable?"

"If the boat does not come back," Eduardo replied, "we can go up river to Tambo in my canoe and wait for a boat there. But he will come. He needs money. You are not the only visitors to come here, but there are not many. I do not like to have visitors unless I invite them."

"We need to go back to the pool where we came in and get our bags now," Annie explained to Eduardo.

"We will all go together," Eduardo insisted. "You must begin your instruction at once. Seven days is not enough." As if echoing Eduardo, the little monkey chattered in agreement, scrambling down from the roof of the hut to perch on Eduardo's shoulder. Sarah and Annie clapped their hands in delight, enchanted with the tiny creature's theatrics.

"We don't have to meet the monkey, too, do we Eduardo?" I asked, envisioning a monkey on my shoulder.

"No. But the monkey wants to meet you. She's a little devil. She'll climb up on you when you're not looking. You must learn how to say no to her and chase her away if she bothers you. Don't leave any food where she can get it either or it will disappear. So will your tools, clothes, and anything else she can get her paws on. Keep everything in your bags at all times," he cautioned us, scratching the monkey affectionately behind her ear.

We started down the footpath toward the boat at a leisurely pace. Wasting no time, Eduardo kept up a constant conversation to prepare us for our stay. "And always shake out your shoes before putting them on," he said.

"For heaven's sake, *why?*" asked Annie.

"You probably don't want to know," I replied sarcastically.

"Scorpions. They live in the thatch roofs. Sometimes they drop down at night and climb into your shoes. Always shake out your bedding before climbing into your hammock, too. The mosquitera should keep out the scorpions and snakes, but you should check your bedding and clothes regularly."

"More snakes?" asked Sarah in disbelief.

"If you see a bright red snake, a small one, it is a deadly viper. Avoid it. The other snakes will leave if you hit at them with a stick."

"That's your job, Joe," Annie offered, laughing nervously. "You can be in charge of hitting the snakes."

"And checking the shoes and beds, too, Dad," Sarah added.

"Anything else we should know, Eduardo?" I hesitantly asked.

"The mosquitoes can carry malaria. There are about seven kinds of mosquitoes, but only the big ones carry the disease. Try to avoid being bitten. They will all be out preying on us after the sun sets. We will liven up the fire then and the smoke will keep them away until we sleep. Also, sand fleas and some flies carry disease, too. Keep a long-sleeved shirt and long pants on and keep your skin covered unless you're in your mosquitera, or swimming underwater."

"Where can we swim?" asked Sarah. "Our guide said

there are crocodiles in the water." We were walking single file through the jungle with Eduardo leading the way. I brought up the rear.

"He is correct," Eduardo said over his shoulder, pushing aside a huge fern frond as he passed by. "But the crocodiles will not hurt you. They are small, no bigger than two meters long. But you must never swim anywhere if you are bleeding. The blood will attract dangerous fish to you. Tomorrow, we will go to a place back the other way, through the bush, where I swim and bathe. It is a large lake and the shore is sandy, like a beach. We will catch fish there for dinner tomorrow."

My mind drifted as I became totally engrossed in the surrounding flora. The ferns scattered over the mossy ground were unbelievably huge, like in a fairy tale. Vines hung everywhere. Liana "air plants" were nestled in every tree crotch like leafy spiders, thriving without roots in the soil. The trees we walked between towered overhead and seemed to disappear into the sky. Walking behind my family down this path through the Amazon rainforest with a strange shaman in the lead suddenly seemed totally incongruous to me. Three days ago we were home in Pennsylvania, now we were having anacondas wrapped around our necks and thinking about scorpions in our shoes. I thought about the circumstances that had led us here, and I desperately needed some clarification on this matter. "Why did you want my Aunt Lucy to come here, Eduardo?" I asked. "Why did my aunt come down here to see you? And why did you send for us?"

"Lucita came here many times. She needed my guidance. There are things to learn that you cannot learn in your society. So she came here. I was her teacher."

"Why you?"

"I am a shaman. A healer. Lucita wanted to learn how to heal, but didn't know where to start."

"How did she know about you?"

"I summoned her, like I summoned you. I am bound by an oath to teach the ways of the shaman. If someone can learn the ways, I will teach them. But they are ways that very few people can learn, and therefore few ever will. For example, can you hear that insect?"

"What insect?" I stopped in my tracks and listened, but heard nothing.

Eduardo stopped, too, pointing above him, off to the right. "Listen closely," he instructed. "Even though the insect is there and it is speaking," Eduardo continued, "you do not hear it. You do not know what it sounds like, and so you do not know what to listen for. You can walk past it day after day without hearing it. The voice of that insect is like the way of the shaman. Your people cannot learn such ways for the same reason you cannot hear that insect. Although everything a shaman knows is knowable by anyone else, most of your people will never gain that knowledge because they do not know how to listen. Like the insect, the knowledge could be right in front of them, and they would not recognize it. Lucita was different. She was open to knowledge. She could listen and hear things others couldn't. That is why I could contact her. Most of your people are deaf and blind. They cannot be contacted because their minds are closed and their heads are already full."

"What do you mean, 'my people'?"

"Your people who are destroying the Earth mother."

"But aren't your people also destroying the Earth?" asked Sarah. "What about all the rainforest that's being cut down?"

"They are not my people. They are your people. You are all the same. You think the Earth mother is to be taken. So you take and never give back. Your souls are lost. Your hearts are misplaced. You suffer from a sickness." Eduardo suddenly stopped and pointed. "There is the water ahead."

We arrived at the tributary and took a seat on the bank to rest. The little waterfall made a soothing sound like tinkling glass. It started to rain. Eduardo quickly stepped into the jungle and came back with four large leaves. "Hold this over you to stay dry. It rains every day here. Several times.

It will pass soon."

"I guess that's why they call it a rainforest," Sarah said. "Look! There's a rainbow!" A display of colored light arching across the tributary pond disappeared into the trees.

"It really *is* beautiful here," Annie said.

"The Earth is beautiful everywhere," replied Eduardo. "Except where she is being hurt. Then she cries in pain. A shaman feels the pain as if it is his own. The Earth mother is sick. Your people are killing her. You must stop before it is too late."

"Stop what, exactly?" asked Sarah. "How do we stop hurting the Earth?"

"We will discuss it more later. Now is not the time," Eduardo waved his hand as if to dismiss the subject.

"How is it that you speak English so well?" I asked, perplexed.

"I was born here in Peru, but I grew up in Belize. I received an education in English there at the university. My father was Spanish, my mother Peruvian."

"Belize is an English-speaking country in Central America, Dad," Sarah explained. "It was a British colony for a long time. They have a small English college in Belize City, the capital."

"I came back here to apprentice under my grandmother," Eduardo continued. "She was my shaman teacher. She learned from her own grandmother. My grandmother passed into the Great Mystery several years ago. I still call on her if I need her. The spirit of a shaman, like the spirit of the Earth mother, never dies."

"This is all very interesting. Fascinating, in fact," I said. "But I don't see how we can be of any use to you. If Lucy came here over and over again and couldn't help you, how can we possibly do anything?"

"You will be of no use to me. I will be of use to you, but you must learn quickly." Eduardo tilted his head back and scanned the treetops, as if looking for something in particular. "We should return now," he abruptly announced.

We strapped our packs on our backs and marched back

toward the camp. On the way, Eduardo paused at a large ant nest that hung from a tree branch. It looked similar to a hornet's nest. He poked it with a stick, opening a small hole to reveal the tiny ants inside. "These make very good food for chickens," he said, then he started off down the path again. Before long, he stopped at another tree. A vine twisted its way up the trunk. "You should learn to recognize this vine," he said, pulling his machete out of its canvas case strapped at his waist. "If you need water to drink, this vine will give it to you." He gave the vine a solid whack, cutting it in half. Water poured out, and he placed his mouth underneath and drank his fill. "Here, drink." I drank from the vine next, surprised that it tasted just like water. I passed the vine to Annie and Sarah to try. Eduardo removed a skin vessel strapped over his shoulder and filled it with the water. Then he quickly took off down the trail as we followed closely on his heels.

"You must never wander off the path," he warned us.

Eduardo teaches us the ways of the jungle

"It is very easy to get lost. Let me show you. Joseph, walk in that direction twenty paces." He pointed to the right of the path. "Then stop, close your eyes, turn around twice, and then open them. We will wait here."

Fine, I thought. I walked the requested twenty paces, pushing my way through the thick undergrowth, counting my steps out loud. At the count of twenty, I stopped, closed my eyes, turned two times, and opened them. I recognized absolutely nothing, and was surrounded by tree trunks, vines, and leaves on all sides. Vegetation crowded all around me. I desperately looked for the group and for the footpath, but I wasn't sure which way I had come, and I didn't want to start wandering off in the wrong direction. Back in the woods of Pennsylvania, if all else failed, I could at least look at the sky to gain a sense of direction. Here, any view of the sky was blocked by the canopy of towering trees. Damned if I wasn't already completely lost. "OK!" I

Visibility was limited to fifty feet or less

yelled into the green thicket. "I'm lost! Where is everybody?!" I could hear Sarah's loud laugh behind me, so I spun around and made a beeline toward her, shoving my way through tall philodendrons and ferns.

"Jesus H. Christ in a chicken basket!" I yelled. "I was lost! I hate it when that happens! Everything looks the same when you walk into this goddam jungle. Let's not do any wandering alone in the jungle, OK? I don't want anybody getting lost, especially me!"

"C'mon Dad, let's go," Sarah laughed as she started down the footpath. "You can hold my hand if you want to."

We eventually made our way back to camp, completely exhausted from our travels and hoping for an early night. Sarah became increasingly worried about Michael as dusk filled the jungle with shadows and mosquitoes began their evening browse. We were wondering if we should go down the footpath with flashlights, when we heard someone trampling through the underbrush. We were relieved to see that it was Michael carrying two plastic mesh sacks filled with fruit and other provisions. He set the heavy bags down with a groan of relief as Sarah jumped into his arms. Annie and I stashed the goods in our hut while Sarah told Michael all about our afternoon in the jungle with Eduardo.

Annie quickly prepared some food for us all and then we spent a few minutes around the campfire swatting at mosquitoes until Eduardo urged us to get some sleep. He could tell we were weary and he said we were in for a long day tomorrow. Relieved, and at the same time slightly apprehensive, we crawled into our hammocks under our mosquiteras. The serene silence of the daytime jungle had been replaced by the increasing crescendo of night sounds. We laid in our makeshift beds, silently listening to the cacophony of insects, tree frogs, and nocturnal monkeys that soon serenaded us into dreamland.

24

Eduardo's Lake

THE RATTLING OF PANS AT THE CAMPFIRE WOKE US JUST
after dawn. As Eduardo boiled water in a pot, we ate our
imported breakfast of dried fruit and homemade granola.
Eduardo, who ate with us, seemed delighted with the
unusual fare, but annoyed at the plastic yogurt containers,
which he demanded we take with us when we left the jungle. Lifting his blackened pot from a hook over the fire, he
poured us steaming mugs of a thick, dark liquid while
complaining of the garbage he frequently sees floating in
the Madre de Dios. We hesitantly peered into the cups.

Eduardo was amused at our reluctance to sample his
drink. "It's cacao," he assured us. "Chocolate. It grows wild
in the jungle. I roast and grind the seeds, then mix them
with boiled water, and sugar, too, if I have it. Without
sugar, it's very bitter." Eduardo explained that this drink
was once reserved only for Incan royalty and that it was
traditionally mixed with very hot peppers. He said that the
seed of the cacao plant is very special and it will enable a
person to have extraordinary strength and stamina. Even
though he could tell by the looks on our faces that it was a
little too bitter for our taste, he urged us to drink all of it.

As we ate, Eduardo began teaching us about some of
the plants and herbs he gathered and used from the surrounding jungle. Apparently, there was a wealth of local

plant life that could be used for medicine, for clothing, construction, rope, cord, insect repellent, and food. He explained that some plants could give a person strength and stamina and enable one to prowl through the jungle like a panther. Cacao was one of these plants. Other plants could put one to sleep, rid one's self of parasites, heal skin problems, kill bacteria, poison prey, or enhance dreams. He told us that he would show us some of these plants on the way to the lake, our destination for the day.

Soon after we ate and brushed our teeth, we set foot on a path leading from the camp in a direction opposite the path to the boat. After a full hour of winding through flat, heavily wooded terrain broken by meandering rivulets, which we had to jump over or wade through, Eduardo stopped and pushed aside some thick philodendron bushes. He nodded his head toward the opening in the leaves, inviting us to take a peek. Through the bushes we could see mangroves overhanging the edges of an enormous lake, and an impossibly blue sky reflecting on the water. We continued on the path, past the vegetation, and soon arrived at the lake shore, where Eduardo led us to a wide beach. Huge white birds flew from tree to tree and waded near the water's edge. We could just barely spot the reptilian shapes of crocodiles basking in the sun on the distant banks. The light brown sand was fine and clean and felt good under our feet. A dugout canoe, almost identical to the one at the tributary pond, floated at the water's edge. It was carved of a single log in what I assumed to be a traditional style. Crude fishing equipment lay on the beach near the canoe, including a bamboo rod and a long, barbed fishing spear.

Eduardo stripped off his shirt and pants and waded into the lake. He motioned for us all to follow. "It is good to bathe every day. I come here every morning. Lucita bathed here many times." In no time Sarah was in the water, and we were right behind her, grateful for the opportunity to wash several days of dirt off our bodies. We even scrubbed our grimy clothes and draped them on mangrove branches to dry in the sun. While Michael and Sarah splashed in the crystal clear water, Annie dried on the sand, soaking up the warmth. In the meantime, Eduardo gathered his fishing gear and ventured alone out onto the lake in the canoe.

Our clothing soon dried and we all dressed, then decided to go exploring. Annie and Michael went one way around the lake on foot, and Sarah and I went the other. We walked slowly at first, for fear of flushing a crocodile or snake or something else that would startle us, but we weren't afraid of getting lost because we had the lake to use as a point of reference. The mangroves made walking difficult in some spots, but we could climb through their elevated roots over the water's edge when we needed to get past a challenging place. Occasionally an iguana would jump out of a tree and splash into the water, scaring the

*Michael in the dugout canoe
at Eduardo's Lake*

hell out of us. Most of the time we were too busy looking at every little insect and plant to make much progress. Sarah was particularly interested in the snails that we found near the water's edge on the dry land, which were the size of softballs. She picked one up and decided to take it back to show Michael. I continued to explore the lake on my own, trying to see how close I could get to a crocodile. They always managed to sense my presence and glide into the lake before I could touch one with a stick.

After a couple hours of exploring, I meandered back to the beach, where Sarah was speaking with Eduardo as he cooked a large fish on a bed of coals. I could see Annie and Michael still wandering along the lake shore in the distance. I walked over to the water's edge and sat alone in the sun with my feet submerged. I couldn't help but overhear Eduardo's and Sarah's conversation.

"What did you mean when you said you could hear the Earth mother." I heard Sarah ask.

"I said I could feel what the Earth mother feels. I can know what the Earth mother knows."

"But how can you do that?"

"I can do it, you can do it, anyone can do it."

"How?"

"We are all of the Earth. She is in us and we are of her. There is no separation. We are born from the Earth, we live from the Earth, and when we die, we will return to her. That is how we know."

"Then why don't *I* know?"

"You do. The Earth mother speaks to you at all times. You would hear her if you would listen. You cannot hear her because you have allowed her quiet voice to be drowned out by the loud noises of those who would destroy her."

"What noises?"

"There is no noise here, in this place. This is a good place to hear the Earth mother. To listen to her heartbeat. But you are not here normally. You are usually in a place that is noisy with people who can only think of taking from the Earth mother and not giving in return. They are lost. They have lost their spirit. They have lost sight of the Great Mystery. They think only of themselves."

Sarah paused, still confused. "Uh, what exactly do you mean by 'the great mystery,' anyway?"

"The Great Mystery cannot be explained in words, *señorita*. It is called Great because it is large beyond comprehension. It is called Mystery because it cannot be understood. If you would listen, you would hear the voice of the Great Mystery as well as the voice of the Earth mother. The Earth mother is part of the Great Mystery, the stars are part of the Great Mystery, you are part of the Great Mystery, I am part of the Great Mystery. We are all connected. We are all the same. When someone harms the Earth, they harm all of life. You cannot pluck a hair from a great being without sending a shudder of pain throughout the whole body. We are all the body of the Earth mother, and she is the body of the Great Mystery. We all feel the pain of the Earth. Unless our spirit is dead. Then we feel nothing."

"How can our spirit be dead? What do you mean?"

"Our spirit is what connects our human mind to a higher mind. When our spirits are dead, we are not aware of our connection at all. We think we are separate from the Earth, and we deaden ourselves to her pain. The more we develop spiritually, the more we are aware of our connection to the Earth mother and to the Great Mystery."

"That's not what I learned about spirituality. I was taught that we develop spiritually in order to be closer to God."

"What you call 'God' *is* the Great Mystery."

"But that's not what I learned. The church I go to says God . . ."

Eduardo interrupted. "Let me tell you a story, Sarah, *sí?*"

"Sure."

"Look at this beach." Eduardo swept his hand in front of him, along the entire expanse of beach. "How many

---

Searching for a Spiritual Missing Link   189

grains of sand do you think are here?"

"I have no idea."

"Billions and billions. Many, many more than anyone could count. And on a single one of those grains is a population of animals that are much too tiny to be seen."

"You mean microorganisms? Microscopic organisms — too small to be seen with the naked eye, like a microbe?"

"Yes, that's what I mean. Microbes, as you say. Well, a population of these microscopic animals has lived on a grain of this sand for a hundred thousand years. If we walked down this beach, we could probably find that single grain of sand buried somewhere, if we knew where to look. But a grain of sand is so small and there are so many we would probably never find that particular one."

"But why would we want to find *that* one?"

"Because it's very special. You see, the microbes on that grain of sand have evolved over a hundred thousand years and have developed their own simple intelligence. They can communicate with each other. They have their own microbial form of language. Some of their more evolved ones wonder why they exist at all. They have become self-conscious. They question their existence in their own primitive microbial manner."

"Microbial manner?"

"Well, they don't talk like we do with mouths and vocal cords, but they *can* exchange information between each other. So they wonder why they exist."

"Why would they wonder that?"

"*Don't ask me!*" Eduardo laughed. "I'm just telling the story! Let me finish. Then one day, one of the microbes thought of an answer to that great existential Question. It suddenly figured out why they all existed. The microbe declared to the other microbes that it knew the answer; it said, 'We are the most intelligent form of life on this grain of sand. Since we know of no life more intelligent, we must be the most intelligent form of life that exists. We must exist, therefore, because a very Great Microbe, like us, created us!' This explanation seemed good enough for the microbe population — a Great Microbe made them and their grain of sand, and everything else, too. So the microbes accepted this as the true nature of their existence, and they have believed it ever since."

"So what's the point?" Sarah asked in exasperation.

Eduardo laughed. "What do you think the point is?"

"Microbes aren't very smart?"

"Microbes are limited in understanding, limited in intelligence, and limited in what they can know. They create explanations that allow difficult concepts to become understandable to them. They create myths to help them understand the nature of their existence. As they evolve over the next hundred thousand years, their myths will evolve too. Their ability to describe what they are aware of will change with time, because their awareness will also change."

"This is an analogy, right?"

"Yes, of course. People look at those microbes and see how they think the world was created by a Great Microbe, and laugh. It's silly. The microbes have no idea of the true extent and nature of existence. They don't have a clue. Well, people are like microbes too, only on a larger scale. There are hundreds of billions of stars in our galaxy, just like the sand on this beach. Each star may have numerous planets and moons. We inhabit one tiny grain at one edge of our galaxy, as if we ourselves were microbes on the edge of a cosmic beach. We've evolved enough to wonder about the nature of our existence, but our awareness of the true extent of life is very limited. So we have created myths to explain it all. And, like the microbes, we want to believe that one of us, a Great Human, a human God, created us, our planet, and everything else."

"But that's the basis for most religion, isn't it. That myth?"

"Perhaps. And it would simply be laughable if the myth weren't considered truth by so many humans. But we have reached a time in our coevolution when we need our existential myths to evolve."

"Coevolution?" Sarah asked.

"Yes, there is no such thing as evolution. There is only *co*evolution. We evolve along *with* the other living things on this planet. We are not separate. As I was saying, the 'Great Human' myth was fine for a long while, but now it's doing more harm than good. It is deluding us, impeding the spiritual development of the human species," Eduardo explained.

"How?"

"Humanity is worshiping *itself* when it believes that a human created everything, when it believes in a human God. We are like the microbes believing in their microbe God. True spiritual development occurs when we realize that we are a part of something *greater* than us, and we strive to understand the true nature of that greater Being. As long as we cling to the myth of the Great Human, as long as we believe that the larger level of Being is just another level of human-ness, we convince ourselves that there is *nothing* greater than us. Then we spiritually stagnate. We cannot coevolve without cooperating with the rest of Life. The Great Human myth makes us believe we are superior to the rest of Life, that we don't have to cooperate. However, we are not superior, and we must cooperate with the Earth mother if we are to survive."

"But what difference does it make if people are like microbes? How can we ever understand the true meaning and nature of existence?"

"Perhaps humans will never fully understand *anything*. But our understanding *does* grow. It does develop and evolve. We know now the Earth is not flat, although we once believed it was. We understand that the Earth is not the center of the universe. But as long as we continue to blind ourselves to the connection between us, as humans, and the Earth as a greater Being, then we will remain self-centered, deaf to the voice of the Earth mother, whom we are harming. We will never come close to understanding our true position in the Great Mystery. We will suffer spiritual imbalance. Spiritual stagnation and impoverishment.

That's what's happening now."

"What's happening?"

"I must not be a very good storyteller!" Eduardo laughed.

"No, that's not it. I just don't understand, Eduardo. What is our true position, as humans, in this thing you call the Great Mystery?"

"*Señorita*, you have asked the right question. You are learning. *Bueno*. Now it is up to *you* to find the answer. Before you can even ask that question, you must realize that there *is* a Great Mystery. You must understand that we humans do *not* have the answers. You must come to realize that we, like the microbes, are just *one* life form in a vast, universal, continuum of life. Our individual consciousness is one drop in an ocean of consciousness. We have our place, and it is not at the pinnacle of life, even though some humans may think it is, the way they once thought the Earth was flat. There is no pinnacle of life. There is no hierarchy — there is only life. Where is our place? By asking that question, you have set foot on a true spiritual journey."

"Can you give me some more clues?"

"Ha! Alright. Let me try to sum it up for you. We humans have an awareness of ourselves, each of us. We are all self-centered, to some extent. You are Sarah, with your dyed blonde hair and your friends and everything else that defines your sense of self."

"Sure," Sarah agreed.

"The more spiritually evolved we become, the more we are aware that we are also a part of everything outside and beyond ourselves; we are just a tiny piece to a greater whole. We become more selfless. If we were to become completely selfless, as some mystics do, we would perhaps no longer care at all about our individual self and maybe just wander off and die. Either extreme, whether too self-centered, or not self-centered enough, makes us spiritually out of balance. It's a *balance* that we must maintain in order to live in a productive and fulfilling manner. That's what spiritual development does, it refines the balance between us as individuals, and the rest of life."

"I think I'm following you."

"There is a point in your consciousness between self-awareness, and selfless awareness. When you have reached a balance between the two, you have reached a place of spiritual fulfillment. It's that simple, *señorita*. The people who are harming the Earth mother are out of balance. They have developed their self-awareness with little or no *selfless* awareness. They, like the microbes, are not aware of the Earth mother, or the Great Mystery. These people believe they are the pinnacle of life. They spend their time counting their money and their other material possessions. Although this is an age-old problem, it has now progressed to a level that threatens the Earth mother. Your people are destroying the continuum of life, as if your people were, in fact, a disease."

Although I hadn't been involved in the conversation, I had been hanging on to Eduardo's every word. It reminded me of my conversations with Cynthia, Lana, Tom, Cecilia, and Dr. Gaulton. How could I be hearing the same theme from a Peruvian shaman so far away in such a foreign world? I casually wandered over to the fire. Eduardo was poking at the huge fish which lay on the hot coals, wrapped in thick green leaves. "Nice catch," I said.

"We will eat soon."

"Eduardo, I couldn't help but overhear a lot of your conversation with Sarah," I admitted. "You were saying there is a point in our consciousness between our 'self' and a 'greater self,' or something like that?"

"That is correct. Your consciousness is not something separate from the greater consciousness. You are a part of it. That is a fundamental lesson of shamanism. When we learn that we are part of a greater being, we can also learn how to raise our own level of awareness within that greater consciousness. We all have that capability at all times. Sometimes people have premonitions. Sometimes they see the future. Many people call it intuition. They are simply allowing their consciousness to tap into the greater consciousness, which knows all. A shaman, with many years of practice, can do so at will."

"But what about this consciousness point you were talking about?"

"It is your place of spiritual balance. At this place, your individual consciousness will not dwell on itself too much, nor will it dwell on the greater consciousness too much. The point is different for each person."

"And when we arrive at that point, you're saying that we have achieved spiritual fulfillment?"

"*Si, amigo*. When we arrive at a point of balance between the two. That is what I said. You will know when you have found it. We are all connected to the Great Mystery at all times. There are no exceptions. We know this in our hearts. Because of this connection, we have a natural yearning to understand that connection more fully. We yearn for spiritual awareness. It is a natural human trait. It is that yearning that fuels your religions, although your religions may not approach the issue in the right manner."

"We're all connected to this thing you call the Great Mystery at all times, you say. And the Great Mystery is, in fact, the world around us? Is that what I'm supposed to be understanding here?" I asked.

"The world around us is only the part of the Great Mystery that is knowable to us. The true nature and extent of the Great Mystery is quite beyond anyone's grasp. We are like microbes. Our understanding is very limited."

"I still don't understand this balance thing you're talking about."

"Imagine that you're walking on a tightrope," Eduardo said. "If you fall off one side, you fall into the pit of self-worship. If you fall off the other, you fall into the pit of selflessness. If you are balanced, you remain on the wire, neither worshipping yourself, nor denying your self-worth. That is spiritual balance, a balance between you and the rest of existence. My analogy may sound precarious, but, in fact, spiritual balance is normal."

"Normal? Not just for religious people?"

"Of course not. Spiritual balance has nothing to do with religion. Nor is it exhibited as unusual behavior. A spiritually balanced person cannot necessarily be picked out of a crowd. He or she does not need to wear any unusual costume or act in any unusual manner. Spiritual balance is the natural state of the human being, and of all beings. It is normal. It is abnormal when we are imbalanced. We are spiritually balanced when we live in harmony with the greater whole — with each other, with all of life, and with the Earth mother. When entire societies such as yours become spiritually imbalanced, wallowing in the pit of selfishness, great harm plagues the Earth mother."

"And to achieve this spiritual fulfillment you speak of, we need to find the point in our consciousness between selfishness and selflessness?"

"*Si*. Otherwise, you will remain lost. The point is like the North Star. It constantly reminds us of the Great Mystery and our position in it. Most of your people are not consciously aware of it. Most of your people are still trying to establish a point in their consciousness between themselves and a mythological Great Human, a point that doesn't exist because the Great Human doesn't exist. That is why they are lost, wandering in a spiritual desert. They must instead look for a point in their consciousness between themselves and the Great Mystery. It is not difficult to find. It would happen on its own if you would simply allow it to do so."

"Tell me Eduardo, would you call that point we're speaking of a *balance point*, by any chance?"

"*Si*. That is what Lucita called it."

I was elated. Finally, I was discovering the meaning of the balance point! Maybe I would solve this mystery after all and cash in on that half million dollar estate! Damn, that Lucy was a clever one. But how did she know I would ever meet or talk with Eduardo? Was this just a huge stroke of luck on my part, even though I wasn't sure I understood what the shaman was talking about?

Eduardo scraped at the fire with his stick and then wandered off into the jungle to find more firewood. Still somewhat confused, I continued the conversation with Sarah. "The whole thing seems rather abstruse to me," I said to her. "I don't think I understand what Eduardo's saying."

"I think it's simpler than it sounds, Dad," Sarah responded. "Eduardo's saying that spiritual growth means having an increasing awareness of the relationship between yourself and a greater being, which, to him, is 'everything else.' He's saying that 'everything else' adds up to something he calls the Great Mystery, and it's probably most evident to us humans as the natural world around us, which he calls the Earth mother." Sarah squatted beside the fire and raked some coals against the sides of the fish bundle. "Religion, on the other hand," she continued, as she poked at the fire with Eduardo's stick, "is often based on a relationship between oneself and an imaginary creator deity that people call God. Eduardo's saying that since a human creator isn't any more realistic than a microbe one, any relationship we have to such a deity is only *imaginary*. If I understand him correctly, a *true* spiritual relationship can only exist between yourself and something that actually *exists*. You can't have a realistic relationship with an imaginary being. He says the Earth mother is a greater being that actually exists, and by extension, so is the Great Mystery, which is the totality of the universe as we know it today."

"So, you think the guy's an atheist?"

"No, I wouldn't say that. He believes in a supreme being, but it's a natural one rather than a human one. A real one rather than an imaginary one. To him, 'God' is the totality of existence, not just another human male. And by maintaining a reverence for that greater Being in his life, he tries to live in harmony with the natural world around him. That's why he says we're spiritually lost. We don't have reverence for the natural world. Instead, we worship dead humans and, in the meantime, ignore our destructive effects on the planet. It does seem really silly when you think about it."

"So the mysterious balance point is actually some kind of equilibrium between me and the world around me."

"Yes, something like that. I think he means it's a balanced awareness. We realize we're actually a real part of a greater Being and then we adjust our consciousness to accommodate a more humble position in the web of life. More humble than the dominator mentality we currently cling to."

"It's a lot to think about," I said. "It'll probably take a while for it to sink into my calcified brain."

"Well, it makes sense to me."

"Your brain cells are younger than mine."

"I probably have more of them too, Dad."

"I'll pretend I didn't hear that! Where did Eduardo go? I need to ask him some more questions. There's suddenly been an alarming increase in the number of things I know nothing about!"

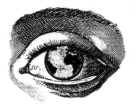

25

The Door

EDUARDO WAS SURPRISINGLY WELL-EDUCATED, articulate, and a bit cerebral, despite his relaxed appearance and his crude style of existence in this tropical world. For a "witch doctor," I was impressed. He was proud of the extensive garden surrounding his encampment, which blended so well with the enclosing jungle that it was not immediately apparent that a cultivated garden existed there at all.

On a walking tour, he pointed out his small cacao trees, with fruits like acorn squash. Eduardo split one open with his machete and we ate the sweet, spongy pulp in the center, sucking it from the slimy seeds. We washed and saved the seeds to roast later. Eduardo also showed us his banana trees, heavy with small red fruits, coffee bushes, covered with tiny berries, and one towering Brazil nut tree, seventy meters high. The abundance of his forest garden was amazing; he harvested mangos, pineapples, oranges, tangerines, and many other exotic fruits. One fruit looked like a red golf ball with fish scales. Peeling off the scales exposed a large, round seed underneath, covered by a dry rind. The seed was inedible, but the rind was tasty. There was no shortage of food in this year-round garden.

Our wanderings through the jungle gave us plenty of opportunity for discussion. I was intensely interested in getting back to the conversation we had initiated the day before at the lake, particularly the issue of the "balance point," but Eduardo refused to discuss it further. I had a half million dollars resting on that issue, and I wanted to know as much about it as I possibly could. He said it should sink in slowly. So instead, I barraged him with questions about my Aunt Lucy — why had she come to him, and what had she gained from it? We were all together on a food gathering expedition in the jungle when I started asking questions.

"Lucita needed a teacher. I taught her about the spiritual side of life," Eduardo explained, plucking a breadfruit from a small tree. He put it into a mesh sack.

"How do you define the word 'spiritual'?" I asked. "It could mean a lot of things, like ghosts."

"It means only one thing," he replied without hesitation. "We are all part of a Greater Being. We are linked to it. Everything is connected. Awareness of that connection is spirituality. Nothing more, nothing less." He dropped two more fruits into his bag.

"Can you describe the Greater Being again?" Sarah asked, jumping into our conversation. "My Dad has trouble understanding that concept."

"Well, I wouldn't put it exactly like that," I replied defensively. "It's just not something I think about much."

Eduardo stopped gathering fruit and looked around. He pointed to a towering tree, covered with a thick mat of vines. "See that tree?"

"Yes," we answered.

"Do you really *see* that tree?" he asked.

"Of course, it's right there. What do you mean?" I asked.

"Not all of the tree is visible to the eye," he said. "Half of the tree is under the ground. That is a part of the tree that many people do not acknowledge. That huge tree began from a tiny seed. An invisible spark of life caused the seed to sprout, the same life energy that permeates the Great Mystery. The seed then sent a tiny root into the earth, and at the same time, opened a tiny leaf to the sky. Over time, the young plant absorbed the earth through its roots, and it absorbed the sky through its leaves, until it became the huge living being you see there now. The earth, the air, and the sun combined to create this tree. Because it is a tree, it is easy for you to see that it is physically connected to the earth through its roots. The connection to the air and the sun is not as apparent. If the tree is uprooted from the earth, it would die. If it is removed from the sun or the air, it would also die. The Earth mother is a Greater Being in relation to the tree. The tree is made from her and cannot live without her. Humans are no different. We are like walking trees. We start as a seed, then we absorb the earth and the sun through our food, and the air through our lungs. If we are uprooted from the Earth, we will die. But even our Earth mother is only an insignificant speck of dust in comparison to the Great Mystery. We are mere humans and can know only very little about the ultimate nature of Being."

"So as a spiritual teacher, you taught Lucy to better understand her connection to the Earth, is that what you're saying?" I asked.

"Not to the Earth only. Our Earth is almost nothing in the overall scheme of things, just a grain of sand in the universe, but it is a critically important grain to those who live on it, like us. It is not a dead rock revolving around the sun, as some of your people believe. It is a living thing, a Being. We sprout on its surface, as does the tree. Yet, humans have become so self-centered, arrogant, and insensitive, they are making the Earth mother sick. We are becoming like parasites. Lucita was very concerned about this, so I tried to help her understand."

"And what did you tell her?" I asked.

"I told her many things. And she learned much on her own. I told her the Earth mother will only tolerate human foolishness for a while. Then she will shrug us off like a dog scratches a tick from her back."

Eduardo glanced to his right, abruptly ceased speaking and beckoned for us to stop and stand still. Then he crouched and sneaked toward a nearby tree very slowly, almost on all fours, as we watched in silent bewilderment. Suddenly, he jumped up and lunged toward a big Iguana resting on a low horizontal branch. In one lightning-quick motion he grabbed the lizard by the tail and swung it in a full circle over his head, dashing its skull against the heavy tree branch. Eduardo held the dead creature up by the tail for all to see. "This will make lunch for all of us," he announced. We were speechless. Annie and Sarah covered their mouths with their hands and stifled quiet gagging sounds. "It is quite delicious," asserted Eduardo, noticing our reaction. "And it is easy to skewer with a stick for roasting over a fire."

Back at the camp, Eduardo gutted the lizard, impaled it with a long stick, then slowly roasted it, head, legs, tail, and all, over the fire.

"Tastes like chicken," I commented to Annie and Sarah, neither of whom would touch the carcass. They were content to gnaw on dried provisions from home, mostly oatmeal and raisins, and to scowl at me with frequent sideways glances as I ate the Iguana with gusto. Michael was more adventurous than the ladies and was also happy to eat his fill of lizard. I'd have given anything for a cold beer to wash it down.

"You must eat nothing else today," Eduardo informed us after we ate. "Tonight I will show you a door that will lead you into the higher consciousness. You must fast the remainder of the day, taking only drink, but no solid food." I groaned out loud, remembering the last time I had fasted, for the Sisters of the Sacred Circle. I could hardly believe someone else was asking me to do it again. I was intrigued by Eduardo, but not exactly thrilled to be missing yet another dinner.

"What do you mean, you'll show us a *door*?" asked Michael, who perked up with a sudden keen interest. We were all sitting on the ground under the lean-to between the two thatched huts. The fire had died down to a bed of coals. Eduardo always kept the end of a long log in the fire so it wouldn't go out. Every so often, he'd push the log in a little. When he wasn't tending the fire, he'd throw a huge green leaf over the smoldering log's end. The leaf kept the intermittent rain off the fire and when the leaf dried up, it was simply used as kindling to get the fire stoked.

"I will show a door only to those who want to see it," he said, looking in my direction.

"What door?" asked Sarah. "How do we know we want to see it if we don't know what it is?"

"You already know what it is. Lucita sent you here. You are here for a reason."

"Can you explain what this door actually *is*?" asked Annie.

"I will try, but it is very difficult. There are some things for which there are no words. The door I speak of is one of them." We were all sitting around he fire spot. The little monkey came running out of nowhere and climbed onto Eduardo's lap. He began stroking her head as he continued speaking. "I have explained already that we are part of the Earth mother, although you may *think* that you are separate from her. Your concept of being separate is only an illusion. It is, to some extent, a necessary illusion because it helps you to recognize that you are important, too. We must take care of ourselves. We must have some degree of self-respect and pride. That is the human condition. Little Pepita here is part of the Earth mother too."

He squeezed her arm, and she chattered as if in agreement, then climbed onto his shoulder and grabbed his hair with her little fists. "Everything is connected," Eduardo grimaced, as Pepita tugged at his hair. "Nothing is separate. That is the Great Mystery. When we think we are separate and apart from the rest, then our spirit becomes ill. In indigenous cultures, when a person's spirit is sick, they seek the help of a shaman. The shaman asks the Earth mother herself to provide the necessary healing." Eduardo carefully removed Pepita from his head and set her on the ground, shooing her away. He rubbed his scalp and brushed dirt off his shoulder.

"How do they do that?" asked Sarah. "How does a

shaman ask the Earth mother for help?"

"The shaman can ask for help in many ways. One is to ask the spirits of the sacred plants. The Earth mother has given us plants that will unlock the door that imprisons human consciousness. It is like releasing a caged animal and allowing it to taste freedom, perhaps for the first time. Only outside the cage can the animal realize that its life has been extraordinarily limited. What it thought were its boundaries were only the walls of a small box. When the animal sees that the actual extent of reality is huge beyond imagination, it gains a new perspective on its own limited existence. It understands then that its reality is only a small part of something much greater. It is thereby humbled, enthralled, amazed, and enlightened, and its spirit is renewed."

"So you're saying our consciousness is limited, like it's in a cage?" asked Annie.

"No. That's not what I'm saying. I'm saying that our consciousness is *unlimited*. Incredibly unlimited! But we *choose* to box it into a small room because only then can we function as human beings. Everybody's room is a different size. Some bigger, some smaller."

"So if we need to limit our consciousness, why bother opening any doors?" Sarah shrugged.

"If the room has windows, and I'm speaking metaphorically now, you understand? These concepts are difficult to put into words. If there are windows in your room, then you can see that there's an entire world out there beyond the limited scope of your space. When you are comfortable with that awareness and understand it, you will be able to open the door to your room at will. You will be able to wander into the higher levels of consciousness. But you will always come back to your room, because that is the framework that enables you to function as a human. That is where you belong. Lucita could open the door of her room at will."

"I still don't get your point," replied Annie. "Why not just stay in the room, if that's where you belong?"

"There is nothing wrong with staying in your limited consciousness. You can spend your life within that room and it would be fine. If, that is, you can also see through a window. If you understand that there is more to reality than just the walls around you. Instead, people line the insides of their rooms with things that reflect themselves. These things could be called mirrors, because everywhere the caged person looks, they see only themselves."

"What do you mean?" she pressed.

"For example, a person sees a tree and they think of how much money they can make from it. They're not seeing the true tree as a living entity, they're only seeing themselves, their desires, superimposed on the tree. Such a person thinks they are the world, forgetting that they are only one miniscule part of an infinite puzzle. They remain unaware of the true nature of what exists beyond themselves. This is when they need to be reminded that there is a door, and that it leads out to the rest of reality — the world they have forgotten or denied. If a person cannot see beyond the confines of his or her own self, their spirit shrivels and, eventually, dies."

"So how do plants enter into this picture?" I asked.

"Humans have evolved over many hundreds of thousands of years. Even millions. Many other life forms have coevolved with us, some of which complement human beings here on Earth. Plant helpers come in many forms, but the most important ones are the spiritual helpers, the sacred plants. These plants coevolved with us, and some contain chemical substances that are otherwise found only in the human brain. When we ingest the plant helpers, they communicate with us. It is one of the Earth mother's ways of speaking directly to us. Some plant helpers can open a door for us, exposing us to a greater level of consciousness. Tonight, we will ask the plant helpers to speak to us. I will ask them to introduce you to the Earth mother. You must see through the door, once and for all. Then you will understand what I am saying."

At that, Eduardo stood up, walked a few paces, and

turned to face us. "I must go off into the bush to find the plant helpers. I must go alone, but I will return in a few hours. It will take some time after that for me to brew the drink, which should be ready by nightfall. Eat nothing until then and don't wander off." He climbed up the ladder into his hut, and soon jumped out with an empty sack. Then he took off into the jungle leaving the four of us alone.

Well, not entirely alone; we had a small, black monkey to keep us company. She had grabbed Sarah's half-eaten bowl of oatmeal and had almost gotten away with it, but Sarah wrestled it back, offering the monkey a banana as a trade. Pepita took it and ran off, chattering like crazy.

"That monkey is a pain in the ass," Michael complained. "The damn thing took my toothpaste this morning."

"You should keep everything zipped in your bag,"

The author and Pepita
(author on left)

Sarah suggested.

"It was *in* my bag. The friggin' monkey unzipped it."

"Tape the zipper down. I have some duct tape in my bag. That works," I offered.

"I don't know about this plant helper stuff," Annie said, shaking her head, ignoring the monkey.

"What're you worried about? This is a once in a lifetime opportunity to learn something from a South American shaman in person, not in your books! What more could you ask for?" I replied.

"But he's talking about taking *drugs*. Probably hallucinogens," she countered.

"Ah, that's not exactly accurate," Michael offered, forgetting about his Pepita problems for the moment.

"What do you mean?" she asked.

"Well, number one, he's not talking about drugs, he's talking about *plants*. Drugs are things people make in laboratories. Pills, capsules, crystal powders, synthetic chemicals. Indigenous peoples don't even have a word for 'drug' in their language," he explained. "It's a concept created and embraced by our culture; it's not a concept indigenous cultures even understand. Nature gives them their cures, but there is no stigma attached to using them. There is only respect. Most of the cures are medicinal, but some are spiritual. In fact, they say that all diseases have a spiritual cause."

"What makes you such an expert on this?" I asked.

"It's a research specialty of mine. Ethnobotany. I've studied it in Mexico and in Central America. So I agree with you, Joe, this is a great opportunity," he continued. "As I was saying, number two, the word *hallucinogen* is a misnomer. The correct word is *entheogen*. It's derived from the root words *en*, meaning within, *theo*, meaning divine, and *gen*, meaning to create. Entheogens are plants that enable a person to find the divinity that dwells within — to find the link to the Greater Being that Eduardo talks about all the time. So Eduardo is apparently speaking of entheogenic plants, not hallucinogenic drugs. There's a world of difference between the two."

"Well, it seems wrong," Annie said.

"What seems wrong?" Michael asked.

"Taking drugs."

"Really? Then don't take any. But you'll be un-American if you don't."

"What's *that* supposed to mean?"

"Drugs are big business in the United States. There are drugstores on every corner. There are drug commercials all over TV, in the magazines, in the newspapers, on radio. Drug use is fully encouraged and supported by both the government and by American society. Americans are the biggest drug users in the world."

"That's not what I mean by drugs. I mean *illegal* drugs."

"The vast majority of drugs are both dangerous and perfectly legal," Michael continued. "They're big, big business. And many of the so-called illegal 'drugs' are not drugs at all. They're plants. Some of the world's most valuable sacred plants, those used by indigenous peoples since prehistory, have simply been labeled 'illegal drugs' by American law makers and banned, despite thousands of years of beneficial use. Americans have been subjected to decades of brainwashing on this issue, and now they can't even distinguish between a drug and a plant. The so-called 'war on drugs' itself has become another huge business. But there is no war on 'drugs,' there's only a war on *people*. When beneficial plants are made illegal, people's basic freedoms have been stripped away."

"But don't you think, Michael, that the illegal drugs are dangerous *too*, and that's why they're illegal?" Annie countered.

"I can only speak of plants. I know little about pharmaceutical drugs. The most dangerous plants in the world, plants like the fungus called the Death Cap, are perfectly legal to grow, possess, and eat. If plants were illegal because they were dangerous, then dangerous plants would be illegal. They're not. Only an idiot would intentionally poison himself. So why make laws that tell people not to poison themselves? People already have enough sense that such laws are unnecessary."

"Why are substances illegal, then?" she questioned.

"Substances? You mean plants? It depends on the plant. Virtually all of the plants that have been made illegal in the states have hundreds of years of beneficial use in other cultures. So why are they illegal? That's a good question, and one we've been conditioned to *not* ask. We're told to 'just say no,' as if asking questions, or even *thinking*, is wrong. Well, if a plant can enable a person to see things from a different perspective, if it can enable us to communicate with nature, with the Earth mother as Eduardo calls it, then maybe our government feels threatened by that. Maybe our government doesn't want us to be able to hear what the Earth mother has to say. Maybe our government wants to control our minds, control what we think. No doubt we're much better consumers that way."

"For *chrissakes*, Michael. That sounds like paranoia to me," said Annie dismissively. She rolled her eyes at him.

"Oh? Then why do you have such a knee-jerk reaction to so-called 'drugs'?" he pressed. "Why do you call plants 'drugs'? Why are you so quick to obey restrictions against plants, or even to assume they exist when you don't even know if they do? Could it be that your mind has been manipulated? That's thought-control by *my* definition. It starts in the schools, it's reinforced by the media, TV, radio, print media, and then, by the time you're an adult, you're cheering on the sidelines as innocent people are being dragged off and crammed into overcrowded prisons because of the *plants* they use. That's not paranoia, that's the real world today."

Seeing no end in sight to their heated debate, I abandoned camp and wandered off to take a nap. Sarah had left the conversation long ago, and was underneath Eduardo's hut, tossing raisins and nuts to the chattering monkey, who was scooping up the treats and stuffing them into its mouth. I climbed the ladder to our hut and settled into my hammock, trying to forget about the loud protests of hunger coming from my stomach. My next meal would be, according to Michael, an entheogenic one. I don't know if I was ready for that, but it sounded interesting, to say the least.

26

Plant Helpers

I MUST HAVE SLEPT FOR HOURS. IT WAS NEARLY DARK when Annie came up the ladder to wake me. "Joe, wake up," she whispered, shaking me gently. "Eduardo's been out there all afternoon, cooking some plants in a clay pot over the fire. He says it's almost time for the ritual."

"Ritual?" I mumbled, groaning as I tried to twist my way out of the hammock.

"That's what he called it. He said it's time for us to start."

"I'm coming."

I followed Annie down the ladder, stopping to stretch once I had my feet on the ground. Eduardo sat beside a blackened pot, stirring its contents with a stick. He beckoned to me.

"I have collected parts of two sacred plants. They are very special," he said, gesturing toward the pot. "They do not grow together; they grow very far apart. One is a vine. I have chopped and pounded it and then added it to the brew." He stirred a thick, green liquid; dark, woody strands of bark floated to the top. "The other plant gives us a leaf. It also has been crushed and added to the brew. The drink is almost ready. I must strain the brew, and then we will let it cool. After that, we may begin."

Sarah, Michael, and Annie had gathered around to

watch. The sun was setting and the twilight called out the mosquitoes and other night insects. We made sure we were covered up and had citronella oil on our bare skin. We all had net hats nearby. The mood of the evening was quiet and serious.

Eduardo strained the liquid through a piece of white cloth into a smaller clay pot. He covered the small pot with the cloth, and asked us to get our cups. He then poured a portion of the drink in each cup, and instructed us to set the mugs on a rock beside the fire. Everyone had apparently decided to participate in this experience, even Annie. She must have changed her mind after her long debate with Michael.

Eduardo passed his water flask around and told us to drink our fill. "Can you tell us what your brew is made of?" I asked.

"He already told us all about it," Michael responded. "While you were sleeping. He's gathered plants of two species, a vine and a leaf. I believe the vine is a *liana*. He calls it the 'vine of the soul.' I can probably determine the genus and species after we return to the States."

"This is an ancient shamanic brew," Eduardo added. "I learned how to make it from my grandmother. No one knows how long it has been used, or exactly how the first person knew how to make it. It is said that the Earth mother led someone to the plants in a dream, and that is how it was first made, perhaps a thousand years ago."

"He told us he makes the brew about once a year," Michael added, "and has been using it for thirty years."

"What's it called?" I asked. "Does it have a name?"

"*Si. Natema*," Eduardo replied. He said it could not be translated into English.

We all sat together by the fire. "We will all drink at the same time," Eduardo instructed. "You may feel ill for a while. If so, just lie down on your back. You may lie in your mosquitera if you prefer. It is alright to be by yourself. It may even be better to be by yourself. I will remain here by the fire all night and I will watch over you so you do not wander into the jungle. There is nothing to be afraid of. I will make sure that you are safe at all times."

"How long will this last?" Sarah asked.

"Most of the night," he replied. "You will not be able to sleep, but you will be able to rest. Time will be meaningless. Eventually you will fall into a deep sleep. Traditionally, only men drink the brew. But Lucita drank it more than once." He glanced at the cups. "It is time. Take your cups and begin to drink. Sip the brew slowly and try to drink all of it. It may take you an hour or more to do so."

We each took our cups from the rock and held them in our hands, as if offering a reluctant toast to each other. I hesitantly took a sip and sputtered. It was extremely bitter. "Whew! I can see why it would take an hour to finish a cup of this stuff," I said, taking another small drink, letting the heavy liquid sit in my mouth and slowly seep down my throat. Sarah and Annie both winced when they tasted their brew, their faces curling up in disgust. Michael imbibed without expression. Eduardo drank nonchalantly, watching us closely. We continued in this manner for about ten minutes, then Annie was the first to succumb.

"Oh no!" she cried suddenly. "I'm gonna throw up!" She set her cup down quickly and jumped into the dark bushes behind us, vomiting fiercely.

"Oh god, oh, god," Sarah moaned as she rocked back and forth on her log seat, holding her hands over her ears. Then she jumped up and disappeared into the bushes too. The sounds of two vomiting women could be heard amidst the orchestra of night insects. We three men stared at the fire in silence, each cradling a cup of the bitter brew in our hands. I clenched my teeth, trying hard to ignore the retching and gagging sounds for fear I would be joining them.

Several minutes later both women returned, wiping their mouths on their shirtsleeves. "I've had enough," Annie announced abruptly. "I can't drink this stuff. It's horrible. I'm going to bed. Sorry guys, you'll just have to go on without me. You can tell me all about it tomorrow."

"Me, too," added Sarah. "Have fun."

We watched them disappear into the darkness. Minutes later, faint fingers of lamplight could be seen piercing the stick wall of our hut. Aside from the glow of the dwindling fire, the light from that kerosene lamp was the only thing visible in the inky blackness of the jungle night.

We drank more. I was feeling very nauseous and clammy and had begun to sweat profusely. Nevertheless, I sipped the brew as Eduardo instructed, a little at a time, stopping whenever nausea overcame me, or when I knew I would vomit if I even caught a whiff of the drink. Eventually, I couldn't force myself to drink another sip. Just the thought of it made me want to puke. I had sipped almost two-thirds of the cup, so I set it on the ground beside me. I felt so awful that weakness and shaking overcame me and I had to lie down. Fortunately, the log I sat on was long enough for me to lie on my back with my feet propped on either side for stability. I couldn't have walked anywhere. I felt utterly weak, sick, and dizzy, and had to either remain horizontal or else go somewhere to throw up. The log was hard and would have been uncomfortable under any other circumstances, but now it felt extraordinarily soft and warm.

Minutes, maybe hours passed, and then, suddenly, I noticed sharp flashes, slivers of colored lights, appearing at the edges of my field of vision. Faint sounds rushed through my ears as if they were coming from a long distance away. They seemed to be moving closer. The chorus of nocturnal amphibians and insects took on a new dimension, filling my head and developing into a richness I had never experienced before, a symphonic splendor that would have shamed any philharmonic orchestra. I could hear individual human-like voices in the sound, first low baritones, then high sopranos, as if they were each, in turn, singing directly to me. I could *feel* the sound entering my ears. Incredibly intricate, colorful patterns bloomed before me, convoluting and folding into themselves against the backdrop of the night.

The mysterious baritones in the distance seemed to merge with the nocturnal orchestra and boom louder, and with each pulse, a transparent red sphere emanated from nowhere and passed over me. I could *see* the sounds that I heard as well as feel them. I sat up effortlessly, or I was pulled up — I don't know which.

Eduardo was still sitting in the same place on the ground beside the fire, crosslegged. He was motionless except for his right arm, which slowly tapped a gourd rattle against his thigh. Each shake of the gourd poured sound over me like rain, draining into my ears. Each sweep of his arm left a blur of light and color by his side, phosphorescent. As I stared at him, he turned his head and looked at me with eyes like deep, luminescent pools. It was as if I was looking into his body through windows. I had the thought that I was peering into his soul. I knew that I looked the same way to him.

When our eyes made contact, I instantly knew that we were both the same entity, without separation. The He and I disappeared. There was no us, we were one. I had no concept of Self. My individual personality had vanished. There was nothing separating me from what was around me, because there was no *me* to segregate things. I was what Eduardo was, and what Michael was. Pure awareness, nothing more. I saw everything, and I understood everything.

It was as if I had been spending my life inside a semi-translucent bubble, unable to clearly see the world around me. Everywhere I looked, I had seen my reflection on its curved walls, distorting my view of the world outside. My every view of life was a reflection of *myself* transposed upon all of my surroundings. I hadn't realized that what I was seeing was actually only a meager reflection on the sides of my bubble, and not a true representation of reality. Now the thin walls of the bubble had burst, and I could see the world clearly, without reflections or distortions. My consciousness was a drop of water that, having lost its surface tension, dissolved into an ocean of consciousness. For a period without time, in a place without boundaries, I was not there, and yet, I was everywhere. I became the Earth Mother. I *became* the Great Mystery.

I remember eventually seeing the first glimpse of dawn light filtering through the jungle canopy and knowing that it was the most beautiful thing anyone could possibly ever see. I was not bitten by a single insect that evening. We three men never exchanged a word between us all night. Eventually, I climbed into my hammock and fell into the deepest sleep of my life.

27

Oneness

BOTH ANNIE AND SARAH SEEMED ONLY CASUALLY
interested in the experience that Michael and I had shared
with Eduardo the night before, and that was probably for
the best. We three had traveled everywhere, and nowhere,
but we didn't need to say a word to each other about it —
we fully understood what the other had experienced.
Besides, no words were available that could adequately
describe what had transpired that night. Nevertheless, we
made feeble attempts.

"So, did you see the 'door'?" asked Annie, skeptically. I
had slept until late morning and was brushing my teeth
with a cup of water outside the hut, trying to remove any
lingering taste of the previous night's potion. Michael and
Sarah were nearby, eating breakfast underneath a banana
tree.

"Door, hell, I didn't even see the *room*," I mumbled.

"I think Eduardo was right, Annie," interrupted
Michael, between mouthfuls of granola. "Consciousness
probably *is* unlimited. At least that's the way it seemed to
me last night."

"Or maybe it would be more accurate to say we're *part*
of an unlimited consciousness," I offered, putting my
toothbrush in my breast pocket and hoping Pepita would-
n't steal it. She had already wandered off with several of
Michael's possessions. "The brew seemed to cause the

boundary between me and everything else to disappear. It's hard to describe. And it made me sick as hell, too."

"It's fantastic to know that we can tap into that infinity," Michael said, philosophically. The four of us found seats around the smoldering fire.

"But what did you guys tap *into*?" Sarah asked. "How do you know it wasn't just all in your *minds*?"

Michael and I both shrugged. "I don't know if I can explain it," I said. Michael agreed.

"First, I know I got sick as a dog."

"So did I," added Michael.

"Then, I started seeing lights out of the corners of my eyes."

"Me, too."

"After that, I saw *everything* differently, and *heard* everything differently. I could actually *see* sounds, and feel them, too. I could hear the individual voices of the tree frogs. They sounded human. I could almost understand what they were saying. Then each voice took on a shape and color of its own. It was incredible. Each croak rolled over me like a gigantic magenta bubble. I could even see things with my eyes closed."

"Like what?!" asked Sarah.

"Patterns. Moving shapes and forms in three dimensions. Lots of colors. It was amazing, and it didn't matter if my eyes were open or closed. Did you see stuff like that, Michael?"

"Kind of. At one point I bent over to throw up and the stream of vomit turned into a huge snake that curled around my feet. I wasn't afraid, though. It was fascinating."

Annie closed her eyes and shook her head.

"I saw a person," I interjected. "I felt like it was Lucy. A woman stood in the shadows, staring straight at me, glowing white. I could feel a warmth radiating from her. I couldn't see her face, but I knew she was looking at me."

"How did you know it was a woman?" Annie asked doubtfully.

"I just *knew* it. I don't know how. The moment I

noticed her, she disappeared, and so did I."

"What do you mean, *you* just *disappeared*?" asked Annie, incredulously.

"I just did. I wasn't here anymore," I tried to explain. "Well, maybe physically I was here; you probably would have seen my body sitting here if you looked. I don't know. But my sense of *self* disappeared. I just can't explain it. I went to the same place the woman did. A place where everything is one thing, where there was no separation between my consciousness and everything surrounding me. I didn't just see the trees around me, I *was* the trees. I didn't hear a sound, I *was* that sound."

At that moment, we heard a stirring from Eduardo's hut, and saw a pair of feet searching for the rungs of the ladder. Eduardo climbed down, looking a little bedraggled. He had probably been up most of the night too. Pepita scrambled out of nowhere and climbed up onto his shoulder. They walked off into the bush, and returned with a bunch of red bananas. Eduardo passed us each a banana, including Pepita, then sat beside us at the fire spot. The bananas were remarkably delicious, with a rich and tangy flavor that made the commercial bananas back home seem insipid. Pepita gleefully took her banana and scrambled off into the forest.

"Eduardo," Michael broke the silence, "I think I found the door last night. I think I had some sort of religious experience! At the risk of sounding trite, I felt I was 'one' with everything!"

"Oneness is the essence of spirituality," Eduardo responded. "There is only one thing — the Great Mystery. We are only a very small part of it. We can sense the oneness beyond ourselves in many ways, not just by plant helpers. It can be a daily exercise, even a normal state of mind." He rested his chin on his hand and stroked his beard thoughtfully. "But, *religion* can have little to do with spirituality. Religion separates. It separates people from each other, it separates people from the Earth mother. Religion is based upon *belief*, whereas spirituality is based upon *awareness*. You can believe *anything*, but you can only be aware of what is real."

"Are you saying the snake that came out of Michael's mouth last night was *real?*" asked Annie.

"Michael was aware he saw a snake in his mind's eye, but he didn't believe he saw a *real* snake. Awareness is flexible. It is always changing according to the information it is receiving from the senses. Belief is inflexible. It is reluctant to change. It requires no senses. That is why the spiritual person relies on awareness, and avoids belief."

"But you believe the Earth mother is sick, don't you?" Annie stressed.

"I am *aware* that the Earth mother is sick. You can also gain that awareness through observation of real things in the real world. I don't have to believe it; I can see it with my own eyes. I can hear it in the silence that now blankets the night in many areas of the bush that once thrived with life. I can feel it in my heart when I see the poor, the malnourished, and the unfulfilled people in the villages."

"When we rigidly believe things for which there is no proof," Eduardo continued, "*that* is religion. Religion will show you the ephemeral nature of truth, because whatever you believe will be true, for you. No matter how ridiculous, no matter how foolish, no matter how harmful. If you believe it, it is true, and you will live your life by it. That is the danger of religion. So Michael, no, you did not have a religious experience. Instead, your awareness was expanded. You saw a truer nature of your total self. You had a *spiritual* experience."

"Incredible," Michael whispered.

"But what difference did it make in the whole scheme of things?" asked Sarah, always the analytical one. "What *good* did it do you?"

"Well, Sarah," I spoke up, finally feeling like I was beginning to pull some of the pieces of Lucy's puzzle together. "Let me tell you what *I* think happened last night. I think I understand now what Lucy meant by the 'Eco and the Ego.' My ego was stripped away last night by

Eduardo's rank brew," I turned to him, apologetically. "Sorry Eduardo, but it did taste horrible." Turning back to Sarah, I continued, "Somehow, the brew made my ego disappear, like popping a bubble. I had absolutely no feeling of self-importance. My *self* was like the air in that bubble; it simply merged with the surrounding atmosphere when the bubble burst. Lucy might say that the atmosphere is the Eco, the Earth mother, or the Great Mystery. When the bubble is popped and the Ego disappears, all that's left *is* the Eco. It all became crystal clear last night. I can see now why Lucy said there's a battle waging between the Ego and the Eco. The Ego is merely human self-interest and —"

"No!" Eduardo abruptly interrupted. "It is *not* human self-interest to destroy the very life support systems that humanity depends upon. The 'Ego,' as Lucita calls it, is human self-*importance*. That is a big difference. Human self-*interest* demands that we protect the Earth mother. But it is human self-*importance* that wages a war against the Earth mother. When we believe we are more important than the rest of life, our belief blinds us to the awareness that we are harming not only the rest of life, but also ourselves, our children, and our future, even as we poison the Earth mother under our feet. Your people suffer from spiritual blindness. They must be made to see for the sake of us all."

"What about the 'balance point'? How does that figure into all this?" asked Annie.

"What about it?" I asked.

"What does it mean?" she persisted.

"Annie, I think I can explain," Michael offered offhandedly. "Let me make a stab at it at least, if you don't mind. The 'balance point' would be when we realize we're only part of something bigger — a part of something that's real, something knowable by our senses, a 'living universe' as Eduardo said earlier. If we place too much importance upon our individual personalities, let's call it self-aggrandizement, we can do damage to that greater Being by overconsuming, creating waste, squandering resources, destroying species, and so on, all so we can have a home that's ten times bigger than we actually need —"

"Like a castle?" interrupted Sarah. "Some people want to be a king or queen, don't they? It's an ego trip."

"Yes, and we'll eat ten times more than we need," continued Michael.

"And get bloated and fat," Sarah chimed in. "While people all over the world are starving."

"And so on," Michael added. "But if we find a balance point between ourselves and the living universe, we'll live harmoniously with the greater whole. We'll still place enough importance upon ourselves to lead healthy, productive, rewarding, and fulfilling lives. But it'll be without the waste and pollution and greed that's come to be the trademark of our culture."

"Yes," added Sarah, "a culture that obviously denies that there *is* such a thing as a future."

"The balance you are speaking of, Michael, is spiritual fulfillment in the truest sense of the word," replied Eduardo, "and it is different for each person. Some will remain imbalanced toward self-importance, and some imbalanced toward selfless devotion, but most will be somewhere in between. It is the natural condition of any creature to be in balance with the Earth mother; we know we are at a place of balance when the Earth mother is content and healthy." Eduardo frowned, and looked pensive. "She is now ailing, though. She is sick. Too many of your people are imbalanced toward the ego, as Lucy would say, toward self-importance. They are locked in their rooms with mirrors on their walls. They forget they are part of something much greater than themselves. In their self-absorption, they are harming the world. When so many people have lost sight of their spiritual balance point, the entire planet is thrown off-kilter. For all of us to survive, your people need to change their obsession with self-importance into a focus on self-interest. They need to grow beyond their blind beliefs to become aware of the greater reality around them."

"But how can you say that religion has nothing to do with spirituality?" asked Annie, who seemed to be hung up on this issue. "Isn't that what people go to church for? Are you saying people should denounce their religions? Leave their churches?"

"Annie, you must understand that spirituality is not religion," replied Eduardo. "Spirituality is *everything*. It is our connection to the Totality. I am simply saying that religion is not necessarily spirituality. A person can be very religious and not spiritual at all. They can have no awareness of their connection to the greater being — the Earth mother. They can engage in all sorts of *religious* rituals and practices, and cling to all sorts of religious *beliefs*, yet have no *ethical* connection to the *real* world. Do you understand?"

"I think so."

"Many of your people who are making the Earth mother sick are very religious. On the other hand, a person can be totally non-religious and still be very spiritual. A person can be both spiritual *and* religious too, if they so choose. Many people are."

"How's that?" asked Annie.

"It's quite simple. Religion is based on belief. Do you remember me saying that?"

"Yes."

"And people will believe almost anything," Eduardo continued. "But a spiritual person can participate in a religion without actually *believing* the myths. They are *aware* that the theological stories are only myths."

"Myths? Such as?" Annie demanded, somewhat defensively.

"Religious leaders try very hard to make people believe that the universe was created by one mythical creature or another. The very concept is absurd — quaint, perhaps, but unrealistic. Nevertheless, people do believe it. There is nothing spiritual about believing in myths; that is religion, dogma, and nothing more. Perhaps we believe in myths because we no longer want to think, we no longer want to sharpen our awareness or evolve our understanding."

"Then who created the universe?" Annie asked, somewhat smugly.

"Why do you think the universe was created by someone?" replied Eduardo.

"Because it exists."

"And you believe something created the universe, then, because it exists?" questioned Eduardo.

"How could it exist if it wasn't created?" she asked.

"If you think the universe was created, Annie, then who do *you* think created it?"

"God created the universe, of course," she responded, defiantly.

"Does God exist?"

"Absolutely."

"Then who created your God?"

Annie opened her mouth to speak, and, realizing that Eduardo had just checkmated her line of reasoning, shut it just as quickly.

"If everything that exists had to be created, then a Creator, if one exists, had to be created too, following your line of reasoning," explained Eduardo. "And if a Creator can exist without having to be created, then, by the same logic, the Great Mystery could also be self-created. It makes just as much sense to think that the Great Mystery is not limited by time and space, even though *we* are, and therefore the Great Mystery has no beginning or end. A Creator, under those circumstances, is not necessary — its only purpose is to provide a basis for religion. 'Creators' are myths used to explain the unexplainable. In many cases, such myths simply amount to humans worshipping human deities, which again unnecessarily swells our sense of human self-importance."

"What about the Big Bang?" I countered. "How can the universe have no beginning if scientists say it began with a bang?"

"Lucita, a nuclear physicist, was quite amused by this topic. She agreed that we humans are like microbes on a grain of sand. We know very little about the nature of the universe. For some reason we want to believe there was a beginning, so we make up a theory. We don't know what happened twenty billion years ago any more than a microbe on a grain of sand can recite Shakespeare. Eventually, the Big Bang theory will develop into another theory. But they are only theories, beliefs, if you will. Sometimes science itself is like a religion."

"Let's get back to *real* religion," persisted Annie. "So people should denounce their churches? Is that what you're saying?"

"No. That's not what I'm saying. Please don't misunderstand me. Religious institutions have their purpose. They provide charity, social support systems, inspiration, and revitalization for many people. Now all they need do is adopt a more spiritual perspective based on *reality*. People need to feel a real connection within themselves to the greater life force they are *part* of. You cannot have a connection to a mythical human figure except in your imagination. That is not good enough anymore. We must evolve beyond that limited scope of awareness and realize we are part of something that is real, not imaginary. We are part of a living universe, a Great Mystery, and our minds are part of a universal mind. Our consciousness is part of an unlimited consciousness. The religious frameworks can remain as they are, but the hearts and minds of the people must change. Then, everything else will also change."

"But what about the afterlife?" asked Annie. "Is that only fantasy too? Are we supposed to throw out everything we learned in church?"

"He's not a doctor of theology, Annie, jeez, give the guy a break," implored Michael.

"She actually asked a very important question, Michael," replied Eduardo. "Look carefully around you, Annie. What do you see?"

"Well, I see trees and bushes. I see Pepita swinging on a vine over there, like a maniac. I see two huts. I see smoke rising from the fire in front of us."

"What you are seeing, Annie, *is* the afterlife," Eduardo replied.

We all looked at him with blank expressions on our faces.

"*This* is the life that will continue after you have passed away. Religious people tell you to prepare for life after death. They do not understand that the life that exists after death is the life that continues on this Earth. *That* is what a spiritual person prepares for. It is our descendants who will live here after we are gone. We must prepare the afterlife for *their* sake. We, as people, will all die, Annie, but Life will never end."

28

Balance Point

ALTHOUGH LIFE NEVER ENDS, AS EDUARDO HAD SAID, time also never stops. The days had slipped by rapidly, and we had arrived at our last full day in the rainforest. We had all become rather adept at making our way through the thick vegetation, which was good, because we now had a fourteen mile hike planned, through the immense and ancient jungle.

There were no hills to climb in this flat, green Amazonian basin, but lots of moss-lined, meandering rivulets to wade across. And there were always new wonders to marvel at — snakes thick as a person's leg that seemed to take minutes to cross our path because they were so long (Eduardo cautioned us to avoid them); flying, crawling, and buzzing insects, some the size of your fist; birds with long, sweeping tail feathers and sharply curved beaks; unbelievable fungi, as big as elephant ears; snails as round as grapefruits; towering ferns everywhere; and, of course, the ubiquitous mosquitoes. Our net hats and insect repellent were lifesavers — we found that the natural oils of the citronella grass worked remarkably well in keeping the bugs at bay.

And the rain showers — intermittent, but certain — poured on us at any unforeseen moment, and then passed over, allowing the sun to filter through the canopy once again. We learned to ignore these drizzles, perhaps even to find some pleasure in them. The most striking feature of the jungle, however, remained the utter silence. Unless we were near running water, the deep, daytime forest was completely quiet and still. Our conversation was the only sound to break the silence, other than the trampling of our feet.

Our final day's hike into the jungle allowed us ample opportunity to discuss the issues that had drawn us there. I was still somewhat obsessed with the "balance point" concept, recalling that a half million dollars with my name on them were burning a hole in an escrow account somewhere. Relentlessly, I questioned Eduardo about it. He kindly endured my persistent barrage, although he often preceded his answers by telling me that the concepts were difficult to put into words. He insisted that my awareness would develop in its own time.

"You have seen your greater self, *amigo*. You know that you are much more than just a man, you are a part of a greater being, as we all are. Now you must take that into consideration with every act you engage in, for the remainder of your life. Everything you do affects everything else. You know that now."

"That's right, we're all strands in the web of life," Michael added.

"You're so *trite*," chided Sarah, poking him in the back.

"So I'm trite, but it's true!" retorted Michael. "You can't damage one of the threads without eventually fraying the entire tapestry."

"But how does that translate into *normal* life, in the *real* world?" asked Annie. We had paused to rest on a bed of moss beside a huge tree trunk. "What's that have to do with average Americans like *us*? We can sit here in the middle of the Amazon jungle and wax poetic all day long, but we still have to go home tomorrow. Back to the real world."

"Look around you, Annie. *This* is the real world!"

Michael exclaimed, standing up and spinning in a circle with his arms outstretched. "This world has been here for eons, and will continue to be here for eons more if we don't destroy it. The world we're going home to tomorrow is an artificial world, one we've created — very recently, in comparison, I might add. And who knows how long it will continue the way it is. Not very, if we have any hope to survive as a species."

"So what're we supposed to do? All go and live in a cave? Go live in huts in the woods and eat lizards? If our American world is going to change, it isn't going to change *that* way. No one would go along with that. No one is going to give up their hot showers and their cars and their washing machines and their toilets!"

Michael apparently had a knack for pushing Annie's buttons.

"I'm afraid the problem is more dire than that," interrupted Eduardo, who was seated beside us, weaving some fibers he had stripped from the stem of a plant. It looked like he was making a short cord of some kind. "Your people could make the necessary changes without going back to the dark ages. You could use your intelligence to solve the problems, and if you don't ignore your true spiritual nature, your sense of oneness, it will work. But first you have to admit that the problems exist. So far, your people haven't even done that. Instead, they rush to feed their egos — to line their cages with more mirrors, to cloud their awareness, to stifle their spiritual selves. They are desperate to make money. Money has become their god. It is blinding them, leading them to their doom. Your people don't want balance. They could not care less about spiritual fulfillment. They want money, the more the better."

"So what's the solution, Eduardo?" I asked. "What can we do about it? The problem is too great, it's too big; there's nothing that one person can do!"

"Ah, *amigo*, this is where you are dreadfully wrong. There is one thing that everybody can do, and as more and more people do it, the Earth mother will heal."

"What's that?" asked Sarah.

"Seek and find your point of spiritual balance. That is something no one can do for anyone else, but it is something that each of us can and must do for ourselves," continued Eduardo. "Religion is not necessary to do this, and religious leaders may even lead you away from spiritual balance. Government is not going to help you; money is not necessary. Spiritual balance is actually quite a simple thing, a natural state of being."

"Well, it all sounds a bit too philosophical to me," remarked Annie. "Too abstract. I want to know how to translate that into practical terms. What does that mean with regard to my day-to-day living?"

"Today is our last day in the bush together," Eduardo replied. "Tomorrow we will meet the boat and you will be taken to the airport at Puerto Maldenado. Stop your questions and just sit with what you have learned and discussed

*Annie crosses a downed tree
in the heart of the jungle*

so far. You will understand it all soon enough. And, Annie, I have one suggestion only. There will be someone waiting for you when you return. She may have the answers that you seek. I suggest that you talk with her."

"Waiting where? In Lima? In Pennsylvania? Who, for heaven's sake?" asked Annie.

"The one who sent you to me."

"Melissa Berger?"

"Yes, her. She waits for you in America. You must speak with her."

"How do you know that?" asked Annie, still skeptical. "I talked to her and she was *not* at all friendly. In fact, she would barely speak to me."

"She will be waiting for you. Enough questions, though. We have spent too much time talking. If we start back to camp now, we will just get there by nightfall. You do not want to be hiking in the bush after dark, believe me."

At that mild admonition, Eduardo started working his way back through the jungle rather hurriedly, and the rest of us were right on his heels.

29

Going Home

THE FOLLOWING DAY WE WOKE AT DAWN, PACKED, AND walked with Eduardo down the footpath. It was hard to believe that a week had already passed. The boat wasn't waiting for us, as we had hoped, when we arrived at the pond on the tributary. We assumed that it would be coming soon, so we found a little clearing by the waterfall and waited. Sarah was tearful at the thought of parting with Pepita, whom she had become rather fond of. The little monkey had accompanied us down the footpath, and waited with us. Sarah fed her peanuts from her backpack, talking softly to her. Pepita chattered right back to her, as if they were carrying on an important conversation.

"Finally found someone you have something in common with, huh?" I remarked, jokingly.

"Funny, Dad," Sarah retorted. "She's smarter than you!"

"She'd be great in soup," Michael said, only half joking. Pepita had a particular penchant for Michael's belongings. On our return trip, his pack was decidedly lighter, and not at his own choosing. He was obviously not as taken with the furry little primate as Sarah.

"Shut-up! She's *sweet!*" The monkey gently took another peanut from Sarah's outstretched hand.

Eduardo had a little surprise farewell gift for each of

---

us. He asked us, one at a time, to hold out our left hand. Tying a section of a soft, brown cord around each of our wrists, he explained that the cord contained the spirit of the jungle, and that it signified we would be taking the spirit with us. He said the plants that he stripped the fiber from on our hike the day before were very special ones, and that they had given of themselves for our benefit. He instructed us to wear the bracelets until they fell off on their own, which, he assured us, they would in time. When he tied Michael's bracelet to his wrist, he looked Michael straight in the eyes and said, cryptically, "The spirit of the jungle will wait for you here." Michael just looked at Eduardo and nodded, saying nothing.

After waiting about an hour, we started to worry that our ride wasn't going to come. Eduardo suggested we throw our bags into the dugout canoe that was tied there, and then row down the tributary toward the river. He said it would be a lot faster than taking the boat out, and maybe we'd meet the boat on the way. We all thought that was a great idea, offering us one last chance to enjoy the jungle splendor before our return to Lima.

We rowed the two miles down the placid, black tributary, ducking down in places where the overhanging jungle crowded the river. The canoe was remarkably easy to row, especially downstream, and we made good time. When we arrived at the river, there still was no sign of the boat, so we rowed on up the churning Mother of God River to Tambo, hugging the shoreline. This rowing was much more strenuous. By the time we reached Tambo, we were all sweaty and completely exhausted, all except Eduardo, who was apparently accustomed to this sort of exertion.

We anchored the canoe to some bushes at Tambo, and climbed out onto the bank. Annie, Sarah, and I sat under the shade of a tree and watched the swollen, muddy river drift by. Eduardo and Michael made small talk with the residents. Before long, we could see the white roof of our long-awaited boat making its way down the river. Soon our smiling guide was tying his little boat beside the canoe.

Michael threw our bags from the canoe into the boat, and we all said our good-byes to Eduardo. We had made a friend. Even Annie, for a split-second, was reluctant to say farewell.

"Only a couple days away from a hot shower," she sighed as she stepped onto the bow of our boat, as if to remind herself to focus on her destination. "Puerto Maldenado, here we come."

"There aren't any hot showers in Puerto Maldenado," Michael reminded Annie.

"I don't care, I can wait," she said haughtily.

"There weren't any at Nellie's either," he said, rubbing it in.

"There is a hot shower *somewhere* in this world, Michael, and I will find it!" Annie assured him with daggers in her eyes.

We were off, churning upriver in the little boat with the wind blowing through our hair, and the turbulent Madre de Dios dancing beneath us. Our shaman friend stood on the bank with a dark shape perched on his shoulder and watched us drift away until we were out of sight. The rainforest, Eduardo, Pepita, and what seemed like an entire universe, disappeared into the distance behind us.

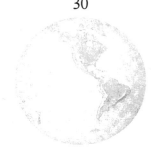

The American Dream

OUR FLIGHT OUT OF PERU WAS LONG AND TIRING, BUT
we were happy to be homeward bound. The culture shock
upon landing in Pittsburgh was more than we had bargained for. In Peru, we had grown used to one dollar meals
that were ample enough for two people to eat, and now,
back home, we were paying more than a dollar just for a
glass of iced tea. We were amazed at how the streets of
America looked so barren and abandoned after being in
South America only two weeks. There the streets bustled
with activity all day long. People interacted in throngs
from dawn until late at night, and a large portion of people's lives took place outside of their homes. Most of the
people there didn't have televisions and therefore had no
reason to stay indoors. In contrast, our two hour drive
home from the Pittsburgh Airport seemed like we were
driving through uninhabited territory. If there were people
living in the small Pennsylvania towns we passed through,
they were hiding somewhere. Perhaps this is the effect of
TV on America's social life — people no longer need to
seek social interaction outside of their homes when it can
be provided electronically, however artificially, in the comfort of their living rooms.

We arrived home in the evening, a bit weary, but nevertheless embracing an entirely new and refreshing perspec-

tive on life. Such is one benefit of traveling outside one's own culture. As soon as we pulled into the drive, Annie jumped out of the car and, like a possessed woman, made a beeline straight for the shower. Michael and Sarah took their places in line behind her, leaning against the bathroom door and chattering about one thing or another as they waited their turn. I rummaged through the refrigerator, desperate for a cold beer, and a taste of home.

I had cracked open my second beer by the time I called Annie's mother to let her and Penelope know that we were safely home. Although I'd arranged earlier to pick Penny up, Annie's mother offered to make the two-hour drive herself. I didn't argue with her — after traveling thousands of miles, I didn't want to go anywhere. It was good to be home and I wanted to stay put. I rifled through the stack of mail that had accumulated, called the neighbors to let them know we were back, and then checked the messages on our answering machine, making a mental note to give Cecilia Tomasso a call. It was her information that led us to Berger in the first place, and then to Eduardo. I thought she would probably like to know that we had gone to Peru to see the "witch doctor" and that we had returned safely.

As I scanned through the messages on my answering machine, there were two that quickly reminded me that Lucy's adventure was not yet over. The Montana attorneys had called to determine whether any advances were being made by me toward claiming Lucy's estate. They said I didn't have to wait the full year to do so and that it would be better for me to claim the estate as soon as possible. Evidently, they didn't have a clue what I was going through because of the damned inheritance; they just wanted to get the paperwork off their desks.

The other phone message was quite interesting. It was from the mysterious Melissa Berger in Montana. She called to say she wanted to meet with us as soon as possible. She was traveling on the east coast and could be reached at a phone number in New York state. I was surprised that she sounded so cordial on the phone, almost friendly.

Something must have changed for her to be so outgoing with us. Maybe she felt bad about acting so rude to us on the phone. Whatever the case was, I wanted to find out what caused her sudden and radical shift in personality. After scribbling her New York number on the back of a used envelope, I stuffed it into my shirt pocket, too exhausted from our trip to deal with it at the moment.

The next morning I called Berger, but she wasn't there. The person who answered said she'd have Berger call me back. Later that afternoon, she returned my call. We made arrangements to meet the very next day at my home. She was heading back to Montana and the interstate highway would take her within a few miles of our house. She mentioned that she had heard from Eduardo and knew it was important to see us. This all sounded mysterious and improbable to me, but by this time I wasn't going to second guess anything. I gave Berger directions to our home, asked her to come for lunch, and she was delighted to accept the invitation.

Annie was in the kitchen chopping onions for a broccoli quiche when Berger arrived late the next morning. I was at my office desk sorting through the mountain of papers and bills that had accumulated in our absence when I heard her car rumble down our gravel lane. From my office window, I was surprised to see two passengers in the car. Berger had mentioned nothing about having a guest with her.

When I met her at the door, she introduced herself and her husband. I addressed them as Mr. and Mrs. Berger, but they insisted I call them Melissa and Max. They appeared to be in their late sixties or early seventies, both graying and slightly overweight. She had the poise and appearance of a university lecturer, or perhaps an opera singer — her voice was unusually deep for a woman. She carried a brown leather briefcase. Max had a neatly trimmed beard and appeared stout and solid, a cannonball of a man. Both were casually dressed.

They were enthralled with our rustic home, insisting I

show them around outside even before they set foot in the front door. I was happy to oblige them, and I showed them our garden and orchard, our chicken coop and root cellar, my workshop, roof slate stockpiles, and other things they weren't accustomed to seeing in Montana. They explained that they had some acreage in the mountains there, and had built their own home many years ago. The Montana countryside, they noticed, seemed much drier than Pennsylvania's, and they were amazed at our garden's tropical feel.

"In the summer, northwestern Pennsylvania is similar to a rainforest," I explained, "because we have more rain than almost anywhere in the continental United States, except the Pacific northwest. In the winter it's barren and cold as hell. Lately, though, it's been unusually dry, and the winters have been extraordinarily mild."

"Global warming," the Bergers stated, nodding almost in unison as we walked into the house. I introduced them to Annie and Penny, who were putting the finishing touches on the quiche. Michael and Sarah had left in the morning to spend the day swimming at a nearby lake, and hadn't yet returned. Annie shoved the quiche into the oven and wiped her hands on her apron. She was delighted to be back in civilization again and acting as a hostess. She gave the Bergers the "grand tour" of our home, which, admittedly, wasn't much, as our house isn't big. Then she ushered Max and Melissa outside to the deck. We all gathered our wrought iron chairs around the round glass table, under the blissful shade of an overhanging red maple tree. I pulled out several iced beers from a metal bucket that Annie had set in the center of the table, and passed them around. I was happy to share Annie's homebrew with someone who could appreciate it, and Max quaffed it down rather readily. Ruby-throated hummingbirds buzzed over our heads like giant bees, shooting to and from a bright red feeder hanging on the patio. The languid summer afternoon lent itself to casual conversation and hospitable formalities, but my curiosity very soon got the better of me.

"Melissa, tell me something," I asked her, taking a deep drink from my bottle. "How do you fit into this picture? How do you know Lucy? Or Eduardo? And how did Eduardo contact you to tell you to call us?"

"One question at a time, please," Melissa laughed, in her matronly voice. "I was probably your aunt's best friend. I've known her for decades. She discovered Eduardo first, about ten years ago, and then she introduced *me* to him. She visited him every year, but I've only been to see him twice. You just came from there, didn't you? Quite a place, huh?"

"I'll say. What a trip!" Annie commented.

" I was just *fascinated* by Eduardo," Melissa added. "Anyway, he has a special connection with things, as you probably know by now. I actually *dreamt* that he told me to come and see you. The dream was so real and so vivid that I felt compelled to contact you. So here I am!"

"Don't ask me how she does that," interrupted Max. "That dream stuff, it's all Greek to me."

"So you don't go to Peru with your wife?" I asked.

"*Hell*, no. That's her thing, not mine," he replied, smiling. "When she's gallivanting around Peru, I'm hiking in the Montana mountains. That's where I like to be."

"As fortune would have it," Melissa continued, "I was going to attend a conference in Philadelphia anyway, and we wanted to visit Max's son in New York. So it all worked out beautifully."

"Speaking of Eduardo," Annie said, looking warily at Melissa, "he said something funny before we left Peru. He said you'd be waiting for us, that you'd have answers."

"Ha! Answers? Maybe yes, maybe no. It depends on what the questions are," laughed Melissa.

"Well, here's one. What're your backgrounds?" I asked, curiously, looking at both of the Bergers with raised eyebrows.

"Well, I was an accountant all my life," replied Max. "Not a very sexy or exciting job, but you really get to know money and how it works in that business. I retired about ten years ago."

"We were a match made in a banker's heaven," Melissa joked. "I'm an economist."

"Love at first sight," interjected Max.

"Lucille and I worked together at the University of Montana," continued Melissa, ignoring her husband's quips. "Of course, we were in different departments — she taught physics and I taught economics — but we got along well because neither one of us could identify with the other people in our own departments. We were both pretty progressive thinkers. Most of our colleagues were pretty stuffy people."

"Still are," Max said.

"Stuffy?" asked Melissa.

"Well, yes, but that's not what I meant. You two are still non-conformists," replied Max.

"Maybe you and I are, but Lucy, the poor woman..." Melissa's voice drifted off into silence. She stared at her beer.

"My wife, by the way, thinks Lucy's death was suspicious," Max confided, in a soft voice.

"*Suspicious*?! How?" Annie asked, obviously disturbed.

"I'm not certain *how* she died," Melissa explained. "Her corpse disappeared before I even saw it. And I know for a fact there were very powerful forces wanting to stop your aunt," Melissa explained.

"Stop her from doing *what?*" Annie frowned. "What forces?"

"Business interests," replied Max. "Lucy was trying to expose how businesses are destroying the planet. Very big corporations that make a lot of money. Believe you me, they were, and still are, making money hand over fist. The fossil fuels industry immediately comes to mind. And there are many more."

"What's wrong with making money?" I asked. As a self-employed business person myself, I was a little uncomfortable with the idea that making money was bad.

"Why, nothing," Melissa answered. "Nothing at all. It's not making money that's bad, it's *how* it's made."

"That's right," added Max. "Money in and of itself is not a bad thing. It's simply a mechanism for trade between people. Money is not the problem."

"Then what is?" asked Annie.

"Environmental destruction. Social degradation. Resource depletion. The undermining of our life support systems," replied Melissa, "and all of the things that breed from these problems — violence, disease, poverty, biodiversity loss. It's not money that's the problem, but it's the obsessive desire for it and the resulting faulty economy that's the problem. This is what I taught in the classroom for years. A sound economy is never based on destructive practices. A sound economy recognizes two basic tenets that our present American economy, incredibly, refuses to acknowledge." She held up two fingers.

"Which are?" I asked.

"A *future*." She folded down one finger with her other hand, leaving one finger up. "A sane economy realizes that there will be a future. Future generations must be accounted for. Our economy doesn't do that. The future can be damned in our present economy — it doesn't exist. Businesses work for today's profits; they're not concerned with tomorrow's generations."

"And what else?" I pressed.

She folded down the other finger and set her clasped hands on the patio table in front of her. "That natural resources have value in and of themselves, in their natural, *unused* state. A coal seam, in our economy, has no value until we dig it up and sell the coal. Then we only acknowledge the value of the money someone's made from the *sale*. We won't admit that when we use our resources up, we've actually *reduced* our wealth, especially when the resources are non-renewable. It's as if we're taking money from a bank account that nature has endowed us with, and never putting anything back in. This is a collective bank account, mind you, for the entire human race, a bank account for all people, for all time."

Penny joined us on the deck and was immediately recruited to help. "Excuse me for a moment, Melissa," Annie interrupted. "Penny, please set the table for lunch. We'll be ready to eat in ten minutes. We'll just use paper plates." Penny spun on her heels and went back into the house to get the table settings. "Sorry to interrupt, Melissa, please go on."

"As my wife was saying," interjected Max, "some of the people alive today are withdrawing from our natural bank account as fast as they can get away with it, getting incredibly wealthy in the process, and no one's stopping them. Our economic system doesn't account for the loss of our non-renewable resources. It only accounts for the *gain* derived from the sale of the resources, as if the resources themselves have no inherent value. Our economy uses Gross Domestic Product as a measure of its health. That's like saying the person with the best economy is the one who spends his money the fastest, even when he's depleting his savings. This would only make sense if the savings were either infinite, or considered to have no value as a savings in the first place."

"I don't understand," Annie said, shaking her head.

"Okay, let me explain it this way," answered Max. "If you have money in the bank and you withdraw it, you deduct, mathematically, that amount from your balance, don't you?"

"Of course."

"If you took a thousand dollars out of your bank account, would you then say you've 'earned' a thousand dollars?"

"No. Because I already had it."

"That's right," said Melissa. "Although you now have a thousand dollars to spend, you also have a thousand *less* dollars in your savings. When you spend the money, you're actually a thousand dollars *poorer*. Proper economics requires the complete accounting of any withdrawal. Most people understand this because they worked hard to put the money into savings in the first place. If they were to *inherit* the savings, though, then they're less apt to understand its true value and may spend it foolishly. Easy come, easy go. That's what we're doing with the Earth's resources. We've inherited them, and we're spending them foolishly."

Penny busied herself setting plates and silverware on the table in front of us. "Don't forget napkins, honey, and a hot pad for the table so we can set the quiche on it," Annie reminded her.

"In our present economy," Melissa continued, ignoring the interruption, "we withdraw non-renewable resources from nature's 'bank' — resources that have been saved for eons to conceivably benefit all humanity for all time — and then we call the spent resources *earnings*. We ignore the fact that we're withdrawing from an account that can't be replenished. We ignore the fact that, as we burn coal and oil and gas, our natural resource wealth is going up in smoke, never to be replaced. Our natural bank account is being depleted, and only a few people are getting rich from it. Most people aren't. In fact, despite the extravagant cashing in of the Earth's non-renewable resources, most people on this planet are poor. It's bad economics, economics literally without a future."

"You keep saying the economy has no future. According to Wall Street, the economic future looks pretty damn good," Annie countered.

"It should be obvious, but it isn't," Melissa replied. "Our economic attitude of 'get rich quick at any cost' is ultimately a dead-end road. It might look good right *now*, but let's assume for a moment there will be a long-term future for humanity, along with many hundreds of future human generations. If we realize that there is a future, we also realize that we don't *own* this planet, we only temporarily *borrow* it from future generations. We understand that we hold the Earth's wealth in *trust*. We realize that we have no right to squander the Earth's wealth for the short-term gain of a few people in the present."

"Let me put it another way," Max added. "In the past sixty years, we Americans alone have used up as many of the Earth's minerals, for example, as have been used by all of the other people on this planet since the beginning of time. When an accountant like me sees a statistic like that, alarms go off. Something's wrong with that picture."

"But that's the American way, isn't it?" I asked. "What about the American Dream? Aren't we supposed to be able to get rich in this country? Isn't that what sets America apart from the rest of the world? This is one place where a person can go from rags to riches, don't you think? What's wrong with that?"

"The American Dream has become a nightmare," Max answered. "We no longer want happy homes, healthy families, solid communities, clean environments, decent jobs, and stable relationships, which is what the American Dream initially promised. We want to get rich. And everybody and everything that gets in the way can be damned. The environment? It's a joke. The future? Who cares? That's what the less ethical elements of America's business community has warped the American Dream into. And unfortunately, they've succeeded. So far."

"Thank heavens for evolution," Melissa said. "If not for evolution we'd still be hanging from trees. Thanks to progressive change over time, we gradually and incrementally improve. The American Dream, as you put it, must progressively evolve too. And soon."

Symbiosis

ANNIE BROUGHT OUT THE BROCCOLI QUICHE AND SET IT on the deck table as the conversation with Max and Melissa broke off into small talk about the weather. She returned with a green garden salad and another round of beers. "Anyone for some iced tea?" she asked.

"Beer's fine," Max replied. "This is homebrew, you say? Not bad."

"Annie's been making beer for about ten years," I told Max. "She makes the beer and I make the wine, and so far, we've lived happily ever after."

Annie and Penny sat down at the table with us, and we dove into our lunch. "Great quiche," Max told Annie with a smile as he gobbled it down.

"The eggs are from our own chickens," she replied. "And the broccoli is from our garden. So is the salad."

"This food's as fresh as it can get," I added."

"It's wonderful," agreed Melissa.

Between mouthfuls, Max steered the conversation back to their favorite subject: money. "The few people getting rich from the squandering of our non-renewable resources," he said, "don't want anyone to realize what they're doing. They don't want anyone to know that no one's minding the store, that they have their hand in the cash register drawer. By convincing everyone that the economy is good because the money is being spent, they take our minds off the fact that our bank account is being systematically depleted," explained Max, who paused to chug his beer.

Melissa continued the conversation for him. "He means our natural resources are being pilfered, squandered."

"Unfortunately," Max added, wiping his mouth with a napkin, "the robbing of our resources is causing severe problems for our biosphere —"

"That's the Earth," Melissa interrupted.

"I think they know what a biosphere is," Max chided. "The biosphere is being damaged, our basic global life support systems are being undermined, because the cash drawer is being robbed and no one gives a damn! A tiny minority is profiting at the expense of the majority! I'd say it's unbelievable, I'd suggest that people in general are incredibly stupid. How can a few people claim the Earth's non-renewable resources, extract them, and then sell them for their own personal profit? These are resources that have taken millions of years to create, then have laid in the ground under the feet of humanity since time immemorial, and now someone comes along and claims them? That's what I mean about no one minding the store."

"Are you aware of the power of the media and advertising to influence people's decisions?" Max continued. "Well, the media are controlled by the same wealthy minority that has our government representatives in their pocketbooks. A minority that's using up our resources as fast as they can. It *appears* that we have a good economy, but it won't last — it can't. It's a one-way ticket to bankruptcy. Any accountant worth his salt can tell you that. You can't just withdraw, withdraw, withdraw, and spend, spend, spend, forever. Our resources are limited. The future generations are going to look back at us and shake their heads in disbelief. Why would a couple of generations of Americans want to spend *everyone else's* resources? Why would they want to waste them so flagrantly? What conceivable rationale could there possibly be for that sort of behavior?"

"Greed and ignorance," answered Melissa. "The greed

of the people who can get away with it, and the ignorance of the people who could put a stop to it. That's where *we* come in," she said, looking at Annie and me pointedly. "Max and I are *idea* people. We suggest alternatives. We try to wake people up. An economy is necessary, but we must have one that has a future. One that recognizes the value of natural materials in their natural state. One that understands that we only have one natural bank account, an account from which all wealth is derived, an account for all people for all time, an account that can't be replenished. We need an economy that is not destructive and wasteful. Our economy must become benign with regard to this planet."

Just then a dim light bulb went off in my head. As I sat there forking spinach into my mouth, I remembered eating dinner with Professor Gaulton in Newfoundland a couple months earlier, and his robbing frenzy scenario raced through my mind. "Melissa, have you ever heard of a theory called the *robbing frenzy*? That was one of Lucy's ideas."

"Of course I have. Lucille was very interested in that concept in the last months of her life. There was a professor up in New Brunswick who she talked to about it, wasn't there?"

"Newfoundland. Yes, Brian Gaulton," I replied. "As the professor explained it, according to Lucy's theory, humans are acting like disease organisms on the planet. Do you think disease organisms could be said to have an economy of sorts? I don't mean a money economy, of course. But would you say that the over-consumption of resources would be a characteristic of a pathogen's economy?"

"Exactly," Melissa replied. "You've hit the nail on the head. Damn, I wish my students could have been so perceptive! The word 'economy' simply refers to the management and exchange of goods, services, and energy. For humans, that means manufacturing, construction, food production, and every other aspect of life requiring goods, services, or energy. Any organism has an economy, no matter how rudimentary. Even a colony of bacteria requires the flow of nutrients and energy, and thus has a simple sort of economy. A disease organism overconsumes its resource base without regard for the future, and it therefore has an economy without a future. That's why diseases kill their hosts. But diseases go on to infect other hosts. That's how they survive. Humans can't kill their host and move on to another one like a disease organism does. Unless we're going to find another planet in the galaxy and infect it, too. Lucille and I discussed this at length. She loved this analogy."

"From what I gathered, though, I don't think she thought it was necessarily an analogy," I insisted. "I think she thought humans were actually exhibiting *real* disease potential in relation to the Earth. Anyway, if we currently have an economy that parallels that of a disease organism, do you think there's an alternative?"

"Yes, yes, that's what I've been trying to say!" replied Melissa, excitedly, slapping her hand on the table. "That's what I've been trying to say all along! A disease organism has a *destructive* economy, an economy without a future. But a *symbiotic* organism, on the other hand, which is an organism that lives in harmony with its environment, also has an economy. An economy *with* a future. Both types of organisms have their own economies, both require the flow of materials and energy, but the disease organism progressively *undermines* its economy through over-consumption and waste, and eventually destroys it. Destroys its own economy and destroys itself in the process! The other, the symbiotic organism, knows how to maintain a benign economy by managing its resources properly and avoiding overconsumption and waste. It will live on indefinitely. Humanity, if we are to survive, *must* develop a symbiotic economy!"

"And that's not even the most important aspect," added Max.

"What do you mean?" Annie asked.

"It makes sense that the symbiotic economy would be

much more *preferable* for the organism involved, especially humans. Preferable in many ways. A human symbiotic economy could last indefinitely, it could allow for goods, services, and energy to be distributed among people equitably, it could guarantee prosperity, peace, meaningful and rewarding jobs, and fulfilling lives for everyone, without a sacrifice in our standard of living."

"I'm not following you," Annie eyed him skeptically. "How would it *not* sacrifice our standard of living?"

"The people who are robbing our store, who are promoting a destructive, wasteful economy, argue that if we stop squandering our resources, our economy will take a huge nose dive and we'll all be back to washing our laundry on scrub boards in our back yards," explained Max. "So people's natural reaction is to think we can't do *that*, therefore we must continue to squander our natural bank account like there's no tomorrow. But this is ridiculous. Symbiotic economies, by definition, involve the exchange of goods, services, and energy in a manner that allows everyone to benefit over the long term. It's a balanced, equitable economy. There's no reason to believe that our average standard of living would drop simply because we shift to a more conscious economic system. Our standard of living would more than likely *improve*. We'd have cleaner air, cleaner water, better quality food, less disease, less poverty, more rewarding employment, healthier societies, and more fulfilling lives."

"But wouldn't we be paying a lot more for gas and oil and coal?" argued Annie. "Wouldn't our prices go up and therefore our disposable income go down?"

"Sure, if we're dumb enough to rely heavily on those non-renewable resources. A symbiotic organism would phase out or minimize the use of polluting, non-renewable resources as quickly as possible while finding ways to use the same resources efficiently, cleanly, and, perhaps most importantly, wisely. The people making wads of money selling gas, coal, and oil, are singing a different song. They're telling us that we have to buy their products in large quantities or suffer a drastic drop in our standard of living."

"By centering our lifestyles around non-renewable resources like fossil fuels, we've painted ourselves into a corner," Melissa declared. "But the people extracting and selling these resources force us, through media influence, to keep consuming them mindlessly. After all, that's how they make their money. It's a downward spiral, like being hooked on heroin. We're the addicts, they're the pushers. They steal the heroin from nature's bank account, get us hooked on it, make a pile of money in the process, and in the meantime, our ecosystem slowly dies. It's frightening."

"That's right," Max added. "The business people goading us into consuming huge quantities of non-renewable resources aren't motivated by altruism, they're motivated by greed. But the truth is just the opposite of what they tell us — if we continue to burn the huge amounts of fossil fuels we're currently using, we'll pollute the planet beyond repair and everyone's standard of living will plummet. We have to summon up some good old-fashioned ingenuity and find *new* ways to meet our needs, and we have to learn to see *past* the industry hype and propaganda. As a culture we have to change, to evolve, and thereby shift our direction."

"How? How would a shift like that take place?" I asked.

"That's the intriguing part," answered Melissa, dabbing at her lips with a napkin. "Our personal consumptive habits must change. It's intriguing because it puts a lot of power to make the necessary changes into our *own* hands, as individuals."

"What sort of changes?" Annie wondered.

"Well, as symbiotic beings, we have to learn how to work *with* nature, not against it," Max responded. "Let me give you some examples. Take light, for instance. We currently produce most of our light by generating electricity and then burning it in light bulbs. That usually requires huge amounts of fossil fuels, with an incredible amount of pollution. In any case, our lighting devices produce a lot of heat, which is waste energy. It's the light that we want, not the heat. Lightning bugs, or fireflies, on the other hand, produce light without heat. Their source of energy? Other smaller insects. Obviously, it's possible to produce cool light directly from natural, organic ingredients, at room temperature. That's the sort of thing we humans need to be figuring out. Another example is the common spider. Its silk is one of the strongest fibers known. It spins its silk from what it ingests — house flies, crickets, and other bugs. Obviously, very strong fibers can be made using only natural, organic, renewable, raw materials, at body temperature. Humans instead make fibers in ways that are very dirty, wasteful, energy intensive, and polluting. We could learn nature's ways too, if we wanted to. And if we humans were half as smart as we think we are, that's exactly what we'd do."

"But don't you think that's unrealistic?" asked Annie. "We're not going to be able to do anything like that in the immediate future, wouldn't you agree?"

"Why not?" Melissa challenged. "Besides, there are lots of other things we certainly *can* do immediately." By this time we had finished lunch and were leaning back in our chairs watching Penny gather dishes off the patio table.

"There's dessert, by the way," Annie reminded us.

"I am *stuffed*," Melissa replied, patting her stomach contentedly.

"Count me in," Max said. "I can't refuse dessert." Annie asked Penelope to serve the last course. Delighted to be playing hostess, she rushed inside and immediately came back out balancing a tray of dishes set with golden slices of cake and fresh red strawberries. Beside each slice, I noticed with amusement, she had placed a small, purple pansy. As soon as Melissa eyed the decadent dessert, she changed her mind and decided she'd have some as well.

"As I was saying, Annie," Melissa mumbled, spooning the shortcake into her mouth, "there's a lot of stuff we can personally do immediately to shift toward a symbiotic economy. In fact, a lot is already happening. Max and I are not fringe kooks crying alone in the wilderness. There are lots and lots of people around the world who are aware of the dire problems facing us today and are trying to do something about them."

"Yes, we heard about the World Scientist's Warning to Humanity," I remarked.

"Besides scientists, though, there are people in the business world too, who are trying to make products that are more symbiotic," Max said. "Cars don't have to be the big, heavy, wasteful things they are today. They're being redesigned to be light, energy efficient, and recyclable. Although, admittedly, American car makers are way behind the rest of the world in this regard. They keep cranking out big gas guzzlers like they don't have a clue."

"And people keep buying them," added Melissa. "Advertising obviously works."

"Some people are learning how to phase out the need for petroleum through the use of hydrogen fuel cells," Max continued. "Appliances are being reengineered to be recyclable and much more energy efficient. And made of recycled materials, as well."

"Building materials can also be manufactured without waste, pollution, or toxic chemicals," added Melissa. "We could be recycling our buildings instead of demolishing them and dumping them in landfills. Wood can be harvested sustainably; structures can be designed to be energy efficient and recyclable; fibers and fabrics don't need to be processed with environmentally damaging chemicals and poisons. Of course, none of these things will ever happen if people aren't aware of the need for them. And that awareness probably won't come from TV. Just the opposite — it seems that the more people are exposed to commercial media, the more convinced they are that they should buy wastefully."

"Take food for example," continued Max. "Food can be produced in sustainable, non-toxic ways. Natural soil fertility can be protected and built up through the recycling of organic materials. There are an endless number of beneficial alternatives that we can support today, right now, if people only knew how critically we need to switch to a symbiotic way of life on this planet."

"For example," explained Melissa, thumbing through some papers in her brown briefcase, "did you know that in the United States, ah, here it is, we throw away so many aluminum cans that we could rebuild our entire fleet of commercial airliners every three months with the wasted metal? Did you know that we now use 98 tons of resources to make only one ton of paper, or that a laptop computer, when manufactured, produces four thousand times its weight in waste?"

"Incredible," we agreed.

"And we're not sitting here trying to sell you anything," Max added with a smile. "What do *we* have to gain by telling you this stuff? We're just glad to have someone who will listen to us. So many people have closed minds when it comes to issues like this. Media personalities have convinced the average American that anything resembling environmentalism is bad, and that anyone who offers any criticism of our economy, no matter how constructive, is a quack. The wool has been pulled over America's eyes, big-time. That's what's incredible to me!"

"We probably wouldn't be so sympathetic ourselves, Max, if we hadn't recently been through these Lucy escapades. They've been real eye-openers for us. For example, you say that Americans aren't aware of these issues. Well, Eduardo said something about 'our people' being deaf and blind," Annie said.

"How can you hear anything with a set of earphones blaring commercial media into your ears?" asked Max. "How can you see anything with your eyes glued to a TV set? Your Eduardo fellow was right in that sense. Many Americans have loaned their eyes and ears to commercial interests. They're no longer aware of the real world around them. It's time they take their eyes and ears back."

"Think of it this way," Melissa said. "A clam can make

one of the hardest organic materials known, its shell, simply by sucking in sea water. We humans are so far out of touch with nature, and so damned self-centered, that nature's miracles may be right underfoot, but we wouldn't see them even if we tripped over them. We already live in a sustainable world — it's all around us. *We're* the ones out of sync. Did you know that four million pounds of raw materials are required to meet the *yearly* needs of the average American family today? Four million pounds!"

"Not to mention that the average American individual requires a *ton* of water every *day*," added Max. "Literally. Two thousand pounds. And when they're done using that water, it's polluted!"

"We produce over fifty *trillion* pounds of waste every year in the United States! Imagine that!" continued Melissa. "That's fifty thousand *billion* pounds. It's mind-boggling. And when you think that the *rest* of the world has twenty-one times as many people as *we* do in the United States, and they think *they* need to live like *us*, then you can see that we have an impending disaster now developing on this planet."

"What we're telling you is only the tip of the iceberg, folks," added Max, solemnly. "We haven't even mentioned the loss of topsoil, climate change, species extinctions, and the many, many, other symptoms of a poorly planned economy."

"So what're we supposed to do?" implored Annie. "It's overwhelming. Where do we start?"

"Start right here, right now," Melissa said. "Life is short and then you die. You must act now if you're going to make any difference in this fragile world. Perhaps Eduardo taught you that. There are lots of things you can do."

"Such as?" she pressed.

"Well, for example, there are really simple things," Melissa explained. "Read the ingredients in the food you buy. Avoid anything artificial. Companies that put artificial flavors and colors into their foods are doing it only for their profit, certainly not for your health. Instead, buy organically grown foods, foods without harmful chemicals. Here's another thing: avoid household cleaning agents that don't clearly state they're non-toxic. Some of the most common household cleaners contain chemicals that have been proven to cause cancer. If we stop buying these products, the companies will either improve them or go out of business. That's the power of the consumer."

"Of an *informed* consumer," corrected Max. "People buy bad products because they see them advertised. Because the advertisements are slick, and the ingredients are never discussed in the ads."

"That's right," continued Melissa. "Why just the other day, I heard an ad on the radio for disposable storage containers for storing leftovers. Can you imagine? So now, when you forget about your leftovers, and they mold in the refrigerator, you just throw them out — containers and all. And it's not like the containers are being recycled; they're just going directly into landfills, along with the food. Ludicrous! We shouldn't buy things in containers that have to be thrown away in the first place."

"Every damned thing nowadays comes in a plastic throwaway box," huffed Max. "Where's the economic wisdom in that? You know, this stuff we're telling you should be taught at every level of our educational system, from kindergarten up through graduate school. Churches should be on the bandwagon too, encouraging symbiotic living among members of their congregations. There could be more civic groups dedicated to restoration of the planet. Boy scouts, girl scouts, fraternities and sororities, the PTA, everyone can pitch in."

Melissa continued, "We should all be supporting businesses that are trying to shift toward symbiotic practices. Boycott the polluters — don't buy their products. But most of all, be informed, be aware. All of the necessary information is out there, and if you expend only a small amount of energy to look for it, you'll find it. It's mostly common sense. And you can begin to shift your lifestyle toward a symbiotic one without anyone even knowing it. And who knows? Maybe your friends, neighbors, and relatives will catch on too. It has to start somewhere. Why not with you?"

"That reminds me of one of the basic rules of life," I said flippantly. "You can't judge a person by their relatives! Not to change the subject or anything."

Annie laughed, dry as dust. "Does that go for spouses too, dear?"

"Yes, and speaking of rules of life," added Max, "here's another: you should never criticize someone until you've walked a mile in their shoes. Do you know why?"

"Well, because you don't really know them until you've lived like them?" Annie offered.

"No. Because then you'll be a mile away and you'll have their shoes!" Max laughed uproariously at his own joke. The rest of us looked at each other straight-faced, then broke out laughing too.

Back to Montana

JUST AS ANNIE WAS STACKING OUR EMPTY DESSERT
plates on the table, Michael and Sarah came strolling down
the lane, wet towels draped over their necks. They joined
us at the table, sharing a small bench that I had fashioned
out of some barn wood, and grabbed the last of the straw-
berry shortcake.

They were thrilled to meet Melissa and Max. The four
of them got along famously, and became immediately
immersed in more discussions, which carried on late into
the afternoon. Both Michael and Sarah were fascinated to
explore ecological principles from an economic perspective, something that they hadn't been exposed to in the
classroom. That a misguided economy was largely responsible for the environmental problems we were faced with
was an idea that hadn't occurred to them. Furthermore, the
notion that such an economy could be transformed into a
benign and symbiotic one through the actions of consumers was empowering to both of the young adults who
had their entire lives ahead of them. It made them feel that
it was within their power to make positive changes for a
better future.

Before we knew it, dusk was upon us. Fireflies glowed
in the dim light, and the stars began to glimmer against
the darkened sky. Melissa and Max exchanged looks with
each other over the table, and explained regretfully that
they had a long drive ahead of them. We loitered around.

their car as they packed up and buckled in. Rolling down the driver's side window, Melissa passed me a stack of papers — copies of reports, research materials, and statistical information supporting their view that our "pathogenic" economy could, and should, be transformed into a "symbiotic" one. I assured her I would review the material and return it to her, but she insisted that I keep it.

Sarah and Michael lounged around our house for another week, and then decided that they needed to return to Minnesota and settle in for another year of college life. Shortly after they left, I phoned Cecilia Tomasso in Halifax. She was thrilled to hear about our trip to Peru and our meeting with the Bergers. Coincidentally, she had just received Lucy's death certificate from Montana the day before. She said the cause of death was attributed to heart failure, but admitted that heart failure can be caused by unnatural things such as medications or drugs, or even sudden and unexpected fear. She said that only a thorough investigation could determine if foul play was involved in Lucy's death, an investigation that was beyond her scope, especially if Lucy's corpse had been cremated. Cecilia made me promise that I would let her know as soon as any new developments occurred in the Lucy saga. I promised.

Annie and I spent the next few weeks describing our Peruvian adventure to friends and family. We were no longer reluctant to discuss Lucy's quest and our improbable role in it. We had finally come to realize that there was a solid foundation of reality underneath the façade of fantasy that I had originally referred to as Lucy's Goose Chase. The more we talked about it, the more we processed it, and the more we seemed to understand it. However, we were left with a nagging feeling that we weren't finished with our escapades, and we wondered what to do next.

We visited with Cynthia and her family again, and met with Tom and Lana. Fascinated by our detailed account of Peru, they hung onto every word. Our story of the introduction to the snake had them in stitches, wiping tears of laughter from their faces. But it was Cynthia who once again steered me in a direction that I would ultimately decide to follow. She gently reminded me that Lucy had expected me to find my point of personal equilibrium — my balance point. After hearing about my experiences with Eduardo, she thought that maybe I *had* found it. If that were the case, Cynthia suggested, I should contact the law firm in Montana and claim Lucy's half million dollar estate. This certainly gave me a lot to think about, and Annie and I bounced the idea back and forth at home for another week or so after that.

"I *do* think I understand what Lucy meant by finding a personal balance point," I told her as we sat in our hickory rockers one evening.

"What did she mean, then?"

"It's like that tree Eduardo showed us in tne forest. We only see what's above ground, but we don't see the rest of it — the roots, the great amount of water that's being sucked into those roots and up the trunk, the earth dissolved in solution entering the roots, the microorganisms on the root hairs that help the tree to live, the huge volumes of gases being sucked in through the leaves and transpired out again, the sunlight being absorbed through the massive canopy. When Eduardo explained it to us in this way it became obvious to me that there's much more to a tree than meets the eye. A tree, if we could actually see all of its connections, would look like a spider web with strands extending in all directions, some for great distances. A tree is not a separate, independent entity on this planet; it's inextricably linked to most of the world around it. We humans are exactly the same. We're connected to the world around us in many ways."

"Sure," she agreed. "I can see that too."

"With that in mind, I now realize, for example, that whenever I throw something away, there is, in fact, no such place as 'away.' It just goes out into the world, to some-where else. For some crazy reason, we've come to believe that we can just throw garbage over our shoulders, so to speak, and walk away from it, as if our actions have no consequence on the rest of the world. Like no one in the future is going to have to come along and clean up after us. Like there is no future, as the Bergers would say. I know now that anything I do, no matter how inconsequential I may think it to be, has ramifications for the rest of the world. For future generations, including all life, not just humans. The way I view things is different now," I explained.

"But what about the balance point? Your *personal* balance point?" Annie stressed.

"I'm getting to that. Every move I make tugs on a strand in the web of life, a strand that's connected to something else. That would be Lucy's 'Eco,' or Eduardo's 'Earth mother.' Then there's the time element. I think the native North Americans referred to the concept of 'seven generations,' didn't they?"

"You mean they thought we should consider the effect of our actions on the next seven generations?"

"Yes, that's it. I understand what they were saying now. The native Americans had an economy with a *future*. Anyway, I now have to weigh all of my decisions — my personal choices as a consumer and as a business person — against the ramifications those choices will have on the world around me. Not just today's world, but the future world. I can refuse to buy stuff that I know pollutes the world, or creates waste, or harms our social fabric, or supports violence. I can no longer pursue my business for the simple goal of making a profit. I have to think about the rest of the world and about posterity when I have any interaction with our 'economy.' And I know I won't be at peace with myself unless I do these things. On the other hand, I want to be happy and comfortable and enjoy life while I have it. That puts me at a place in my consciousness that I would definitely call my personal balance point. If I move toward careless selfishness, I feel out of balance. If I move too far the other way, I'm off-kilter, too. Eduardo's right, it *is* a spiritual phenomenon. Something you feel *inside* you. And when you allow that feeling to surface, when you get in touch with it, you just *know* it's right. Remember when he kept telling me that for some things, there are no words? Well, this is one of those things. I can't explain it very well."

"You're doing a pretty good job of it, I think. So you're a changed man, then?" asked Annie, cocking an eyebrow at me. "You're seeing the world with different eyes? Would you say you've turned a corner in your life?"

"Yes, and I hope you have too," I told her.

"What's *that* supposed to mean? How do you know I wasn't already at *my* personal balance point?" she said with a half-smile. "Eduardo said it's different for everyone, and it's the natural state of being, anyway. Maybe I'm a little more evolved than you!"

"Ok, *whatever*. The point I'm making is that we need to do this together. We need to support each other."

"I agree."

"I think you should come with me to Montana to meet with the lawyers up there."

"Okay," she said, after hesitating a moment. "But are you sure that we have to go there? Can't we do it by phone or by mail?"

"I think I have to sign papers in person, in front of their notary. The estate is worth a lot of money. A half million bucks is nothing to sneeze at."

"I was just thinking that we would be wasting energy and fuel to transport our bodies around, that's all," she shrugged. "But if you think it's absolutely necessary, fine, let's make the arrangements. If you're ready, that is."

"I'm ready."

"You're ready to claim a half million dollar estate?" she asked, somewhat incredulously.

"I'm as ready as I'll ever be," I replied unequivocally.

Lucy's Gift

I HAD THREE WEEKS TO WAVER, WHICH SEEMED LIKE endless days for doubt to creep back in, like bees sneaking in the back door of a beehive and stealing my resolve, bit by bit. The attorneys were tied up in court, consumed with an auto accident lawsuit, and I was not their top priority. In the meantime, I wrestled with my conscience about greed, about honesty, wondering what I would do with a half million dollars, knowing that a sudden influx of money could skew my sense of judgement and tilt me spiritually toward selfishness. Self-importance, as Eduardo called it. I couldn't just claim a half million dollars for myself, then run out and buy a yacht or something, now aware of the effects of mindless consumerism and the impending threat of ecocide. I no longer saw the inheritance as a bonus that would enable me and my family to gain new luxuries in life; instead, I viewed it as a burden of responsibility. The things we valued most in our life couldn't be bought. I had a healthy, loving family, a cozy home that was already paid for, and we were comfortable with the middle class income of a roofing contractor. Annie refused to make suggestions about what to do with the money. "Don't count your chickens before they hatch," she'd say to me, or, "It's your money, not mine. You inherited it. You decide what to do with it."

So it was with this degree of uncertainty that we traveled to Bozeman, Montana, to settle Lucy's estate. The law office of Stainbrook and Halforth was richly appointed: thick leather-bound books lined oak floor-to-ceiling shelves; the carpets were deep and plush. Everything was done to excess — the place reeked of money. When we arrived, we were immediately whisked into a large windowless side room where two starchy lawyers and a young female secretary sat with us at a huge rosewood conference table. They checked my photo identification, my birth certificate, and my passport, all of which they had asked me to bring. One of the lawyers, a grey-haired gentleman in a blue pin-striped suit, opened a large briefcase and removed some papers.

"Mr. Jenkins, Dr. Lucille Boggs, whose estate we represent, has named you the beneficiary of the estate, under certain specific conditions. Do you understand that?" he asked me in an official manner.

"Yes, I do."

"The estate is worth approximately one half million US dollars, and includes some real estate, namely her personal home. Here is the copy of her will." He pushed the document across the table to me.

I quickly scanned it, noting that it simply stated that I would be the beneficiary of the estate under conditions set forth by an accompanying letter. "So, where's the letter?" I asked.

"The letter is here." The lawyer waved it in his hand, but didn't offer it to me.

"May I see it?"

"I'm afraid you may not at this time, Mr. Jenkins." He opened the letter and began to read from it. "Mr. Jenkins, I am bound by legal duty to ask you for the following information in front of witnesses before we can proceed with this transfer. Sir, please state your full name for the record."

"Joseph Jenkins."

"Please state your full address, for the record." I did so.

"Mr. Jenkins, was Dr. Lucille Boggs your great aunt by blood, your father's aunt?"

"Yes, she was."

"Finally, Mr. Jenkins, have you found your personal balance point?" The look the attorneys gave each other indicated that they found this whole thing rather bewildering, to say the least.

I took a deep breath and said, "Yes."

"In that case, Mr. Jenkins, please sign these papers at the place indicated by the 'x.' They are simply the transferral papers. The secretary will notarize them for you."

I scratched my signature on the indicated lines.

"Mr. Jenkins, allow me to congratulate you on your inheritance," he said congenially. "I have to admit that this is certainly one of the most unique inheritance settlements I've been witness to in all of my years practicing law. Dr. Boggs instructed us to simply ask you the questions we just asked, and to simply and finally ask if you had found a thing she referred to as a balance point. She seemed to believe that you would answer honestly and that we didn't need to know what a balance point actually *was*. As such, we have fulfilled our obligations and so have you. It is always sad to see a loved one go, but nice when they leave a little something behind."

He handed me a sealed manila envelope. "That's all. We're finished. Take your time and look over the contents of this envelope, which Dr. Boggs asked we give to you at the time of the estate transfer. We'll leave you two alone now." He neatly stacked the papers together and passed them to the secretary, who was waiting by the opened office door. "Ah, but one more thing, Mr. Jenkins," he asked me, hesitating at the entrance. "What exactly is a 'balance point'? We were just curious. Is that something that, say, a juggler or acrobat would look for?"

"No," I replied, suppressing a slight smile while shaking my head. "A personal balance point is a place within oneself where one is spiritually balanced. That's about the closest definition I can come up with."

"Aha! That makes sense. So you found your religion, then, at your Aunt's behest?"

"No, not at all. It has nothing to do with religion," I answered. The lawyers just stared at me with incomprehension. I didn't offer any more information. It just seemed too difficult to sum up the concept of the balance point into a few words that a lawyer would understand.

At that, the two lawyers and the secretary left the room and closed the door behind them. Annie and I just looked at each other, not knowing whether to believe that a transfer of a half million dollars into our names had just transpired. We didn't know whether to jump up and yell, dance around the room, do cartwheels, scream, pinch ourselves, or what. I looked at her, she looked at me, neither of us spoke, then we looked at the manila envelope.

"Open that," Annie said, with a strange urgency. "It's from Lucy. God knows what the hell's in there."

34

Letter to the Living

I TORE THE TOP OFF THE ENVELOPE, BREAKING THE WAX seal. Reaching in, I removed a group of about a dozen letter-sized papers that were stapled together. On the front of the bundle was a letter from my generous and wonderful Aunt Lucy herself, written in pen.

"*Dear Joseph,*" I read, smiling at Lucy's distinctively hurried scrawl.

"*Congratulations. I knew you could do it. In the event that you had not found your balance point, I had ordered my lawyers to divide my estate equally among the charities indicated on the papers attached to this letter.*

However, since you have succeeded in claiming my estate, and since you have honestly and sincerely found your personal balance point, then you quite understand the importance of the attached charities receiving an equal portion of my assets. They are organizations that are working very hard to change the world for the better. I have very carefully chosen them in order to support their work in trying to prevent the approaching Point of No Return. Therefore, I will leave it up to you to see that my entire estate, the one that you now possess, will be divided up and distributed equally to the ten non-profit entities attached.

I'm sure you had no intention of using the money yourself for personal reasons, and I have saved you the trouble of trying to decide what to do with it. Please reimburse yourself for any trouble or expenses. And keep up the good work!

Sincerely,

Lucy

P.S. No doubt you wonder why I chose <u>you</u> to follow my clues and inherit my estate. I picked you because I once saw you, long ago, in a very vivid dream. In that dream you were writing a book — for me. I never fully understood the meaning of that dream until now, as the finger of death gently taps me on my shoulder. And now I understand, without a doubt, that you will write about the Balance Point for me. Although I must now leave this world, it is because of you, dear nephew, that I can leave a little piece of myself behind for the benefit of others. So please carve a little off my estate before you pass it out to the non-profits, and write a book about your experiences. Consider it <u>our</u> little gift to the world, and pray that it makes a difference, before it's too late."

35

Afterword

PERHAPS I SHOULDN'T HAVE BEEN SO SURPRISED THAT Lucy's "inheritance" turned out to be nothing but more work for me. She was a crafty one. Brilliant, perhaps, but crafty. How could I complain, though? I enjoyed writing this book for her, and she paid the expenses. And, as you can imagine, ten non-profit organizations were also very happy to hear from me.

Lucy's notorious Last Will and Testament now hangs framed on the wall of my office, over my desk, reminding me that I was once a half-millionaire for about five minutes. But I have no regrets. Lucy opened my eyes like no one else could have.

Do I believe there's a war in progress between the Ego and the Eco? I think that was Lucy's unique way of saying we humans have to get our act together — soon. But I don't see the outcome of that "war" as being either the Ego or the Eco proclaiming victory over the other. I see the outcome as being a balanced and peaceful partnership between the two.

Do I believe humans are a disease on our planet? Are we engaged in a Robbing Frenzy, as Lucy suspected? Is the Point of No Return looming somewhere between 2020 and 2040? That I don't know. Maybe, but I sincerely hope not. Regardless, I do have a strong feeling that our culture took a wrong turn somewhere in our past, a turn away from wisdom with regard to living on this planet. And I think that Eduardo's assessment of the situation has a ring of truth: the problem is spiritual — we've lost a basic connection within ourselves. And, because of that, we cannot find our spiritual link to the natural world. If the Earth could shed a tear, she would be shedding it for her lost children.

If the preponderance of ecological evidence is correct, if we are damaging our biosphere with increasing severity, and if the time line suggested by the world's scientists is accurate, then it is up to the baby-boomer generation and its children to steer our culture in a new direction. We are the pivotal generations, the ones that must have the vision and foresight to aim for a future that is not marred by environmental collapse. If we don't do it, no one else may be able to. It is an immense and frightening responsibility, and the obstacles are formidable. Perhaps the largest obstacle looming before us is complacency — we just don't seem to care.

Will the human species someday simply become a curious fossil buried in the earth, to be dug up eons from now by more intelligent creatures? Will those creatures wonder why we disappeared? Will it occur to them that complacency, selfishness, and greed could lead to the extinction of a species?

We who are alive today are the people who will determine the future of humanity. We are the ones who must goad the human race to squirm out of an obsolete cocoon of mindless consumerism and metamorphose into something more beautiful, and benign.

As Eduardo said, spiritual balance is our natural state. Humans are capable of incredible beauty. We have the capacity to be the Earth's keepers, and to live together on this planet wisely, fairly, and with foresight. This, I do believe.

NOTES

CHAPTER 13 - HALIFAX

For global warming information see Time Magazine, December 13, 1999, pp. 78-79, "Greenhouse Effects."

For additional information see: Hawken, Paul, et al., (1999); Natural Capitalism — Creating the Next Industrial Revolution; Little, Brown, and Company, Boston, New York and London.

CHAPTER 15 - ECOCIDE

For information on atmospheric composition see Suzuki, David (1998); The Sacred Balance; Prometheus Books, New York.

Egg analogy described in Natural Capitalism, p. 234.

CHAPTER 16 - WARNING TO HUMANITY

For computer modeling information see: Meadows, Meadows, and Randers, (1992); Beyond the Limits — Confronting Global Collapse, Envisioning a Sustainable Future; Chelsea Green Publishing, White River Jct., VT.

Toxic chemicals in body fat: see Colborn, Dumanoksi, and Myers. (1996). Our Stolen Future. New York: Penguin Books, p. 106.

Half the world's rivers are polluted: see World Commission on Water for the 21st Century (as seen in News on Earth, December, 1999).

Almost half (40%) of the water bodies in the US are too polluted for swimming: see US EPA, December 1995.

Cancer is leading cause of death: see Steingraber, Sandra (1997); Living Downstream; Perseus Books, Reading, MA, p. 40.

CHAPTER 21 - PERU

Nellie's hotel is the Hostal San Sebastian at Ica 712, Lima, Peru. Please note: the map to Eduardo's has been altered to protect his privacy. Don't try to find him — you'll only get lost in the very deep jungle.

CHAPTER 30 - AMERICAN DREAM

"Since 1940, we Americans alone have used up as many of the earth's minerals, for example, as used by all of the other people on this planet, since the beginning of time." See The Sacred Balance, David Suzuki, p. 23.

CHAPTER 31 - SYMBIOSIS

"In the United States we throw away so many aluminum cans that we could rebuild our entire fleet of commercial airliners every three months with the wasted metal. We now use 98 tons of resources to make only one ton of paper. The manufacture of a laptop computer produces four thousand times its weight in waste." See Natural Capitalism, p. 50.

"Four million pounds of raw materials are required to meet the *yearly* needs of the average American family today. The average American individual requires a *ton* of water every *day*. We produce over fifty *trillion* pounds of waste every year in the United States." See Natural Capitalism, p. 52.

Aunt Lucy's Tips for Helping the Earth

Now that you've finished this book, you should consider this a *beginning*. Although Balance Point paints a disturbing picture, you are not powerless to act. You can continue your education, for example, by reading through this addendum. Also, keep one eye on the news articles about global climate change, ecological degradation, pollution levels, and consumption habits. Let them be a constant reminder to you that time is running out. What can one person do? A lot. And when that one person inspires another, there are now two, then four, then thousands. Exponential growth can be a disaster, but it can also save us. The world will not change if we do not want it to. As Melissa Berger stated, "Start right here, right now. Life is short and then you die. You must act now if you're going to make any difference in this fragile world."

Consider your efforts to be a shot in the arm for the Earth, and a meaningful spiritual exercise for your soul. Remember that a spiritual act is one that brings you toward a closer harmony with the greater Being, that *totality of existence* that Eduardo referred to as the Earth mother or the Great Mystery, and Lucy referred to as the Eco. So in addition to whatever religious practices you are accustomed to, add some natural spirituality to your life. One simple exercise would be to take an hour a month and contact one of the resource organizations listed at the end of this addendum. Do it with your friends, church members, or school. Be bold: pick up a phone and call them, or email them, or write to them, and then learn from them, and act on what you learn. Or get your hands on one of the books listed at the end of this addendum. Then *read* it.

And please don't forget to enjoy yourself. With one chance at life, we may as well be happy!

Some Basic Principles of Symbiotic Living

We humans need clean air, clean water, fertile land, fresh, nutritious food, practical clothing, resource and energy-efficient shelter, valuable work, caring relationships, spiritual growth, and fun. When we achieve balance, our lives become clearer and less complicated. Practice an exercise used by a Buddhist teacher. Holding up a piece of newsprint, he asks the students to *see* the clouds and forest in the paper, and move their minds into the process of *becoming* the paper: Where did you come from? How many rainstorms did you endure in your lifetime? When we start to think in this manner, we begin to understand our place here on Earth.

Practice the Four Rs — reduce, reuse, recycle, and refuse:

REDUCE — In an ecological household, reducing consumption, conserving water, reducing energy use, and reducing waste is the standard, not the exception. Although American consumption has risen 45% in the past two decades, our quality of life (as measured by the Index of Social Health) has declined by 51%. We have more stuff, but less satisfaction.

Buy in bulk or concentrated form in family-sized containers. Avoid single-use disposable products. Use fewer products. Examine your true needs. Rent or share certain items that you only need to use occasionally (garden tools, sewing machine). Before buying, ask yourself: do I really need this product? Is it safe to use? Is it practical, durable, well-made, of good quality, with a timeless design? Is the product made from renewable or recycled materials taken in a sustainable manner? Is there any information about the manufacturing process? How will I eventually dispose of the product, and what environmental impact will that have? What kind of package does it have? Is it excessive? How far has the product been shipped? Is there another brand that is more environmentally friendly? If there is, buy that one.

REUSE — For every pound of garbage we throw away, we generate twenty-five pounds of waste. Many resources are required to produce a product; its manufacture produces additional waste. Increasing the lifetime of a product is far more effective than recycling, because it doesn't require the product's refabrication. Doubling the lifetime of any product will halve the energy consumption, the waste and pollution, and the ultimate depletion of all the materials used to make it.

RECYCLE — If we would recycle or reuse all of our paper and paperboard (40%), metals (9%), plastic (8%) and glass (7%), we would reduce our garbage by 64%. If we reclaimed our wood (4%), rubber (3%) and textiles (2%), we would be down to only 27% of our current garbage. By composting yard debris (18%) and food scraps (7%), we're left with only sending about 2% solid waste to a landfill. The products that are most recyclable are aluminum, steel, cloth, glass, motor oil, and paper. Plastic, despite its promotion by the plastics industry as being recyclable, is not easily or readily recycled. Plastics that *are* recycled are processed under conditions that endanger workers and the surrounding environment.

REFUSE — Don't buy it at all.

SOME THINGS TO THINK ABOUT

SUSTAINABLE AND SOCIALLY RESPONSIBLE BUSINESSES — Corporations, as defined, are only responsible to their shareholders. In legal terms, they must act primarily in the stockholders' economic interests. This serves to reinforce the idea that they exist purely for profit, at the expense of society and our environment. The alternative to large publicly or privately-held corporations are family-owned businesses and workers' cooperatives. By frequenting locally-owned businesses, money is kept circulating within your community. Small local businesses and worker cooperatives can help build local, sustainable economies and can be easily monitored, held accountable, and truly be "socially responsible."

BUYING GREEN — A popular misconception is that buying green means fewer greenbacks in your pocketbook. Yet, a 1991 study showed that a family who "went green" spent about $155 more per year on environmental products. The few extra dollars spent translates into savings in energy, disposal costs, and pollution cleanup costs. A common product like toilet paper appears to be fairly benign. However, standard toilet paper is made from virgin paper bleached with chlorine to make it look whiter. It is also often dyed with harsh petrochemical dyes. Using virgin paper means using more trees. Chlorine bleaching, and then dyeing, pumps a variety of cancer-causing byproducts into our air and water. Environmentally friendly toilet paper is made with recycled paper, often post-consumer, without chlorine or dyes.

FOOD — Eating reestablishes our connection to people, to land, water, and soil, to the future, and to other species. Our present system of agriculture is among the most unsustainable aspects of our society. Massive inputs of energy are required for food production and transport, nutrients are often not returned to the soil, farming often requires irrigation, and soils are contaminated with pesticides. Increased attention to personal health, as well as the environmental and social impacts of food production and processing are important considerations when eating "green." *Organically grown* means the food has been grown, packaged, stored, and transported without the use of synthetic fertilizers, insecticides, herbicides, fungicides, fumigants, preservatives, hormones, coloring or wax. Certified organically grown products mean that the farm has been inspected and tested by an independent, third-party agency.

Many people are adopting a more healthful lifestyle, which includes adopting a diet low in fat and rich in vegetables and fruit. But despite the nutritional value, most of the produce bought at your local supermarket has tremendous environmental and health implications. It is estimated that over 1.5 billion pounds of pesticides are sprayed on our food crops each year. The EPA has declared pesticide pollution one of our country's worst environmental and health problems.

Besides the higher nutritional content and the fact that you are not exposing yourself or your family to harmful chemicals, by buying organic you are contributing toward the transition to sustainable food production, conserving energy (especially if you're buying locally-grown organic goods), and helping to minimize the dependence on petrochemical based fertilizers and pesticides. More than 200 million tons of pesticides containing more than 100 active ingredients are used annually on food croplands in California alone. Although the EPA regulates pesticides and herbicides, many pesticides were granted tolerances before safety tests were required. Of the 600 principal ingredients in pesticides, only about 120 have been tested by the EPA for their acute and chronic health effects. Pesticides carried by the wind and groundwater become widely dispersed, impacting many other ecosystems.

GROW YOUR OWN — Gardening is one of the best things you can do for the environment, if it's done in concert with nature. Because of the intensive effort that can be concentrated in a small area, the home gardener is by far the most efficient and productive of all food producers. In fact, all the fruits and vegetables for a family can be grown in one-sixth to one-half of an acre. If all US lawns, golf courses, and cemeteries were converted to gardens, they could supply 203 million people with food. Currently, lawns alone consume more fertilizer, more human input, more fossil fuels and more machinery than farming.

COMMUNITY GARDENS — For city dwellers, community gardens are another option for farm-fresh food. It's been estimated that having market gardens located throughout suburbs and cities could cut the dollar cost of food by 70%. Shanghai, which has a population of 11 million, produces 100% of its fresh vegetables. Contrast this to Massachusetts, which imports 85% of its food, a tenth of it from 3000 miles away. Where could these gardens grow? On all derelict and unused land in cities, and on the flat rooftops.

BIOREGIONALISM & SMALL FARMS — Bioregionalism is usually defined by a watershed area, by plant and animal species ranges, and by human cultures, not by arbitrary political boundaries or borders. Acquaint yourself with your bioregion by examining how past peoples used the land. Food that is imported from outside the bioregion comes with many hidden costs. Despite dwindling supplies of US fossil fuels, four calories of fuel are used to produce one calorie of food that is then transported an average of 1300 miles. Small, local organic farms can produce five times as much per unit of energy than conventional farms. Because local produce is also fresher, it is also more nutritious.

COMMUNITY SUPPORTED AGRICULTURE — Local farmers' markets are usually a good example of bioregionalism, if indeed, the farmers are truly local. Community Supported Agriculture (CSA) is a major breakthrough in bioregionalism. In this revolutionary model of agriculture, farmers and consumers join to provide security for the farmer. In return, the farmer supplies his customers with wholesome, local food. By paying a predetermined price for weekly supplies of vegetable produce, fruit, eggs, meat, milk, and/or fiber products (whatever the farmer can produce that is of interest to the shareholders), customers help support the farm's viability. Today, there are about 500 CSAs in the United States.

FOREST GARDENS — Forest gardens are immensely productive and offer many benefits. These systems incorporate an upper story of trees for timber, fruits, and nuts, a middle story of bushes producing fruits and spices, and an understory of maize, beans, and root crops. A community that relies on forest gardens as opposed to tillage systems uses far less energy, reduces soil erosion significantly, and supports more stable and diverse ecosystems.

PERMACULTURE — Permaculture is a design system for creating sustainable human environments. The word itself refers to systems of permanent agriculture and to permanent cultures. Permaculture works with plants, animals, buildings, and infrastructures such as water, energy, and communications, and is concerned with the relationships we create between these elements.

MILK AND EGGS — Buy milk in waxed cardboard boxes, unless your area recycles HDPE plastic. Steer clear from milk and cheeses containing BGH (bovine growth hormone). It can cause cows to develop udder infections, which are then treated with antibiotics, leading to increased levels of antibiotic residue in the dairy products we consume. Buy organic milks and cheeses, or choose a milk alternative: organic soy, almond, and rice milks. Avoid products packaged in aseptic containers made of paperboard, polyethylene plastic, and aluminum foil, as they aren't recyclable. Consider powdered products packaged in recyclable cardboard containers. Purchase eggs in cardboard containers, not foam. Buy organic eggs.

WATER — Bottled water causes extensive energy use and pollution in transport and packaging. Have your tap water tested. If it's substandard, invest in a countertop water filter or use a home delivery service that will bring refillable containers to your home and carry away the empties on a regular schedule.

MEAT — Today in America, there are 7.5 million vegetarians. If you do eat meat, consider reducing your intake. If Americans reduced their red meat intake by only 10 percent, the savings of grains and soybeans could feed all the people who starve to death in the world.

Each year, the US imports over 120 million pounds of beef from Central American countries. Two-thirds of these countries' forests have been cleared to raise cattle. The typical four-ounce hamburger represents about 55 square feet of tropical forest, which could have contained any of 20 different tree species, thousands of insect species, and a section of the feeding zone of dozens of rare birds, reptiles, and mammals. Buy your meat locally from an organic grower.

CONDIMENTS — Examine the packaging. Traditional glass jars and bottles are easy to recycle and less polluting to manufacture. If you must rely on plastic squeezable bottles, don't throw them away. Buy the biggest glass container possible and refill your plastic squeezable.

PRODUCTS TO AVOID — Here's a simple rule of thumb: if there are numbers in the ingredients, don't buy it. Most artificial additives are made from derivatives of crude oil. Some artificial additives to avoid are: artificial colors (also listed as FD&C colors) these are made from coal tar; artificial flavors — also made from coal tar; BHA and BHT — made from coal tar; EDTA — made from minerals, irritating to the skin, can cause allergic reactions and kidney damage; MSG (monosodium glutamate) — derived from glutamic acid, on the FDA list of additives that need further study for mutagenic and reproductive effects; artificial sweeteners (saccharin, aspartame — a.k.a. NutraSweet or Equal); Nitrates and Nitrites — made from mineral salts, can form carcinogenic nitrosamines when combined with amines in food, added to most processed meats and some cheeses; Sulfites — can cause severe allergic reactions, found in many processed foods and in commercially produced wine. Also avoid irradiated foods. Foods that are irradiated are stamped with a "radura" symbol, a benign-looking flower in a circle. Don't be fooled. Certified organic foods are never irradiated.

STORING FOOD — Glass is best; save and reuse jars from food purchases and refill. Plastic bags should be rinsed and reused. A plastic sandwich bag can be used dozens of times.

TRASH BAGS — The increasing volume of trash entering landfills each year produces a massive pollution problem. Although many companies claim that their trash bags "biodegrade," the plastic actually only disintegrates into pieces too small to be seen by the naked eye. The plastic remains in its same chemical composition because living things lack the enzymes necessary to break down these products. The manufacturing of plastics constitutes a major environmental threat, releasing toxic chemicals into the air, which generates acid rain, which then pollutes our water supply. Instead of plastic bags, reuse your paper bags from the grocery store to collect garbage in. Consider not lin-ing your garbage cans. If you've already separated out your food and yard scraps for composting, recycled your plastics, aluminum, and glass, you really should have nothing in your trash to cause odors, anyway. As a last resort, if you must use plastic, buy recycled plastic trash bags. They aren't as energy-intensive to manufacture and don't use as much petroleum.

COMPOSTING — One of the most unsustainable aspects of our society is the almost complete failure to recycle organic materials. The growing of annual crops removes millions of tons of nutrients from the soil each year and trans-ports these nutrients to cities, where they are used and then discarded into landfills or down drains. It would be more appropriate to call this type of agri-culture "soil mining." Our survival depends upon the fertility of our soils. One way to accomplish this is to reclaim and recycle organic nutrients through composting. Compost is the result of degradation of organic materials by micro- (bacteria and fungi) and macro-organisms (earthworms and insects). Besides enriching soil with valuable nutrients, compost helps hold water and warm the soil, degrades toxic chemicals, destroys pathogens, restores the land, and saves money. It also keeps yard debris and food scraps out of landfills, where buried, they would not degrade for many decades. In fact, if everyone in America composted, 15 to 20% of our landfill space would be saved annually.

WOOD PRODUCTS — The term "sustainably harvested" can be applied to any renewable resource, but it usually refers to forest products. In the United States, over 17 billion cubic feet of timber are harvested annually. Of this, 63% goes toward producing paper and pulp; the rest is used for lumber.

Although only about 5% of our primary forests remain, the US is still considered to be "rich" in forest resources. Worldwide, each year, over 35 mil-lion acres of tropical forest (an area the size of Florida) are permanently destroyed. Over half of the Earth's species inhabit these forests, which only comprise 6% of its surface. Over 25% of these forests are destroyed by com-mercial logging operations. Thousands of acres are also cleared for cattle ranching. The destruction of our tropical rainforests are increasing global warming, obliterating thousands of species, and decimating many indigenous cultures.

Although wood is a renewable resource, it is only sustainable if it is managed to ensure that no more trees are cut than the forest can regenerate. Most wood sold in lumberyards is harvested by the clearcut-replant method whereby a large section of forest is cut and then replanted with same-age, same species trees. Clearcutting destroys the protective layer of forest floor vegetation, causes erosion, a loss of soil fertility, a severe decline in biodiversi-ty, and also is a source of pollution, as herbicides are often applied around the replanted trees to discourage competition from other species. Sustainable forestry, in contrast, involves a forest of mixed species and ages, selective cut-ting, sustainable yields, soil conservation, ecosystem preservation, and appro-priate technology.

Consider using reclaimed wood, such as lumber from salvaged buildings. If virgin timber is needed, look to local sawmills. Inquire about their forest management practices. If you don't live in a forested area and need to import wood, consider choosing wood that has been certified from an independent agency as sustainably harvested.

PAPER PRODUCTS — Every day in the US, we use 187,000 tons of paper, or 3,179,000 trees, annually clearcutting an area equivalent to the size of Rhode Island. Each year, the paper industry in America releases tons of toxins into our air and water. Paper also generates more solid waste than any other material in America. Buying recycled paper (with as much post-consumer content in it as possible) is vitally important in protecting our remaining forests. Buy unbleached or chlorine-free products. The most sustainable recycled paper is unbleached, non-deinked, 100% recycled paper with a high percentage of post-consumer material. Tree-free papers are also available. In one year, an acre of kenaf produces seven to eleven tons of usable fiber. In contrast, an acre of forest produces only four to five tons of usable fiber and requires 20 to 30 years to produce it. Bring your own bag when you shop. For every 700 grocery bags not used, one 15 to 20 year-old tree will be left standing. Minimize the use of disposable paper products like paper towels and paper cups.

SHELTER — Over 30% of total US energy usage, 60% of the country's electricity, 60% of its financial resources, and 26% of the contents of its landfills are linked to buildings. Environmentally sensitive design can significantly improve the comfort, aesthetics, and value of properties while mitigating pollution and saving money. The most appropriate materials for building are local materials requiring minimal processing. The most appropriate building style and size should be dictated not by fads, trends, or egos, but by natural factors such as climate and locale. In the 1940s, the average size of a house was about 1100 square feet. In the 1990s, although the median family size had decreased, the average home size had ballooned to over 2000 square feet. Downsizing a house translates into reduced heating and cooling expenses and, of course, less cleaning and work!

ENERGY EFFICIENCY — In our homes, most energy use is devoted to space heating and cooling, water heating, and refrigeration. These tasks account for about 81% of energy use. Lighting, cooking, clothes drying, and other appliances comprise the remaining 19% of home energy consumption.
Conservation is the first step in energy efficiency. Turn off your lights. Turn up your thermostat in the summertime (or turn your cooling system off) and lower it in the wintertime. Insulation is the most important product you can buy to reduce home energy use. It can save you up to 40% of your total energy use and usually has a very short-term payback (within one to two years). About one-third of a home's heat loss occurs through windows and doors. Windows can be sealed with weather-stripping, and, during the winter, covered with insulated drapes. Otherwise, consider replacing your windows with energy-efficient ones. Weatherize your home, use energy-efficient appliances and lights, and shade windows with vegetation or awnings or arbors. Insulate your water heater with a prefabricated blanket. Lower the thermostat on your heater to 120 degrees Fahrenheit. If every household in America lowered their regular temperature by four degrees, 380,000 barrels of oil would be saved each day.

LIGHTING — Use more compact fluorescent bulbs instead of incandescent. And don't let the price tag scare you — they should last about ten times longer than incandescents and use about one-quarter of the energy. Or use halogen bulbs, which last almost three times longer than incandescents. Use natural lighting whenever possible. A three by five-foot window lets in more light than 100 standard 60-watt bulbs. When you leave a room, flip the switch off.

RENEWABLE ENERGY — Renewable energy sources include solar power (photovoltaic cells and passive solar design), biomass (crop residues and animal manures used to make fuel), hydroelectric power, and wind. Studies by the US Department of Energy have shown that we could fulfill almost three-quarters of our energy needs from the sun, wind, water, geothermal, and biomass.

WATER — Although most of our planet is water, the amount of potable (drinkable) water on Earth is in short supply. It is estimated that we will exceed our drinking water capacity within one or two decades. Not only is the *quantity* of available drinking water a serious issue, but so is the *quality* of water. Our waterways receive chemical contamination from industry, and fecal contamination from livestock, and septic and wastewater treatment facilities. Protection and conservation of our water systems is critical to our survival.

Agriculture uses more water than households do: 75% is used for agriculture (25% for produce and 50% for livestock). It takes about three gallons of water to produce one serving of tomatoes, 22 gallons for one serving of oranges, 136 gallons for two eggs, 408 gallons for one serving of chicken, and a whopping 2607 gallons of water to produce one serving of steak.

In the home, the average American uses between 58 and 90 gallons of water per day. The toilet is the largest water user in the household, accounting for anywhere between 25 to 35% of all household water use. The best water saving toilet, of course, is a composting toilet. The low-flush toilet (1.6 gallons/flush) is another option for those who can't make the transition to a waterless toilet. Installing faucet aerators and low-flow showerheads also saves water (and water bills). A low-flow showerhead (2.5 gallons per minute) will save about 30 gallons of water during an average ten-minute shower. Outside the home, if you need to water your garden, do so early or late in the day to avoid excessive evaporation. Apply water slowly to prevent runoff. Water deeply but thoroughly to help your plants develop a deep root system for dry summer months, and use mulch. Mulch protects the soil from erosion, inhibits weeds, and retains moisture.

In many parts of the world, especially in arid areas, water collection is a necessity. Households may collect rainwater in underground or aboveground cisterns, barrels, or tanks. Water recycling is yet another water conservation tool. Rich in nutrients, graywater (water generated from sinks, showers, and tubs and laundry) can be used to water landscapes and even gardens if used properly. A drain is not a waste disposal site. Everything that we pour down our drains goes directly into the environment. Give careful consideration to what you put down your drains. "Living machines" incorporate communities of organisms to purify sewerage.

REDUCING TOXIC WASTE IN THE HOME — Many of us sleep on permanent-press cotton sheets which have been saturated with formaldehyde, on mattresses fabricated from synthetic petrochemicals and treated with polyurethane-based flame retardants, and in rooms where the walls are coated with paints, and the floors are covered with plastic-based carpets. Indoor pollution is one of the most common problems in industrialized nations. We are more likely to breathe in a stew of chemicals from pesticides, aerosol sprays, paints, and cleaners in our own homes than in the air outside. Our first step, of course, is to reduce our exposure to these chemicals by eliminating their use in our homes.

"PEST" CONTROL — Americans douse their homes with over 300 million pounds of carcinogenic insecticides a year. Simple alternatives do exist. First of all, eliminate the source of the problem. Store food in glass jars with tight lids instead of in plastic bags. Most insects are really not harmful, but can be annoying. Fleas can be controlled by pyrethrum powders or soaps or with dips and sprays derived from d-limonine (a citrus extract). Cockroaches can be deterred by scattering bay leaves in their habitat. Garlic mixed with soapy water in a blender can be sprayed in infested areas. Cedar shavings work well to thwart moths.

CLEANING PRODUCTS FOR THE HOME — Over 1000 synthetic chemicals are introduced into our environment each year. Already, about 70,000 human-made chemicals are in use. Many of these chemicals go into everyday products we see on the shelves in our stores. The assumption that because they're on the shelves, they're safe, is a mistake many people make. In fact, almost every product on the market might have some component that could be harmful to one's health or to the environment, and many products utilize toxic substances in their manufacture or packaging. Using simple ingredients to clean your home or for personal care is not only wise from a health and ecological standpoint, but also far less expensive than buying commercial cleaners.

Acute toxicity refers to poisoning as the result of a one-time exposure to a relatively large amount of a chemical. Every year, 5 to 10 million household poisonings occur as a result of accidental exposure to toxic products in the home. Chronic toxicity refers to illness that results after repeated exposures to chemicals over a long period of time. Toxic chemicals are found in nature (deadly nightshade, for instance) and synthesized in laboratories (benzene). The difference is that we don't normally encounter natural toxins in our everyday environment. Yet, we expose ourselves to hundreds of human-made toxins every day. Most commercial products today are made from petrochemical derivatives. Synthetics don't break down in the environment readily or at all, and tend to accumulate up the food chain. At our position at the top of the food chain, we are one of the most bioaccumulative organisms, storing higher levels of chemicals in our fat than that are actually in the environment.

"Signal words," related to a product's potential acute (but not chronic) toxicity, can be found on any product's label. Assume that products marked DANGER/POISON are highly toxic; WARNING, moderately toxic; and CAUTION, slightly toxic.

"FRESHENERS" — Room "fresheners" don't really make a room smell better. In fact, they work by coating your nasal passages and deadening the nerves to diminish your sense of smell. Houseplants act as natural air filters. If you like to scent your home, use essential oils: pure plant oils that can be heated in a candle burner. Candles are wonderful, but be aware that most candles are manufactured with artificial, toxic fragrances and petrochemical waxes. Instead, burn beeswax candles scented with essential oils or herbs.

ANTIPERSPIRANTS AND DEODORANTS — Antiperspirants work by causing the skin to swell and closing off the sweat pores. Although *deodorants* don't inhibit the body's releasing of wastes, they are also made from petrochemicals that are nonrenewable and potentially cancer-causing. It is advisable to shun antiperspirants. If you must buy deodorants, shop for products containing natural ingredients (in packaging that can be recycled or refilled).

SHAMPOOS AND CONDITIONERS — Shampoos and conditioners often come in nonrecyclable containers and contain ingredients that pollute our water supplies. Common shampoos and conditioners can contain petrochemicals, formaldehyde derivatives (like quaternium-15), artificial colors (derived from coal tar), and petrochemically-derived fragrances. Hair colorants and dyes are also a product of the petrochemical industry. Like most commercial brands of shampoos and conditioners, hair dyes are often inhumanely tested on animals. Natural dyes, such as henna (a plant product) are available for darkening hair. For blondes, chamomile tea and lemon juice can lighten hair.

Similarly, most hair sprays, gels, and mousses have a harsh effect on the environment and on your health. Their containers are energy-intensive to manufacture and often are not recyclable. Most rely on synthetic chemicals and resins to hold your hair in a certain position, and their manufacture depletes our supply of nonrenewable fossil fuels and contributes to air, soil, and water pollution. Most people don't realize that hair sprays and gels are mostly plastics (resins) that are micronized. Whenever you spray, you are actually inhaling small plastic particulates.

TOOTHPASTES — As with most commercial personal products, many toothpastes are also derived from petrochemicals and are packaged in nonrecyclable containers made of plastic. They usually contain artificial colors and flavors. Tom's of Maine, for example, is a company that produces toothpastes without artificial flavors or colors, and in tubes made with recycled content.

LOTIONS AND CREAMS — Most commercial brand lotions come from products derived from petroleum (the ingredients may read "petrolatum" or "mineral oil"). They are also packed with harmful chemicals, artificial colors, and artificial fragrances. Avoid companies that don't disclose their animal testing procedures.

PERFUMES AND FRAGRANCES — Major brand perfumes and fragrances are often derived from petroleum-based products and coal-tar derivatives. Animals are often trapped and killed for certain parts of their bodies to enhance the scent of these products (musk, for instance, is taken from a musk deer's naval; civet is taken from the anal glands of a civet cat).

Essential oils, on the other hand, are natural oils expressed from plant parts, such as the flowers, roots, or bark. They are not the same as "fragrance oils," which are synthesized in a laboratory. To produce one pound of essential rose oil, 5000 pounds of fresh petals are needed. Therefore, essential oils always vary in their price: rose oil and jasmine, which require large amounts of materials to produce a small amount of oil, are normally quite expensive, while lemon and orange oils are relatively inexpensive. The best oils are, of course, organically grown, and cold-pressed or expeller-pressed. Avoid oils that are extracted with solvents, because the solvent may be highly toxic and may remain as a residue in the oil.

RAZORS — Americans throw away two billion disposable razors and blades each year. The plastic is not biodegradable and their manufacture consumes high quantities of energy and requires the use of toxic chemicals. Instead of shaving with disposable equipment, use long-lasting metal razors and blades or buy an electric razor. Or don't shave at all.

HARD AS NAILS — Nail polishes and hardeners depend on harsh chemicals to work. They are dangerous to inhale and contain carcinogenic substances, such as xylene and toluene. The bottles are not recyclable, and, once crushed in a landfill, seep toxins into the ground. Red henna is one of the only natural alternatives to nail polish.

CLOTHING — Buy secondhand clothes. Nearly every community has a thrift shop or clothing consignment shop. Donate clothes to your local thrift shop — keep them out of the landfills, where they certainly don't belong. If you must buy new, look for clothing made from natural materials that were grown organically: cotton, linens, hemp, wool, or silks, and which are unbleached or dyed with low-impact dyes.

Although cotton is a natural fiber material derived from plants, it is one of the most chemically intensive crops grown throughout the world. In America, over half of all pesticides produced are applied to cotton alone. Currently, there are some farms cultivating organic cotton, and a few farms experimenting with naturally-colored cottons. Although not organic, "green" cotton is cotton that is minimally processed; it contains no dyes, bleaches, or formaldehyde finishes. Clothing made from synthetic materials are derived from fossil fuels, and are nonrecyclable and nonbiodegradable. Their manufacture is energy intensive and polluting.

CLEANING CLOTHES — Most commercial laundry detergents contain a bevy of synthetic, harsh chemicals, such as brighteners, artificial colors, and artificial fragrances. Until the late 1980s, most detergents also contained phosphates, which contributed to the pollution of many water systems. Many manufacturers still test their products on animals.

Washing soda, an alternative to detergents, is usually available at most grocery and department stores. Add one-third cup washing soda to water before adding clothes to the washer and add pure soap flakes or powder instead of commercial detergents. When switching from a detergent to a soap, wash items once with washing soda only, as the detergent may react with the soap and cause the fabric to yellow. If soap flakes aren't available in your area, look for detergents on the market that contain no phosphates, no artificial colors or fragrances, and which are biodegradable. Read the labels.

Chlorine is one of the most polluting and toxic chemicals in our environment and still commonly used in American households. Instead of using chlorine bleach, add one-half cup of Borax to whiten whites and brighten colors. Non-chlorine bleaches, made with hydrogen peroxide, are now available in most areas, and are far less polluting and hazardous than chlorine.

Fabric softeners are full of petrochemicals, artificial colors, and fragrances. They are also expensive, when much cheaper and safer alternatives exist. Adding one cup of vinegar or one-fourth cup of baking soda during the final rinse serves the same purpose.

BATTERIES — Use rechargeable batteries instead of alkaline ones. Although initially more expensive than alkaline batteries, they pay for themselves quickly. Although rechargeable batteries still contain mercury and cadmium, they last far longer. At the end of a battery's life, seek out a center that recycles them. In a landfill, the toxic metals contaminate the soil and pollute ground water. If incinerated, they release toxins into the air.

PAINT — Each year, Americans buy more than a half-billion gallons of paint. Most of this paint is petroleum-based and contains volatile organic compounds (VOCs) which mix with nitrous oxides (a pollutant from car exhaust, power plants, and refineries) to form ground level ozone, or smog.

Natural paints, which are usually vegetable-based and contain mineral pigments, are available, although they are considerably more expensive.

If you have to use paint, do not pour the leftover paint or rinse out pans and brushes in your sink. Recycle it, or combine it with other leftovers to make a gray or beige primer paint. Donate extra cans to a community organization. Take it to a hazardous waste collection site. Check with your local recycling center or refuse collector to see if such programs are available.

TRANSPORTATION — Automobiles are one of the major polluters in the world today. When purchasing a used or new car, buy a fuel-efficient model. A car driven an average of 20,000 miles a year that gets 40 miles per gallon compared to one that gets 25 miles per gallon will cut your annual CO2 emissions by 6,600 pounds a year, and will significantly reduce your fuel costs.

Go electric — or gas-hybrid. Electric and hybrid cars emit fewer pollutants than standard gasoline powered cars.

Carpool. According to the Union of Concerned Scientists, over 80% of commuter trips in the US have only one person in the car. The best way to cut down the over 200 million gallons of gasoline Americans consume every day is to carpool. Use public transportation. For every 1000 people riding to work by bus or rail, 5 tons of hydrocarbons, 31 tons of carbon monoxide, and 2.5 tons of nitrogen oxide are saved. Bicycling is environmentally friendly and wonderful exercise. Encourage your community to become more bike friendly, to include bike lanes and keep the roadsides clear of obstacles. Walk more.

HEALTH — "Personal" health is a misnomer as there are really no true physical boundaries between ourselves and our environment. Consider that each year 98% of the atoms in your body is replaced by other atoms in the environment. At the end of five years, every single atom has been replaced. The body you now have did not exist five years ago. Likewise, the process of human consciousness is unbounded and not restricted to our idea of self or Ego, but inextricably linked to the Eco, a unified whole. In caring for ourselves, we must accept that the Earth is inseparable from our Selves.

Unlike conventional medicine, natural healing employees naturally-occurring defenses. Health, environmental conservation, and spirituality cannot be separated from each other. The healing of our world, and of ourselves, cannot be accomplished through ever finer analysis, scientific rigor, and technological interventions — although proper scientific work and technology are indispensable to the process — but through the integration of our selves with the World. Natural health care involves educating and empowering ourselves, and being conscious and knowledgeable about how our bodies function. Numerous resources, including books, magazines, and websites are available to help us achieve our independence from the multi-billion dollar health and pharmaceuticals industry.

PLANTS AS MEDICINE — Herbs are the oldest form of medicine as well as the basis for modern pharmacology. Herbs and medicinal plants can be taken in many forms: tinctures (in an alcohol base), teas, capsules, and ointments. Eating fresh, organically grown food, grown in fertile soil, provides the best nutrition for our bodies.

CHILDBIRTH — Although childbirth is a natural process, conventional medicine tends to view birth as a medical emergency. Midwifery acts to support the natural birth process and to address any problems with the least possible amount of interference. Midwives understand the need for women to feel physically and emotionally secure and empowered. Breastfeed your baby.

EDUCATION — Many education systems promote hierarchy, obedience, conformity, competition, and regimentation. The need for educational reform is obvious in our society today — violence in the classroom, boredom among students, vandalism, staff unrest. Problems in schooling are a reflection of societal problems: inadequate parenting, devalued family life, social inequality. Technological developments such as the TV undermine the ability of children to learn to concentrate, or to think for themselves. Technology, as used in the school system, does not teach children how to socialize, cooperate, listen, be creative, or be assertive. Intuition, sensitivity, creativity, and a capacity to understand things holistically are often not fostered in a technologically-based, industrial educational system.

Empowering individuals with creative and practical skills and independent minds is critical to establishing self-sufficient, sustainable communities. Fundamentals and life skills should be integrated to reinforce a holistic way of thinking and to encourage our understanding of our ecological role on Earth.

COMMUNITY — In most industrial societies, the majority of it citizens dedicate their best hours and best years to making an income to exchange for material goods. In the meantime, many of us have lost sight of the fact that our life is more than our work, and our work is more than our job. The commute to and from work and school has undermined community cohesiveness. Today, Traditional Neighborhood Developments (TNDs) are cropping up, especially in large cities. These developments cluster small businesses, private homes, and green spaces harmoniously, and encourage a pedestrian society, which fosters interaction and community.

Living in groups is also a viable solution to problems such as the affordable housing shortage, the dispersal of kin-groups, the disintegration of nuclear families, and the harsh reality of trying to be financially independent. Cohousing is a system of housing similar to the TND, whereby housing is clustered and green space is preserved. In contrast to TNDs, cohousing endeavors are focused on creating "intentional" communities. Groups usually work together to plan, finance, and build the type of cluster they want, although each unit in the cluster may be privately owned. Normally, a common house is also included in the development. This form of housing drastically reduces duplication of resources — commonly used items are shared by community members.

EcoVillages, an expansion of the cohousing philosophy, commit themselves not only to developing a strong, cohesive community, but ascribe to an environmental ethic as well. In many ecovillage communities, housing is confined to 8 to 15% of the total land area, leaving most of the land free for small-scale food production and for the preservation of habitat and biotic diversity. Built structures within ecovillages are designed with resource and energy efficiency at the forefront. Many ecovillages provide their energy locally with the use of renewable energy sources.

ECONOMICS — Our present economic system operates on the premise that growth is infinitely possible. However, on a finite planet, we know this is not feasible. Consider the following : over a 30-year period (1940 through 1970), while the US Gross National Product per person doubled, no increase in the frequency with which people responded positively to quality of life questions was reported. In fact, Americans reported feeling "significantly less well-off." The range of serious social problems over the last few decades has also broadened — homelessness, poverty, unemployment, mental and social breakdown, suicide, vandalism, and crime all have escalated.

BEYOND BARTERING: KEEPING CASH IN COMMUNITY — The key to environmentally-compatible economics is the development of many small-scale local and regional economies that are largely self-sufficient. Communities can create money substitutes for themselves. In a local exchange trading system (LETS), members agree to trade goods and services among themselves. Instead of paying cash, they keep a record of accounts, which enables them to trade, produce, work and receive goods without money. This method of exchange keeps currency within the community and supports community members and local businesses. Establishment of cottage industries, cohousing communities, local recycling and composting centers, and community supported agriculture are all endeavors that favor sound economic and environmental policy.

Eventually, we must get to the situation where producing and consuming have become trivial elements in our personal and social lives, where only a small amount of time and effort goes into providing ourselves with the things we need, where few have any interest in the Gross National Product, and where we can all get on with far more important things such as science, art, communication with each other and with nature, personal development, and play.

SPEAK OUT — Economic growth at the expense of planetary health is not sustainable; we cannot separate ourselves from nature. But we *can* make informed purchasing and investing choices, and favor products and companies that operate in an environmentally ethical and socially responsible manner. Most importantly, we can wean ourselves from the dependence in believing that we "need" certain convenience products.

Write letters to your local newspaper editor to complain about wasteful business practices in your community, or to applaud symbiotic ones. Write to companies that produce wasteful products, such as over-packaged food items, and tell them why you no longer buy their products. Boycott groups with anti-environmental agendas. Exercise your citizenship. Use the Freedom of Information Act to gain access to important information from the government, and know your statutes and rights.

PLEASE CONTACT THESE PEOPLE:

Agroforestry Research Trust, 46 Hunters Moon, Dartington, Totnes, Devon, TQ9 6JT, U.K. www.agroforestry.co.uk. The Agroforestry Research Trust is a non-profit charity registered in England, which researches temperate agroforestry and all aspects of plant cropping and uses, with a focus on tree, shrub and perennial crops.

Alliance to Save Energy, 1200 18th Street, NW, Suite 900, Washington, DC 20036. 202-857-0666; Fax 202-331-9588; www.ase.org; info@ase.org.

Alternative Education Resource Organization, 417 Roslyn Rd., Roslyn Hts., NY 11577. 800-769-4171; Fax 516-625-3257; www.edrev.org; JerryAERO@aol.com. AERO helps people who want to change education to a more empowering and holistic form. It helps individuals and groups of people who want to start new community schools, public and private, or change existing schools. It also provides information to people interested in homeschooling their children, or finding private or public alternative schools.

Alternative Farming Systems Information Center, NAL, ARS, USDA, 10301 Baltimore Ave., Room 304, Beltsville, MD 20705-2351; 301-504-6559; Fax 301-504-6409; www.nal.usda.gov/afsic/; afsic@nal.usda.gov. Provides a listing of Community Supported Agriculture groups.

American College of Nurse Midwives, 818 Connecticut Ave. NW, Ste. 900, Washington, DC 20006. 888-643-9433; 202-728-9860; www.midwife.org. Free midwife locator service.

American Community Gardening Assn, 100 N. 20th Street, 5th Floor, Philadelphia, PA 19103. 215-988-8785; Fax 215-988-8810; http://communitygarden.org; smccabe@pennhort.org. Community gardening improves the quality of life.

American Council for an Energy-Efficient Economy, 1001 Connecticut Ave NW, Ste 801, Washington, DC 20036. 202-429-8873; http://aceee.org/. Publishes booklets on energy efficient appliances for the home, and on energy efficient construction.

American Council for an Energy-Efficient Economy's Greener Cars, 1001 Connecticut Avenue, NW, Suite 801, Washington, D.C. 20036. Publications: 202-429-0063; www.greenercars.org/indexplus.html. Publishes the Green Book: The Environmental Guide to Cars and Trucks (also online).

American Herbalists Guild, P.O. Box 70, Roosevelt, UT 84066. 435-722-8434; Fax 435-722-8452; ahgoffice@earthlink.net

American Holistic Medical Association, 6728 Old McLain Village Dr., McLain, VA 22101. 703-556-9728; www.holisticmedicine.org. Publishes a referral directory.

American News Service, 289 Fox Farm Rd., Brattleboro, VT 05301. 800.654.NEWS; www.americannews.com; info@americannews.com. Has been exploring and reporting on America's Search for Solutions.

American Solar Energy Society, 2400 Central Avenue, Suite G-1, Boulder, CO 80301. 303-443-3130; Fax 303-443-3212; www.ases.org; ases@ases.org. Dedicated to advancing the use of solar energy.

Association of Labor Assistants and Childbirth Educators (ALACE), POB 382724, Cambridge, MA 02238-2724. 888-222-5223 or 617-441-2500; Fax 617-441-3167; www.alace.org; alacehq@aol.com. Helps women reclaim trust in their ability to give birth.

BioDynamic Farming and Gardening Association, Biodynamic Farming and Gardening, Building 1002B, Thoreau Center, The Presidio, P.O. Box 29135, San Francisco, CA 94129-0135; 888-516-7797; Fax 415-561-7796; www.biodynamics.com; biodynamic@aol.com. Biodynamic method of agriculture.

Bio-Integral Resource Center, PO Box 7414, Berkeley, CA 94707. 510-524-2567; Fax 510-524-1758; www.igc.org/birc/; birc@igc.apc.org. Provides practical information on the least toxic methods for managing pests.

Bountiful Gardens, 18001 Shafer Ranch Road, Willits, CA 95490-9626; 707-459-6410; Fx: 459-1925; www.bountifulgardens.org. Sells untreated, open-pollinated seed.

California Certified Organic Farmers, 1115 Mission St., Santa Cruz, CA 95060. 831-423-2263; 813-423-4528; www.ccof.org. Promotes healthful, ecological, and permanent agriculture. Develops standards and certification programs for organic growers.

Center for a New American Dream, 6930 Carroll Ave., Ste. 900, Takoma Park, MD 20912. 301-891-ENUF (3683); 877-68-DREAM (toll-free); Fax 301-891-3684; www.newdream.org; newdream@newdream.org. The CNAD promotes an environmental ethic and voluntary simplicity.

Center for Resourceful Building Technology, PO Box 100, Missoula, MT 59806. 406-549-7678; Fax 406-549-4100; www.crbt.org; crbt@ncat.org. Publishes the guide to resource-efficient building elements, with an emphasis on products made from recycled materials.

City Farmer, Canada's Office of Urban Agriculture, #801-318 Homer St., Vancouver, B.C. V6B 2V3. 604-685-5832; Fax 604-685-0431; www.cityfarmer.org; cityfarm@interchange.ubc.ca. A wonderful resource on composting and urban agriculture.

Coalition for Environmentally Responsible Economies (CERES), 11 Arlington St., 6th Floor, Boston, MA 02116-3411. 617-247-0700; Fax 617-267-5400; www.ceres.org; muzila@ceres.org. CERES dedicates its economic clout to influence corporate behavior.

Companies can use the CERES principles as guidelines for developing more environmentally responsible business practices.

CoHousing Network, P. O. Box 2584, Berkeley, CA 94702. 510-486-2656; www.cohousing.org/. Promotes and encourages the cohousing concept.

Compost Resource Page, www.oldgrowth.org/compost.

Co-Op America, 1612 K St. NW, Ste. Suite 600, Washington, DC 20006; 800-58-GREEN / 202-872-5307; Fax 202-331-8166; www.coopamerica.org and www.socialinvest.org. Publish the National Green Pages, a guide to environmentally and socially responsible businesses in the United States.

Co-Op America Green Pages online, www.greenpages.org; greenpages@coopamerica.org. A directory listing over 2000 socially and environmentally responsible businesses.

Cornell University Resource Center, Business & Technology Park, Ithaca, NY 14850. 607-255-2090; Fax 607-255-9946; www.cfe.cornell.edu/compost/Composting_homepage.html

Cultural Survival, 215 Prospect St., Cambridge, MA 02139. 617-441-5400; Fax 617-441-5417; www.cs.org. Advocates the rights, voice, and vision of indigenous peoples.

Dr. Duke's Phytochemical and Ethnobotanical Databases, www.ars-grin.gov/duke/. Provides a vast amount of information concerning the chemical constituents of plants, the ethnobotanical uses of those plants, and the biological activity or the chemicals.

EarthSave, 706 Frederick Street, Santa Cruz, CA 95062. 408-423-4069 or 800-362-3648; www.earthsave.org; erthsave@aol.com. Committed to reducing both diet-related disease and diet-related environmental degradation. EarthSave provides educational programs, materials, and support for people wishing to make healthier food choices.

Ecological Transportation: www.knowledgehound.com/topics/ecotrans.htm. Offers a variety of links to sites on Alternative Fuels, Carpooling, and Bicycling.

EcoMall, PO Box 20553, Cherokee Station, New York, NY 10021; 212-535-1876; www.ecomall.com; ecomall@ecomall.com. The oldest, largest online green shopping center.

EcoVillage Network of the Americas Central Office, 64001 County Road DD, Moffat, CO 81143. Tel/Fax 719-256-4221; www.gaia.org; ena@ecovillage.org. Grassroots non-profit organization that links together ecovillages and related projects around the world.

EF Schumacher Society, 140 Jug End Road, Great Barrington, MA 01230. 413-528-1737; www.schumachersociety.org; efssociety@aol.com. The Society initiates practical measures that lead to community revitalization and further the transition toward an economically and ecologically sustainable society.

Electric Vehicle Association of the Americas, 701 Pennsylvania Ave NW, 4th Floor, Washington, DC 20004. 202-508-5995; Fax 202-508-5924; www.evaa.org. EVAA is the industry association working to advance electric vehicles and supporting infrastructure.

Environmental Hazards Management Institute, 10 Newmarket Rd., PO Box 932, Durham NH 03824; 800-558-3464; 603-868-1496; www.ehmi.org; ehmiorg@aol.com. Publishes the "Recycling Wheel," and the "Household Product Management Wheel."

Environmental Research Foundation, PO Box 5036, Annapolis, MD 21403. 888-272-2435 or 410-263-1584; www.rachel.org; erf@rachel.org. Provides technical information on toxic substances.

Fairness and Accuracy in Reporting (FAIR), 130 W. 25th St., Eighth Floor, New York, NY 10011. 212-633-6700; www.fair.org; fair@fair.org. Works to provide accurate, unbiased information to the public. Addresses the pro-government, pro-industry stance of the mass media.

FedCo Seeds, PO Box 520-A, Waterville, ME 04903. www.fedcoseeds.com. One of the few seed companies in the United States organized as a cooperative.

Food & Water, RR1, Box 68D, Walden, Vermont 05873. 802-563-3300, or 800-EAT SAFE. Works to educate the public on irradiated foods and other food and water-related issues.

Greywater: www.greywater.com

Health Resource Newsletter, 933 Faulkner St., Conway, AR 72032. 501-329-5272. 501-329-9489. www.thehealthresource.com. moreinfo@thehealthresource.com. A medical information service with an individualized comprehensive research report on your specific medical problem.

HealthWorld Online: www.healthy.net. A comprehensive site addressing both traditional and conventional medicine.

Institute for Earth Education, Cedar Cove, Greenville, West Virginia 24945. 304-832-6404; Fax 304-832-6077; www.eartheducation.org; iee1@aol.com; Dedicated to developing a serious educational response to the environmental degradation of the Earth.

Institute for Global Communications/PeaceNet: www.igc.org: Helps peace, human rights, and social justice organizations communicate and cooperate more effectively.

Institute for Local Self-Reliance, 2425 18th St. NW, Washington, DC 20009. 202-232-4108; Fax: 202-332-0463; www.ilsr.org. ilsr@igc.apc.org. Supports small-scale economic and environmentally-sound development.

International Centre for Research in Agroforestry, PO Box 30677, Nairobi, Kenya. +254 2 521450 or +1 650 833 6645; Fax: +254 2 521001 or +1650 833 6646; www.cgiar.org/icraf/about/about.htm; ICRAF@cgiar.org. ICRAF conducts strategic and applied research in partnership with national agricultural research systems, for more sustainable and productive land use.

International Childbirth Education Association, PO Box 20048, Minneapolis, MN 55420. 612-854-8660; www.icea.org; info@icea.org. Information and referral center for birth information of all kinds.

LaLeche League International, 1400 N. Meachem Rd., Shaumburg, IL 60174. 847-519-0035; Fax 847-519-7730; www.lalecheleague.org. Free referrals to local LaLeche leaders. Call 1-800-LaLeche to connect directly to a breastfeeding counselor.

League of Conservation Voters, 1920 L St NW, Washington DC 20036. 202-785-

8683; Fax: 202-835-0491; www.lcv.org; lcv@lcv.org. A national, nonpartisan arm of the environmental movement. Puts together the Environmental Scorecard, an annual rating of members of Congress on environmental issues.

Local Exchange Trading System, Landsman Community Services, Ltd, 1660 Embleton Crescent, Courtenay, BC V9N 6N8. 604-338-0213; Fax 604-338-7242.

National Association of Housing Co-ops, 1401 New York Ave NW, Ste. 1100, Washington, DC 20005. 202-737-0797; Fax 202-787-7869; www.coophousing.org; coop-housing@usa.net. Promote the interests of cooperative housing communities.

National Center for Appropriate Technology (NCAT), 3040 Continental Drive Butte, Montana 59702. 406- 494-4572 or 800-275-6228 (ASK-NCAT); Fax 406-494-2905; www.ncat.org; info@ncat.org. NCAT's mission is to promote sustainable technologies and community based approaches that protect natural resources and assist people.

National Center for Food and Agricultural Policy, 1616 P St. NW, First Floor, Washington, DC 20036. 202-328-5048; www.ncfap.org. National pesticide database providing estimates on the number of acres treated in each state and the total pounds of active ingredient used by each state and each crop.

National Center for Homeopathy, 801 N. Fairfax St., Ste. 306, Alexandria, VA 22314. 877-624-0613; Fax 703-548-7792; www.homeopathic.org; info@homeopathic.org

National Coalition Against the Misuse of Pesticides, 701 E St SE, Ste 200, Washington DC 20003. 202-543-5450; www.beyondpesticides.org; info@beyondpesticides.org. Information on pesticides, least toxic pest control, database of directories.

National Coalition Building Institute, 1120 Connecticut Ave. NW, Ste. 450, Washington, DC 20036. 202-785-9400; Fax 202-785-3385; www.ncbi.org; ncbiinc@aol.com. Trains individuals to become leaders in building alliances among people of different races, sexes, classes, ages and religions.

National Pesticides Communication Network, OSU, 333 Weniger, Corvallis, OR 97331. 800-858-7378; www.nptn.orst.edu; nptn@ace.orst.edu. Provides an unbiased, scientific information hotline to field questions on the ecological and health effects of pesticides.

National Recycling Coalition, 1727 King Street, Suite 105, Alexandria, Virginia 22314-2720. 703-683-9025; Fax: 703-683-9026; www.nrc-recycle.org. Fact sheets, reports, and directories related to recycling.

New Road Map Foundation, PO Box 15981, Seattle, WA 98115. www.newroadmap.org. Dedicated to lowering consumption in North America. Publishes "How Earth-Friendly Are You? A Lifestyle Self-Assessment Questionnaire" which may be reproduced free of charge and distributed.

Northeast Organic Farmers Association, c/o Hawson Kittredge, NOFA/Mass, 411 Sheldon Rd., Barre, MA 01106. 978-355-2853. Promotes organic agriculture. Provides a map of organic growers in MA, NH, VT, CT, RI, NY, NJ and Ontario and a listing of organic CSAs. An independent certification agency for organic growers.

Ocean Arks International, 176 Battery St., 3rd Floor, Burlington, VT 05401. 802-860-0011; www.oceanarks.org; info@oceanarks.org Information about living machines.

OMB (Office of Management and Budget) Watch, 1742 Connecticut Ave. NW, Washington, DC 20009. 202-234-8494; Fax: 202-234-8584; www.ombwatch.org; ombwatch@ombwatch.org. Free database that you can search to check on corporate activities.

Organic Fiber Council, 5801 Sierra Ave., Richmond, CA 94805. 510-215-8841; Fax 510-215-7253; www.ota.com/ofc.htm; ofc@igc.org. Promotes awareness and understanding of organically grown agricultural fibers by educating consumers and the apparel and textile industry

Organic Trade Association, 74 Fairview Street, P.O. Box 547, Greenfield, MA. 01302. 413- 774 7511; Fax 413-774- 6432; www.ota.com; info@ota.com. Publishes the Organic Pages, a directory of organic growers, and the Organic Fiber Directory, devoted strictly to organic fiber producers, manufacturers, and retailers.

Permaculture Activist, PO Box 1209W, Black Mountain, NC 28711. 828-669-6336; Fax 828-669-5068; http://metalab.unc.edu/pc-activist/; pcactiv@metalab.unc.edu. A monthly magazine discussing permaculture design techniques and implementation strategies.

Permaculture Network: www.permaculture.net

Pesticide Action Network North America, 49 Powell St., Suite 500, San Francisco, CA 94102. 415- 981-1771; Fax 415-981-1991; www.panna.org; panna@panna.org. PANNA links over 100 affiliated health, consumer, labor, environment, progressive agriculture and public interest groups in North America with thousands of supporters worldwide to promote healthier, more effective pest management.

Planet Drum Foundation, Raise the Stakes, Box 31251, San Francisco, CA 94131. 415-285-6556; Fax 415-285-6563; www.planetdrum.org; planetdrum@igc.org. One of the best organizations providing information about bioregionalism.

Public Citizen, Critical Mass, 215 Pennsylvania Ave. SE, Washington, DC 20003. 202-546-4996; www.citizen.org; Founded by consumer-advocate Ralph Nader, this organization addresses consumer, environmental, corporate responsibility, and indigenous peoples' issues.

Real Goods Trading Company, 966 Mazzoni St., Ukiah, CA 95482. (707) 468-9214 or 800-762-7325; www.realgoods.com. A mail-order catalog services that supplies energy-efficient appliances, solar power goods, and other recycled and environmental goods.

Rocky Mountain Institute, 1739 Snowmass Creek Rd., Snowmass, CO 81654. 970-927-3851; www.rmi.org; outreach@rmi.org. Provides consulting and educational information about water, climate, buildings, transportation and other issues.

Rodale Institute, Box 323, RD 1, Kutztown, PA. 610-683-1400; www.rodaleinstitute.org; info@rodaleinst.org. Promotes a regenerative food system that supports human and environmental health. Publishes *Organic Gardening Magazine*, and also publishes a wide array of books on organic farming. An excellent clearinghouse of information.

School of Living, 432 Leaman Rd., Cochranville, PA, 19330. 610-593-2346; www.s-o-l.org; SOL@s-o-l.org. Dedicated to learning and teaching the philosophy, practices and principles of living that are self-empowering for individuals within the general aim of establishing decentralized, ecologically-sound, self-governed and humane communities.

Scientific Certification Systems, 1939 Harrison St. Suite 400, Oakland, CA 94612; 510-832-1415; Fax 510-832-0359; www.scs1.com; gmcpartland@scs1.com. Established in 1984 as the nation's first third-party certifier for testing pesticide residues in fresh produce. In the past 15 years, the company has evolved to become a certifier of multiple facets of the food industry and of the environmentally sound management of forests, marine habitats and a wide variety of businesses

Seeds of Change, 888-762-7333; www.seedsofchange.com. Sells seeds and seedlings that are certified organic, open-pollinated (self-reproducing, non-hybrids), GMO-Free (no Genetically Modified Organisms), chemical-free (no chemicals used to grow or treat), and grown by Seeds of Change and their network of certified organic family farms and nurseries.

Seed Savers Exchange, 3076 North Winn Rd., Decorah, IA 52101. Publishes the "bible" on heirloom and antique seeds.

Simmons Natural Bodycare, Hwy 36, Bridgeville, CA 95526. //home.pon.net/simmonsnaturals/catalog.html. Supplier of some of the purest natural bodycare products.

Sustainability Source, Inc. 11504 SW Woodlee Hts., Portland, OR 97219; 503-244-5808; Fax 650-373-7430; www.sustainabilitysource.com/home; info@sustainabilitysource.com. Sponsors the Sustainability Screen, a listing of manufacturer's environmental and social practices, and provides a listing of green businesses and products.

Sustainable Cotton Project, www.sustainablecotton.org; info@sustainablecotton.org

Time Dollar Network, PO Box 42514, Washington, DC 20015. 202-868-5200; www.timedollar.org; info@timedollar.org. Time Dollars are a tax-exempt currency that people can earn by using their time, energy and skills to help others.

US Composting Council, PO Box 407, Amherst, OH 44001-0407. 440-989-2748; Fax 440-989-1553; www.compostingcouncil.org; info@compostingcouncil.org.

Vegetarian Resource Center (VRC), P.O. Box 38-1068, Cambridge, MA 02238-1068. 617-625-3790; Fax 617-357-2596; www.tiac.net/users/vrc/vrc.html; info@vegetarian.org. Provides the names of local vegetarians in any area in North America. Provides referrals to lists and internet resources for vegetarian questions.

Washington Toxics Coalition, 4649 Sunnyside Ave N, Suite 540E, Seattle WA 98103. 206-632-1545; www.watoxics.org; info@watoxics.org. An information clearinghouse providing education on toxins and their alternatives.

Waterwiser, 6666 West Quincy Avenue, Denver, CO 80235. 800-559-9855; Fax 303-794-6303; www.waterwiser.org; bewiser@waterwiser.org. A branch of American Waterworks Association, Waterwiser promotes water conservation strategies. An excellent resource with articles and links to water conservation, recycling, and reuse issues.

A SHORT LIST OF READING MATERIAL

Balch, James F. and Phyllis A. Balch. 1997. **Prescription for Nutritional Healing.** New York: Avery Publishing Group. A comprehensive resource guide for natural healing. Offers advice on healing from using the least interfering methodologies to the most invasive procedures.

Berthold-Bond, Annie. 1994. **Clean and Green.** Woodstock, NY: Ceres Press. An excellent resource for natural cleaning products. Full of easy to use do-it-yourself recipes that work well. For $10, it's well worth the money.

Campbell, Stu. 1983. **The Home Water Supply: How to Find, Filter, Store, and Conserve It.** Pownal, VT: Storey Books. A well written guide for homeowners.

Chelsea Green Publishing, PO Box 428, White River Junction, VT 05001. 800-639-4099; www.chelseagreen.com. A variety of do-it-yourself books on homebuilding issues, from passive solar design to mortgage-free strategies.

Elkington, John, Hailes, Julia, and Joel Makower. 1988. **The Green Consumer**. London: Penguin Books. Contains a fairly comprehensive listing of "cruelty-free" and environmentally friendly personal care products.

Jenkins, Joseph. 1999. **The Humanure Handbook**, second edition. Jenkins Publishing (www.jenkinspublishing.com). Composter's bible, includes worldwide list of compost toilet sources. 800-639-4099.

Kimbrell, Andrew C. and Edward Lee Rogers. **The Environment, The Law, and You**. In Rifkin, Jeremy, ed. 1990. **The Green Lifestyle Handbook**. New York: Henry Holt and Company. p. 156.

Mander, Jerry. 1991. **In the Absence of the Sacred**. San Francisco: Sierra Books. An excellent treatise on the failures of technology and the survival of indigenous cultures.

Mollison, Bill. 1988. **Permaculture: A Designer's Manual**. Tyalgum, NSW, Australia: Tagari Publications. In bookstores, or on the web.

The Nation, 72 Fifth Ave., New York, NY 10011. Reports on government and corporate involvement in all major current issues.

Schaeffer, John, and Douglas Pratt. 1999. **The Solar Living Sourcebook**, tenth edition. White River Junction, VT: Chelsea Green Publishing. A sourcebook for ecological living technologies and strategies.

Winter, Ruth. 1999. **A Consumer's Dictionary of Cosmetic Ingredients**. Three Rivers Press.

Winter, Ruth. 1999. **A Consumer's Guide to Food Additives**. Three Rivers Press.

GOVERNMENT CONTACTS

Toxic Release Inventory and Emergency Planning and Community Right to Know Act (EPCRA). Free information from the US Environmental Protection Agency. 800-535-0202.

Hazardous Waste is regulated under the **Resource Conservation and Recovery Act**, 800-424-9346.

For information about drinking water contamination, call EPA's **Safe Drinking Water Hotline**, 800-426-4791.

To find more information regarding the health effects of environmental contaminants, call **EPA's Pollution Prevention Clearinghouse**, 202-260-1023. The website for the EPA is: www.epa.gov.

Resource Conservation & Recovery Act (RCRA-7002 (42 USC-6972) Addresses hazardous and non-hazardous wastes. Directed toward companies who transport, store, treat or dispose of waste and violates the Act or fails to perform cleanup responsibilities.

Comprehensive Environmental Response, Compensation, and Liability Act CERCLA or Superfund-310 (42 USC-9659) Addresses hazardous substances or pollutants. Directed toward suppliers or operators of underground injection wells who fail to maintain drinking water standards or violate orders under the act.

Safe Drinking Water Act (SDWA-1449 42 USC-300j-8) Addresses public water systems or underground sources of drinking water. Directed toward anyone who violates permits issued for discharge of pollutants into surface waters.

Clean Water Act (CWA-505 33 USC-1365) Addresses surface and groundwater. Directed toward anyone who violates a permit condition.

Surface Mining Control and Reclamation Act (SMCRA)-520 30 USC-1270. Addresses coal mining during both mining and post-mining restoration of sites. Directed toward anyone who violates a regulation under the act regarding the safe manufacture, use, disposal, and processing of chemicals, including PCBs.
